D1572629

Trogons, Laughing Falcons,
and Other Neotropical Birds

NUMBER TWENTY-NINE
The Louise Lindsey Merrick
Natural Environment Series

Trogons, Laughing Falcons, and Other Neotropical Birds

Alexander F. Skutch

ILLUSTRATIONS BY
Dana Gardner

Texas A&M University Press : College Station

Library of Congress Cataloging-in-Publication Data

Skutch, Alexander Frank, 1904–
    Trogons, laughing falcons, and other neotropical birds /
Alexander F. Skutch ; illustrations by Dana Gardner.
        p.   cm. — (Louise Lindsey Merrick natural
environment series ; no. 29)
    Includes bibliographical references (p.   ) and index.
    ISBN 0-89096-850-0
    1. Birds—Latin America.   I. Title.   II. Series.
QL685.7.S58   1999
598′.098—dc21   98-30287
                                                         CIP

CONTENTS ✿

ILLUSTRATIONS ❀

PREFACE ❧

The beautiful birds with a handicap of whom I tell in the first chapter of this book are trogons. They nest in holes they carve for themselves in tree trunks or other materials, using short, broad bills less efficient for this task than the sharp, chisel-like beaks of woodpeckers. Difficulty in finding a trunk neither too hard for them to excavate nor so far advanced in decay that it collapses leads them to investigate different sites for their nests. I tell of a pair who hatched their eggs in an arboreal ants' nest, the only case I have found of a New World bird's nesting in such a situation. Trogons' search for a place for their eggs led to the most fantastic behavior of a pair of birds that I have witnessed in nearly seven decades of bird study.

Another chapter is about the only raptor known to me that might be called a friend of smaller birds, the Laughing Falcon; widespread in tropical America, it subsists almost wholly on snakes, which devour so many birds' eggs and nestlings. In addition to recent, unpublished observations, I include in this book older studies, published long ago in ornithological journals and updated with new observations and interpretations: the Rufous Piha of tropical forests, which maintains a high population despite laying a single egg in the slightest of nests and having an unusually prolonged nesting schedule; the migratory Piratic Flycatcher, which raises its own progeny in covered nests captured from more industrious birds by a simple ruse that avoids fighting; hummingbirds that learn the songs they repeat in courtship assemblies to attract females, some of which fasten their nests with cobweb beneath sheltering leaves; soaring kites that catch insects with their feet instead of their bills, as flycatchers do; and other notable birds.

I tell of the only wild bird I have raised from the egg, a Gray-headed Chachalaca, and her strong attachment to her foster parents. I have thought it not inappropriate to call attention to the habits of the smallest New World monkeys, the marmosets and tamarins; in several ways their habits resemble those of birds—a fascinating example of ecological convergence by unrelated animals. The final chapter compares the strenuous lives of long-distance migrants with the more leisurely existence of the birds with which they mingle in their tropical winter homes, and calls attention to differences in life histories and temperaments of migrants and permanently resident birds. In the epilogue, I answer a question often asked by visitors to our nature reserve, Los Cusingos, in Southern Pacific Costa Rica and by readers of my books: "What is your favorite bird?"

In this book, probably the last that I shall write about birds, I have tried to blend entertaining reading with solid natural history, including new observations of little-known Neotropical birds.

ACKNOWLEDGMENTS ❀

Chapter 4, "When Less Yields More," is amplified from the account of the Rufous Piha in volume 3 of *Life Histories of Central American Birds,* published by the Cooper Ornithological Society in 1969 and now difficult to obtain. Parts of chapter 6 on the White-eared Hummingbird were contributed to A. C. Bent's *Life Histories of North American Cuckoos, Goatsuckers, Hummingirds, and Their Allies,* published in 1940. Chapter 7 on the Violet-headed Hummingbird contains material that first appeared in my paper in *The Wilson Bulletin* in 1958. Chapter 8 on the Long-tailed Hermit owes much to my paper in *The Auk* in 1964. The accounts of the American Swallow-tailed Kite and the Double-toothed Kite in chapter 13 are based largely upon an article in *The Condor* in 1965, and that of the Plumbeous Kite upon a paper in the same journal in 1947. The epilogue, "The Birds I Love," appeared in the *Bird Watcher's Digest* in 1995. Full citations of sources of information are given in the bibliography. To all whose publications have enriched this book, I am grateful.

LOS CUSINGOS
January, 1997

Trogons, Laughing Falcons,
and Other Neotropical Birds

CHAPTER I &

Beauty with a Handicap

Among the most beautiful of feathered creatures are the thirty-seven species of trogons—stout, pigeon-sized arboreal birds distributed through tropical and subtropical rain forests and lighter woodlands around the world, except in the Australasian region. In the New World, where the family is best represented and best known, males are predominantly glittering green with scintillations of violet and blue on their heads, upper parts, and chests, and with red, vermilion, or yellow on their abdomens. Females tend to be rufous, brown, or gray, with less extensive red or yellow on their underparts. The long tails of trogons are often barred with black and white on the underside. The family includes the Resplendent Quetzal of southern Mexico and Central America, whose iridescent green and rich crimson body, crested head, and long upper tail coverts, flowing behind it like slender, gracefully undulating streamers, have made it famous as the most elegant bird of the Western Hemisphere. Four less ornate quetzals adorn the woodlands of South America.

Trogons are dignified birds. They perch upright, with their tails directed almost straight downward, sometimes slightly forward beneath the branch. In many years spent in the forests where they dwell, I have never seen them fight. At the approach of their nesting season, several individuals of both sexes may congregate in trees, calling and occasionally chasing one another, but avoiding clashes that might knock out many of their loosely attached feathers. Their notes range from soft and mellow to loud and rather harsh. The New World trogons eat both berries and small invertebrates, which they pluck from twigs or foliage on graceful sallies from their perches, without alighting beside the fruit, insect, or spider.

Trogons belong to an ancient family that in past ages ranged more widely, as attested by fossils of Oligocene age from France, where now, as in other parts of Europe, no trogon occurs. Their ability to survive, to adapt to changing climates and habitats, is manifest not only by their almost pantropical distribution but likewise by their persistence amid soaring human populations and expanding agriculture. Like other small, isolated sanctuaries, the modest tract of tropical rain forest in southern Costa Rica that for more than fifty years I have tried to protect from encroaching neighbors has been steadily losing avian species, but the four kinds of trogons that were here at Los Cusingos when I came remain with us, despite brilliant colors that might attract hostile eyes. Nevertheless, of all the woodland birds that I know, trogons have the greatest difficulty finding sites for their nests.

All trogons nest in cavities. As a rule, they carve these for themselves with short, stout, often serrated bills. A male usually chooses a nest site and attracts a female to help him excavate a chamber in a decaying trunk, a termitary, or some other medium, as will presently appear. Long ago, amid pines, oaks, and other broad-leaved trees in the mountains of Guatemala above 8,000 feet (2,440 m), I studied Mountain Trogons; they are known to the local people as *auroras,* apparently in allusion to their red breasts, more intensely colored than Homer's "rosy-fingered dawn." This species, like a number of others, carves, in the side of a slender, rotting trunk, an open niche in which much of the parent bird is visible from the front while it incubates its two white eggs or broods its nestlings. As a wood-carving tool, the trogon's thick bill is less efficient than the woodpecker's chisel-like beak. When I noticed how often a pair of auroras had started to dig into a stub, only to be defeated because the wood proved to be too hard for them, or so far advanced in decay that it crumbled or fell, I was sorry to find such splendid birds so handicapped. But with great perseverance they tried again and again until they found a low stub neither too hard nor too soft, in which they completed their excavation and reared their families. Without laws to protect them, they remained abundant amid an indigenous population hungry for flesh.

THE SLATY-TAILED TROGON

The trogon's stout bill seems best fitted for carving into the black, roughly globular, arboreal nests of certain termites, especially species of *Nasuti-*

termes, soldiers of which have heads like tiny brown syringes that secrete a sticky white liquid to discomfit small enemies. Such nests are composed of thin, hard, curving plates that separate a maze of irregular passages. By seizing the edges of these plates and crunching or twisting to break them off, the birds laboriously excavate, deep in the heart of a termitary, a rounded chamber entered through a short, upwardly inclined tube. Without carrying in any soft material for lining, the female trogon lays two or three white or pale blue eggs on the chamber's hard floor. While sitting inside, the parents are invisible, or at most their heads may be dimly glimpsed by peering up the entrance tube. The termites seal off the passages that abut on the trogons' chamber and seem not to molest them. After the birds depart, the insects may repair their termitary by filling the cavity that their uninvited guests have made. Trogons that occupy termitaries, of which the Slaty-tailed is an example, may carve chambers of the same form in massive dead trunks, but species that nest in open niches are not known to occupy termitaries, which would be inappropriate for this type of excavation (Skutch 1983).

The kind of termitary that trogons prefer is abundant in warm lowlands but becomes rare with increasing altitude, at least in tropical America; here, at 2,500 feet (750 m), where such termitaries are not abundant, Slaty-tailed Trogons usually nest in decaying trunks. Although in the forest at Los Cusingos, as in most unexploited woodland, dead trees are not rare, few of them are at just the proper stage of decay for trogons. Apparently unable to find a suitable trunk in the forest, a pair entered our garden that adjoins it, seeking a nest site, toward the end of the dry month of February. Between the house and the woodland stands a tall African oil palm with a massive crown of huge, feathery fronds and large clusters of fruits with orange pulp for which white-faced Capuchin monkeys dispute with Black Vultures. Woodpeckers, tanagers, and finches come to eat the flesh that the larger animals leave exposed; Agoutis profit by fruits that they knock to the ground, gnawing through the very hard, thick endocarp with sharp incisors to extract the white embryo through a neat round hole. Amid the ferns, other epiphytes, and accumulated debris just below the palm's crown, behind the dead fronds that drape vertically beneath it, the Slaty-tailed Trogons started to excavate a cavity, in a situation such as I had never found any trogon selecting for its nest.

As usual, the shining green, red-bellied male alternated with his dark gray partner in the task of preparing the nest chamber. He was obviously

Slaty-tailed Trogon

the leader, taking longer spells of work in the hole than she did, remaining close to it and calling her back when she flew off into the forest. While she was in the cavity, he perched near the opening, calling softly; while he was inside, she rested farther away, in silence. When the female emerged from the hole after a spell of work, he went more promptly to take his turn than she did after his exit. After enlarging the chamber among the epiphytes until they could disappear in it, the trogons abandoned it. I doubted that they could have reared nestlings amid decaying vegetation that probably swarmed with ants and other stinging creatures.

This pair of trogons continued to frequent our garden. One morning the male, followed by his partner, flew up to an irregular decaying cavity high in the trunk of a dead jacaranda tree on the hillside behind the house. After each in turn had examined this hole briefly and found it unsatisfactory, they flew down to a poró tree by the chickens' shelter, where they rested a long while, the female in silence, the male repeating over and over a low rattle or churr, with each repetition bowing slightly forward and slowly raising his tail from a pendulous to an almost horizontal position. After an interval, he flew to the chickens' roost, to begin the most fantastically inappropriate behavior that I have witnessed in any bird.

The chickens' shelter is a tall, slender structure, with a metal roof and metal bands around each of the four upright posts that support it, to prevent opossums, tayras, and other carnivorous mammals from climbing. On three sides it is open, but to the uphill side I had attached thin metal sheets to thwart animals that might try to jump above the guards on the posts. Over the years, these once-shiny sheets, with nothing solid behind them, had rusted to a deep brown not greatly different from the color of some dead, barkless trunks. The male trogon flew up and struck this wide, vertical expanse with a loud, metallic sound, then flew back to the tree where his mate waited. After he had repeated this several times, she flew to the sheet but did not strike it audibly. The male banged against the metal a few times more, before both returned to the forest.

When, at midday, the trogons returned to resume their assaults upon the unyielding metal, I decided to try to help them out of their predicament by making a nest box for them, although with materials I could promptly lay hands upon, I could not give it the upwardly inclined entrance tube that they prefer. Through most of the afternoon, while I worked on the front porch, I heard the trogons banging loudly against the metal on the other side of the house.

On the following afternoon, they came again to the chickens' shelter. The female was now the more active and flew against the metal twenty-five times before her partner did. In an hour, she hit the sheet thirty-two times; he, nine times; making a total of forty-one impacts. They struck the metal with their underparts—whether with the chest, the feet, or both I could not make sure—rather than with their bills. Exceptionally, they hovered momentarily close beside it, making no sound. I could not decide whether they were confused by the color of the metal, whether they behaved in this extraordinary manner because they were frustrated by repeated failures to find an adequate nest site, or whether, like children with a noise-making toy, they were fascinated by the sounds. They reminded me of a territorial bird "fighting" his reflection in a mirror or some other shiny surface; but the metal they struck was far too rusty to reflect, and their motivation was certainly different.

After the trogons had flown against the metal for two days without denting it, we attached the newly made bird house to the side of the chickens' shelter, above the rusty sheet. The birds returned and appeared to notice the box, but I was not surprised when they disdained it, as I have no knowledge of trogons nesting in a structure made by man. Nor did they occupy the box when we moved it to a neighboring tree. Now they lost interest in the sheet metal and retired into the forest where, a few days later, I found what was probably the same pair, digging into a massive trunk, of the sort they usually choose for their chambers. The male trogon's tail was badly frayed, apparently by his persistent efforts to find a nest site. As often happens, after digging through the soft sapwood of this old stub, they struck heartwood that resisted their bills and abandoned this undertaking. After failing to establish a nest in three quite different sites, they passed from my ken.

THE VIOLACEOUS TROGON

More abundant in our forest than the Slaty-tailed Trogon is the smaller Violaceous Trogon. About nine inches (23 cm) long, the male is largely brilliant metallic green on his upper parts. The black of his head and throat merges into violet-blue on his chest and the back of his head. His underparts are yellow, and his tail, viewed from below, is narrowly and prominently barred with black and white. The female is slate colored, with a yellow abdomen and barred outer tail feathers, much as in the male. Early in the year, when males gather in treetops to compete for mates, their soft, clear *cow cow cow cow*, rapidly repeated at a uniform rate or slightly accelerated toward the end of each sequence, resounds cheerfully through the woodland.

For their nests, Violaceous Trogons choose an unexpected variety of sites. They prefer a large, silvery gray wasps' nest, attached by its broad top to an exposed branch high in a tree, and tapering downward to the doorway through which the insects go in and out. These turbinate, papery vespiaries are most often noticed at the forest's edge or in an isolated tree beyond it. One would never expect birds that seem so mild to capture a nest defended by hundreds or thousands of stinging insects; but tropical wasps tend to be less peppery than northern hornets, and the trogons proceed methodically to reduce their numbers. From nearby perches, the collaborating male and female dart up to pluck the poor insects, one by one, from the surface of their home or to seize them in the air. Apparently, the trogons eat the wasps, but this detail is difficult to observe because the vespiaries are high and the birds are swift. Although sometimes a wasp pursues a trogon, as far as I have seen, the insects make no concerted attempt to defend their nest.

Violaceous Trogons range upward from the coasts to about 5,000 feet (1,500 m) in the mountains of Central America. At the higher altitudes they may begin to break into a vespiary while the wasps are torpid on cool early mornings of the dry season, but in warmer climates they appear not to start excavating until they have greatly reduced the number of the inhabitants, or caused the survivors to abandon the vespiary, which may require a fortnight or more of wasp catching.

Working alternately, the partners prepare a chamber amid the horizontal brood combs, from which they probably extract and eat the tender white larvae and pupae. On these combs the female lays her eggs, which in one nest were three. I have found Violaceous Trogons breeding in vespiaries of the same type, but apparently not always of the same species of wasps, from southern Costa Rica to northern Guatemala, and Alexander Wetmore (1968) watched a pair breaking into a wasps' nest in western Panama. Whether the Violaceous Trogon also occupies vespiaries in the southern part of its range—which extends from tropical Mexico to Peru, Amazonia, and the Guianas—I do not know. Although Carolina Wrens and Yellow-crowned Euphonias occasionally breed in old, abandoned nests of hornets or other wasps, the Violaceous Trogons' habit of capturing active vespiaries for nesting appears to be unique among birds.

In Panama, I found a pair of Violaceous Trogons preparing to nest in a wholly different site. On a thick, ascending, epiphyte-laden branch of a tree, standing on the bank of a road through open woodland with scattered

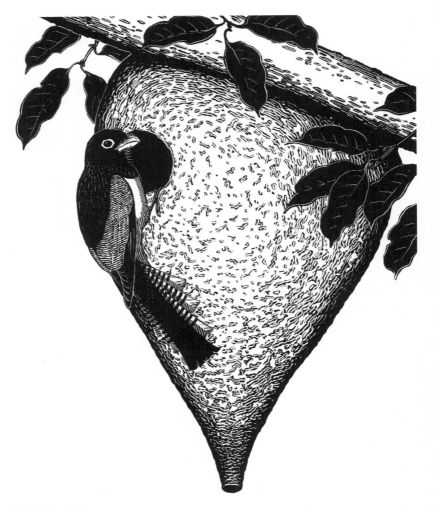

Violaceous Trogon

large trees, grew a vigorous plant of *Polypodium crassifolium* or some closely similar fern. The dark brown ball of its roots, about two feet (60 cm) in diameter, had collected an almost solid mass of decaying vegetation. Into this earthy aggregate a pair of trogons, working alternately, had dug a hole they could enter up to the base of the tail. Movements of the exposed parts of the worker's body and wings suggested that it was vigorously tearing at the roots. When, after a long spell in the hole, the female flew out, much loose material followed her and fell to the ground. We could not stay to learn the outcome of this undertaking, but one of my companions on this occasion, Jaime Pujals, later wrote to me that he had found two other pairs of Violaceous Trogons definitely nesting inside root masses of epiphytes. Others have reported Violaceous Trogons occupying decaying stumps and termitaries, but none of the dozen nests that I have seen was so situated (Skutch 1972, 1981).

In early March, 1984, I had additional evidence of Violaceous Trogons' versatility in the choice of nest sites. In a narrow gap in the forest at Los Cusingos, a targuá tree spread its branches above a tangle of bushes and vines. From a high limb of this tree, a nest of tiny dark azteca ants hung like a thick blackish stalactite. I could not reach the egg-shaped structure, which appeared to be about eighteen inches long and twelve inches thick (45 by 30 cm) and was attached to the tree by its narrower upper end. It might have been mistaken for an arboreal termitary, from which it differed in its covering of small, irregular scales, overlapping downward like the shingles of a roof. Low, soft notes drew attention to a pair of Violaceous Trogons perching near it.

The trogons had just started to dig into this ants' nest, the male at one point, his partner at another a few inches away on the same side—much as, in an earlier year, I had seen a pair begin separate holes in a vespiary. They could have worked simultaneously, each at its preferred spot, but they followed the trogon's usual method of excavating alternately, one partner watching from a neighboring branch while the other worked with its head in the hole, unable to see an approaching enemy. On the first morning that I watched these trogons, their turns at the nest rarely lasted as long as three or four minutes, probably because the ants attacked them. After each spell of work, the trogon dropped out backward from the still-shallow opening and flew to a perch, to shake itself vigorously, twitch its wings and less often its tail, and scratch rapidly with its feet. It appeared to pluck ants from its plumage and legs with its bill, which it often rubbed against its perch. The female, and less often the male, repeatedly flew up to the outside of the nest or to a branch beside it, apparently to pluck off, without alighting, ants too small to be detected through my binocular.

By the sixth day after I found these trogons at the ants' nest, the female's shaft had become deep enough for her to enter up to the base of her tail; the male's was so much farther advanced that he could go all the way in and turn around, to emerge headfirst with a badly crumpled tail. Soon after I began to watch on this day, the female flew into the forest, to remain absent for nearly half an hour, while her companion continued to rest in the targuá tree, softly calling for her. As I have always found with trogons, neither member of the pair would work unless the other was present to act as sentinel; but as soon as the female returned, the male resumed operations. For the next hour the pair continued to carve alternately, in spells that had become much longer, up to eight or ten minutes, doubtless because the ants had ceased to attack them. Now they did not scratch, shake, or pluck things from their plumage after their exit from the nest. While one member of the pair was at work, the other, resting in the targuá tree, continued to call softly, assuring its mate of its continued presence.

At intervals the male, with his body more than halfway inside the cavity, shook vigorously, while a shower of particles fell through the entrance tube. He seemed to be kicking loosened material from the chamber with his feet. While he clung in the entrance, his exposed back and rump appeared green; when he perched upright on a branch well above my head, his tail toward the rising sun, these parts scintillated with deep blue and violet. The dispossessed ants had already started two new nests higher in the same tree.

For at least three weeks, the trogons continued to dig into the ants' nest. Although the male sometimes appeared to try to persuade his partner to enter his shaft, she persisted in deepening hers, until it connected with his excavation. Now the trogons had two doorways for escape from menacing snakes or mammals. Whether this arrangement was intentional, I do not know. Every other finished trogons' nest that I have seen, of whatever species, has had a single doorway; but in Guatemala people repeatedly assured me that Resplendent Quetzals nest in a tree cavity with opposite doorways, so that the male—which, like other male trogons, incubates the eggs and broods the nestlings—could pass through without bending and fraying his elegant train. This may occasionally be true, as though by accident, but the quetzals' nests that I found in Costa Rica had each a single doorway.

By early April, about four weeks after they had started to carve their chamber in the ants' nest, the Violaceous Trogons were incubating in it. Peering upward into the dark cavity with my binocular, I could sometimes detect the yellow rings around the male's eyes and his pale bill, less often the white spots behind and in front of the female's eyes. Much of the time they were wholly invisible. Loud noises did not make them look out, much less leave.

These trogons, like other lowland species of their family, incubated in the manner of pigeons, the male taking one long session covering the middle of the day, the female sitting all the rest of the time. One day my son and I watched alternately from dawn to dusk. No trogon appeared until 8:45 A.M., when the male approached, calling softly. His partner, having incubated through the night and early morning, looked out lingeringly before she darted forth, through his doorway. The male alighted on a branch in front of the nest and churred once, lifting and spreading his tail. Then he flew to his doorway and clung there with his back outward, peering in. At 8:48 he climbed in and the female flew away. During the next six hours we saw no trogon. Then the male's head appeared in the doorway. After looking out for a few minutes he emerged, at 2:53 P.M., and flew away before he called just once. Almost immediately, the female alighted in front of the ants' nest and repeated a few times a subdued version of the *cow cow cow* song. At 2:58 she entered, to remain until daylight faded. On this day the male incubated without interruption for six hours and five minutes. On another day, when we did not watch continuously, he entered at 8:25 A.M. and emerged at 3:11 P.M., six and three-quarters hours later.

Looking up into the nest cavity on April 20, I found the female sitting restlessly, moving around and revealing her yellow belly or her tail much more than on previous days. My surmise that the eggs were hatching was confirmed in the afternoon, when both parents brought small green insects. Since I had found the trogons sitting in the nest, as though incubating, on April 3, the period of incubation was about seventeen days, which agrees closely with determinations of seventeen to nineteen days made directly at accessible nests of several related species. Although I could not see the nestlings, I had no doubt that they were as blind and as completely naked as other newborn trogons.

Both parents fed the nestlings, but their father was the chief provider. During twenty hours of watching, spaced throughout the nestling period, he brought food thirty-three times, she only twenty-one times. Unlike songbirds, which often bring a whole billful of berries or insects to their young, the trogons always brought a single item, held prominently in the bill. Nearly always this was an insect, usually green, small or large, and often winged. I recognized a middle-sized butterfly, a small damsel fly, and a hairy caterpillar. Fruits were rarely brought. Arriving with a meal, the parent alighted in the targuá tree and churred a few times, raising and lowering its tail; rarely it softly voiced the *cow* call. The bird delivered the item

Beauty with a Handicap : 13

while clinging in one of the entrances, back outward, head inside, the female sometimes at the doorway she had made, sometimes at the male's, which he always used. Then the parent either flew directly away or climbed inside to brood. I never saw one remove waste.

While the nestling trogons were only a few days old, both parents brooded them, for periods ranging from half an hour to an hour and a half. When they were eight days old, they were not brooded after their mother, having passed the night with them, flew from the nest at dawn. When ten days old, they were not covered even at night.

The leaves of the targuá tree turned orange before they fell, one by one, while the tree remained green and new leaves expanded. The brilliant male trogon resting among bright orange leaves in the morning sunshine made a colorful display. The descent of one of these large leaves past a perching trogon never made it budge.

On the afternoon of May 3, the nestlings' oft-repeated, soft *cow cow cow*, like the adults' song but much weaker, was faintly audible sixty feet (18 m) from the nest. Two mornings later, sunshine streamed into the nest chamber through a gaping hole in its eastern side, apparently torn by a squirrel or some other small mammal. The young trogons were nowhere to be found. In the next two hours their father thrice took food to the doorway, called much nearby, then flew away still bearing his offering. Their mother did not appear. At nests of other species of trogons, including the Resplendent Quetzal and the Black-throated Trogon, I have found the male more attentive to nestlings about ready to fly than their mother, who might neglect them.

I never glimpsed these nestlings. Years earlier, at one of the lower of the nests in vespiaries, I could see the heads of three by looking up through the doorway. They received more small fruits than the occupants of the ants' nest, and regurgitated seeds, which fell through the entrance. While awaiting their meals, they repeated almost constantly a low, sweet-toned version of the adults' song. Seventeen days after I found them, already hatched, they left the wasps' nest, able to fly weakly and rather closely resembling their mother.

In southern Asia and Indonesia, Rufous Woodpeckers frequently rear their broods in arboreal nests of ants of the genus *Crematogaster;* but except this one pair of Violaceous Trogons, I have no knowledge of any New World bird occupying an ants' nest. Nests of the kind they used, rare at Los Cusingos, are more common at lower altitudes. The nest in which they failed to rear their young fell during the rains. One of the two replacement nests that the ants started higher in the same tree continued to grow; but after two years it was not as big as their original nest and apparently was too small for the trogons. I looked in vain for them to show interest in it. I could not find any other nest of this type in the vicinity, nor any vespiary of the kind that Violaceous Trogons use. As the nesting season of 1986 approached, these birds faced a scarcity of nest sites.

Several years earlier, a swarm of big black guitarrón wasps had built on the wall of our house one of their large nests. Such a structure consists of a single sheet of hexagonal brood cells, closely applied to a vertical tree trunk or wall, and enclosed by a bulky envelope of strongly corrugated gray papier mâché, leaving a wide space between the stout covering and the cells. By successive annexes, these nests may grow to be a yard or more long. As occasionally occurs, this particular vespiary had been raided by army ants and had long been deserted. Lacking horizontal combs, it offered no place for the trogons to deposit their eggs.

In mid-April, a pair of Violaceous Trogons appeared in our garden, searching for a nest site. First, they started to excavate a hole in a short, rotting stub of a carao tree behind the house. When this proved unsatisfactory, they turned their attention to the old, slightly battered guitarrón nest on the wall. Early on a sunny morning, the male called much in the garden. Again and again he flew to the vespiary, hovered an instant beside it, then returned to perch in nearby trees, all the while calling softly. After he had done this many times, his mate joined him in these trees and watched passively, at intervals elevating and lowering her tail, while he continued to fly up to the wasps' nest. After this had continued for about half an hour, the female twice flew to the vespiary, just as he did. Then they departed, and I heard them in the distance.

The next day, when I was not watching, two large holes were torn in the upper part of the corrugated envelope. Before sunrise on the following day, the male again called in the garden, a rapidly repeated, soft *wic wic wic wic* instead of the louder, clearer *cow* note. Then he left, to return with the female later in the morning and resume his flights to the vespiary, often audibly striking the hollow envelope, sometimes only hovering momentarily beside it, then returning with airy, bouncing flight to the tree where his partner rested amid fresh green foliage. Less often he clung to a hole in the envelope and bit off fragments of its edge, enlarging it, or he tore at the empty brood cells in front of him, evidently unaware that they were plastered against hard cement that he could not penetrate. He rarely persevered at this occupation as long as a minute. The female went less often to the vespiary, but four times she visited the same gap, through which she tore at the hexagonal brood cells, once continuing for three minutes. The badly frayed tip of her tail suggested that she had already nested, or tried to nest, elsewhere in the present season. Her rapid notes were much softer than the male's.

For four days the male trogon tried to convince his consort that the old guitarrón vespiary offered a suitable site for her eggs, but she knew better. Then, for several additional mornings he came alone and called, without drawing his partner. After this, for many days, I heard him singing at a greater distance from the house. I found no trogons' nest that year.

Birds that build nests amid the foliage of trees and shrubs have no lack of sites in wooded regions. Birds that occupy cavities of various kinds are more restricted in their choice of sites, for in a flourishing forest, dead trees and branches are much less abundant than living ones. When the birds are not, like woodpeckers, well equipped for carving into fairly sound wood but must choose some more yielding medium, such as a termitary or a vespiary, their choice in many regions is still more limited. They must explore, trying a diversity of sites, until they find one in which they can excavate a chamber. Violaceous Trogons have nested, or tried to nest, in vespiaries with horizontal brood combs well suited for their needs, in vespiaries with vertical sheets of combs that offer no place for their eggs, in ants' nests, in the massed roots of epiphytes, in decaying stubs, and in termitaries. Slaty-tailed Trogons have nested, or tried to nest, in massive decaying trunks, in termitaries, amid epiphytes and decaying debris on a palm tree, and in thin sheet metal. The absurdity of some of their persistent efforts to carve a chamber, especially in unyielding human artifacts foreign to their sylvan abode, should not blind us to the utility of their exploratory behavior. Paradoxically, if they were more discriminating and less persevering, they might more often fail to find a nest site and rear progeny. Their success in spreading through most tropical woodlands before people began to destroy forests on an appalling scale, then in persisting in shrinking habitats, may owe much to habits that sometimes involve them in futile undertakings.

CHAPTER 2 🐚

Glimpses of Wood-Quails

Like the domestic chicken and bobwhites, wood-quails of the tropical American genus *Odontophorus* belong to the pheasant family, which has more species in the Old World than in the New. Unlike bobwhites, wood-quails inhabit forests instead of open fields and light thickets. Except in the most widespread of the wood-quails, the Marbled, which ranges from Costa Rica to eastern Bolivia and central Brazil, the habits of these attractive but retiring birds are so inadequately known that any bit of information about them seems worth recording. Here I tell of an intimate encounter with a family of Black-breasted Wood-Quails, a species that in Costa Rica and western Panama inhabits humid mountain forests from about 2,300 to 6,000 feet (700 to 1,850 m) above sea level. I wrote the account in my journal on March 29, 1938, while I dwelt on the still-wild northern slope of Costa Rica's Cordillera Central.

This morning, in a patch of low, rather open woods that remains amid pastures, I met a pair of Black-breasted Wood-Quails with two newly hatched chicks. They walked through the dense, dark undergrowth uttering a continuous stream of sweet, low, liquid notes that served to guide the little ones onward. Before I could see them well, they vanished like dark shadows into the dusky recesses of the vegetation, so thick and vine-entangled that I did not try to follow. I continued to wander through the woods, circling about, and an hour or so later I again met the family of quails. The undergrowth here was more open and I decided to follow them, for I had never enjoyed a good view of this wood-quail, and I wished first of all to see what they looked like. Cutting obstructing vines with my

Black-breasted Wood-Quail

machete, I gave chase, and in a small open area I nearly overtook them, for the chicks could not travel fast. At this point one of the parents doubled back and ran close in front of me, while the other continued to lead the chicks onward. The one acting as rearguard ran back and forth over the clearer ground where I stood, always moving quickly with many sudden changes of direction, so that I could not distinguish the details of his plumage, and never ceasing until the other parent had led the chicks well beyond the supposed danger, when he hurried after them, guided by his mate's low voice.

The quails now passed through, or rather beneath, vegetation so thickly entangled that I could not have followed without much strenuous work with the machete. Instead of trying this, I circled around, following narrow cow paths, and tried to get ahead of them. When I reached a small opening in the woods that during the wet months was a swamp, I heard the birds among the surrounding bushes. Hurrying up to the edge of the thicket, I caught one of the downy chicks, who had become entangled among fallen branches and leaves and could not follow the others. As before, one of the parents continued to lead away the chick that was able to follow, while the other stayed behind to see what could be done for the little captive. This parent became very excited, ran all around me, sometimes coming within four or five feet, but usually keeping beneath the shelter of the bushes and fallen branches at the border of the thicket, and never pausing more than an instant in one spot. Again he uttered his low calls without cease, but now that he was distressed the notes lost their liquid sweetness, becoming harder and sharper.

While the parent quail lingered near me calling the captive chick, I could see him close at hand in fairly bright light. He was everywhere a dark, rich brown, except where an expanse of black extended from the bill to the belly a short distance forward of the legs, covering the whole face, the front and sides of the neck, and the breast. This area of black was interrupted only by a narrow patch of white on the throat and some faint white marks behind each brown eye. The brown back and wings were marked with large black spots and fine buffy vermiculations. The elongated brown feathers of the quail's crown were sometimes erected to form a low crest. His short, thick bill and his feet were black.

I wished to examine more closely the soft, downy chick—smaller than a newly hatched domestic chick—that all this while I had held in my hand; but I feared that if I kept it too long the parent would become discouraged and follow the others, and the little one would be lost from its family. Accordingly, as soon as I had seen enough of the parent, I replaced the chick on the ground at the edge of the thicket. Subsequent events proved that my misgivings about the ultimate fidelity of the parent were unjust to him. Released from my hand, the chick ran toward its guardian; but directly in its path lay a litter of dead vegetation that was an almost insuperable obstacle to its little footsteps. For many minutes, while it struggled through the obstructing maze and uttered its low, soft peeps, the parent continued to run solicitously around it and to voice subdued calls. Finally the chick managed to find its way to the more open ground beyond and could follow its parent into the depth of the thicket. Guided by the voice of his consort, the parent led the erstwhile captive back to its family, and both parents' calls again became soft and liquid.

Two nests of the Black-breasted Wood-Quail were found at Monteverde in northwestern Costa Rica by David McDonald and Kathy Winnett-

Murray (1989). Both were on steep, heavily shaded stream banks in second-growth woods. Each was a deep hollow or tunnel that appeared to have been made simply by burrowing into the thick litter of leaves and twigs that covered the banks, without additions. The first nest contained, in early June, five eggs of undetermined outcome. In the second nest, also in early June, five eggs were laid in ten days, at intervals of two or three days. They were plain white until stained by contact with the dead leaves on which they reposed. Apparently, only one parent incubated them, while several other quails frequented the vicinity without coming to the nest, suggesting the same close family bonds and caution not to reveal the nest's exact site by a too-near approach that I had observed in the Marbled Wood-Quail. At the second Black-breasted Wood-Quail's nest, the interval from laying the last egg to hatching of four of the five eggs was sixteen to seventeen days, which seems short for the incubation period of a wood-quail.

Two months after my memorable meeting with the wood-quails, near the spot where I had caught the chick, I saw a half-grown bird, apparently chased by a dog, fly up to a thick, moss-covered branch about twenty feet (6 m) above the ground. Here the quail, possibly the same individual that as a chick I had held in my hand, stood for about half a minute, moving a step or two. Then, seeing that it had shaken off its pursuer, it flew down to the ground on the side opposite that from which it had come. Bushes screened from me the point where it landed, but the loud thud that I heard suggested that the poor bird had made a crash landing. Marbled Wood-Quails of lower altitudes also fly to a high perch when chased by dogs. A half-grown individual, hard-pressed by trespassing hounds, took refuge on a rafter above our porch, where it stayed, whistling plaintively, until an adult, probably its parent, came into our dooryard from the adjoining forest and called it down—the only time I ever saw a wood-quail in such an open place.

Another highland species of the genus *Odontophorus* is the Spotted Wood-Quail, readily recognized by its conspicuous orange-tawny crest, often held erect. On the Pacific slope of the Cordillera de Talamanca, I have found it at altitudes of about 3,500 to 8,000 feet (1,070 to 2,440 m); M. A. Carriker, Jr. (1910) met it up to timberline. While passing through the wilderness between El General and Cartago in 1936, I found a flock of five or six of these wood-quails high in the oak forest. They were tame and permitted me to watch them closely. But twenty-eight years later, in

patches of woods amid farms at Cañas Gordas near the Panamanian border, they had become so wary that I enjoyed a more-than-fleeting view of
them only once. While I sat in a blind in the forest, watching a Golden-
crowned Warbler nest, a flock of about half a dozen came walking over the
ground toward me, but on noticing the blind they veered aside before I saw
them as well as I wished. These quails were evidently abundant in ravines
in this region, if I am correct in attributing to them a song that I frequently
heard in the forest. It sounded like *poor-whipporwill-poor-whipporwill-
poor-whipporwill*, very rapidly repeated in a soprano voice that was high
and soft but powerful enough to carry far through the woodland. The re-
frain, which seemed to be given by two or more birds in unison, often
ended with a *poor-whip*. It had the same undulatory character as the twilight duet of the Marbled Wood-Quail that I often hear, which made me
confident that it was a wood-quail voice.

On two evenings at the beginning of June, I watched a pair of Spotted
Wood-Quails go to roost in a medium-sized tree in a plantation of coffee
that had been set under trees of the original forest left for shade, after removal of the undergrowth and thinning of the canopy. In the failing light
the quails flew, one after the other, to a stout, mossy ascending branch
about twenty feet up, drawing my attention to themselves by the sound of
their wing beats. After resting a while here, raising and lowering their orange crests, they continued upward, walking up ascending limbs and flying
from bough to bough, until they were lost to view amid the dense foliage
of the tree's compact crown. Like the Great Tinamou of the forest, these
wood-quails, after passing the day on the ground, fly up at nightfall to the
safety of a high perch. Probably the habit of roosting in trees, as of taking
refuge in them when hard-pressed by terrestrial enemies, is widespread
among wood-quails.

Noteworthy was the devoted attention of the parent Black-breasted
Wood-Quail to the chick that lagged behind the other parent and chick.
Such incautious behavior in the presence of a predatory quadruped or bi-
ped might have cost the brave parent its life. It reminded me of similar behavior that I had observed while watching from a blind the departure from
the nest of four chicks of the Marbled Wood-Quail. Following their
mother, three of the chicks crossed a log lying in their path and vanished
into the undergrowth. The fourth chick was baffled by the low obstruction that stretched far to its right and left. With the pertinacity of a creature whose life from birth depends largely upon its own competence, it

struggled to surmount the barrier, while its father remained behind the others to guard and encourage it. Finally, the retarded chick found a spot where it could scramble over the log, to be led by its parent to the rest of the family. Similarly, when wandering through the forest I have met a covey of Marbled Wood-Quails with chicks, one of the adults has stayed behind to run back and forth through the undergrowth at no great distance from me, trying to draw my attention to itself without incurring too much risk, while the rest of the group led the downy ones away (Skutch 1983). This behavior appears to be an alternative to the widespread injury-feigning distraction displays of parent birds before a flightless animal. I suspect that it is widespread among wood-quails and related birds, but more perilous than typical injury feigning.

Wood-quails, with fifteen species widely distributed through the forests of tropical America, are attractive birds with strong family bonds, whose endearing ways should be better known.

CHAPTER 3 🦋

Snake Eaters in a Garden

On the hillside behind our house, in the Valley of El General in southern Costa Rica, a clump of native jacaranda trees grew tall and slender. After delighting us, during the dry month of March, with splendid displays of lavender flowers on their lofty crowns, they died young, as fast-growing trees with soft wood commonly do, and their spreading naked branches stood gauntly etched against the sky. About the beginning of 1991, a pair of Laughing Falcons, or guacos, as they are more appropriately called in Costa Rica, spent much time on these boughs. They were noisy, calling frequently, long and loudly, alone or in a duet. Sometimes one held a snake.

Silhouetted against the sky, standing erect, these stout birds were striking figures. In both sexes, this falcon has a big, white, loosely crested head, with a broad black facial mask that continues as a narrow band across the back of the head. The upper parts are dark brown, the underparts white or off-white, and the long tail is blackish, boldly barred with buffy white. The birds have large, dark brown eyes, small black bills, and yellowish ceres and legs. Unmistakable in their plain attire, Laughing Falcons are widely spread from northern Mexico to northern Argentina and eastern Brazil. In Costa Rica they range from lowlands up to, rarely, 6,000 feet (1,850 m). They frequent the more open parts of tall forests, their margins, and deforested country with scattered trees, in both humid and arid lands.

The guacos in the jacaranda trees appeared to be preparing to breed. The only nest of this raptor that I had seen, fifty-four years earlier, was in a large cavity, high in the massive trunk of a great, blasted tree at the forest's edge. Framed in the wide doorway, I could from the facing hillside

Laughing Falcon

see much of the brooding female and, when it stretched up to take food from her, a single nestling, softly clad in pale buffy down except on its face, which was black-masked like that of its parents. Morning and evening its father brought a snake, and in a nearby tree delivered this to the mother. After joining him in a prolonged duet, she ate part of the snake and shared the rest with her nestling. While I watched, a large black weasel called a tayra climbed the long, branchless trunk and killed the nestling before my shouts and gesticulations drove the predator to the ground. All this occurred while the mother sat watching in a neighboring tree, making only an ineffectual threat to the sharp-toothed intruder. When, after a long delay, she returned to the cavity, she picked up and ate her nestling's corpse, which the tayra had left intact when I chased it down. In *A Naturalist in Costa Rica* (1971), I described this exciting episode more fully.

From this and a few other published reports, it appears that Laughing

Falcons usually nest in large natural cavities with a wide doorway, high in trees, and that on the unlined floor they lay a single whitish egg, heavily covered all over with dark chocolate-brown blotches and spots, as described and figured by L. R. Wolfe (1954). This pigmentation suggests that the guaco's remote ancestors laid in open nests of sticks, as most hawks and falcons do, for primary hole-nesters, like woodpeckers, have plain white eggs.

From what I then knew, I expected that our guacos would breed in a tree cavity in the tract of rain forest that began close to the jacaranda trees. Early in February, however, it became clear that they had other intentions. In our garden, south of the house, stands a large African oil palm, with a crown of huge, massive fronds rising nearly a hundred feet (30 m) into the air. One or both of the birds rested for long intervals on the broad, spine-margined bases of the lower fronds, sometimes disappearing into a nook among them, where they had apparently chosen a nest site. I thought they were making a bad choice, but perhaps they could find nothing better.

At this season the palm bore great clusters of fruits, each with a very hard seed enveloped in a thick orange pulp, sought by a diversity of creatures. Chief among them were Black Vultures, which every morning came in numbers to feast upon the palm fruits. At intervals a troop of white-faced capuchin monkeys emerged from the forest and chased the big dusky birds from the cluster of fruits that they preferred. Cinnamon-bellied, or red-tailed, squirrels also enjoyed these fruits, as did woodpeckers and a diversity of songbirds. I have known white-faces and squirrels to eat eggs and nestlings, and probably the omnivorous Black Vultures would not disdain them. Moreover, unlike palms with crown shafts, oil palms do not cleanly shed their fronds, but persisting bases of dead leaves collect much decaying vegetable debris, in which small epiphytic plants root and ants and other stinging invertebrates thrive. Amid all these creatures large and small, the guacos' egg and chick (if it hatched) would rest precariously.

After passing much of February 14 on the palm fronds, as night approached the female guaco turned around and disappeared amid them. On the following day, she appeared to be incubating on their broad bases. We could not reach the nest about sixty feet (18 m) up on a thick, branchless trunk, nor learn how many eggs it contained. The sitting female was wholly invisible in her deep recess among the crowded fronds.

The hidden nest did not invite prolonged watches, but at any hour of the day shouts that followed each of the male's arrivals with food would alert us in the house or garden in time to look up and see what he had brought—from a porch both the palm and the jacaranda trees were visible. During the whole course of the nesting, I, other members of the household, or bird-watching tourists saw him bring thirty-eight snakes, which was probably short of the whole number that he delivered. In length these serpents ranged from an estimated foot to a yard or more (30 to 90 or more cm); in thickness, from that of a finger to that of a thumb. All were dull in color, except one coral snake or a mimic thereof. The longest and thinnest appeared to be mildly venomous lance-headed vine snakes. I could not identify the others. I did not see a slender green tree snake, a recognizable fer-de-lance (here called terciopelo), nor any other of the highly venomous species of *Bothrops* that inhabit the vicinity. A mottled black-and-yellow nest-robbing *mica* would have stood out clearly enough, but I did not see one. Possibly the young of some of these serpents were among the guaco's prey, but they often differ in appearance from the adults and I am not familiar with them. All the snakes had doubtless been decapitated before delivery to the female, for a Laughing Falcon's first act after subduing a serpent is to bite off its head, thereby making it innocuous.

Most of these snakes were probably caught on or near the ground; a guaco hunts by perching patiently on a high, exposed branch, or a succession of such perches along the woodland edge, and scanning the ground or low vegetation, to which he pounces when he spies a potential victim beneath him, sometimes so hard that F. Haverschmidt (1962) clearly heard the thud. If on closer view the snake appears too big or powerful for him to tackle, he abruptly departs, as I saw when a guaco pounced down from high in a tree upon a long mica creeping through the pasture grass below him. In addition to the thirty-eight snakes, we saw the male bring one frog, just after I had told a visitor from Canada that I had never seen a Laughing Falcon catch anything other than snakes. Of these only one, which I saw in a guaco's talons years ago, was a slender, green, arboreal snake.

The female guaco's treatment of her partner's gifts was variable. One of the first snakes that we saw him bring to her slipped from beneath a foot and fell to the ground. Diving down in pursuit, she vanished amid bushes, where I could not see whether she retrieved it. Some of the longest, slenderest snakes she swallowed whole, coiling them into herself as though they were overlong pieces of spaghetti. Other serpents, especially the thicker ones, she ate piecemeal, plucking off fragments from the anterior end while holding the body against her perch with a foot. Often her victims still writhed until the tail disappeared in her mouth. After consuming part of a snake, she might balance the remainder across a branch and return to her nest without it. Until the chick hatched, we did not see her take anything into the nest.

At this and other nests, I paid attention to the vocalizations that ensue when a male arrives with food for his consort. He calls her from the nest with a peculiar *how how how* that appears to be a greeting. Leaving her eyrie, she may respond with similar notes. Flying up to him, she receives the serpent. Sometimes she bites its already headless anterior end, as though to make sure that her partner had properly removed the dangerous fangs. Then she lays the writhing body over her perch, holding it with a foot while most of its length dangles limply below. Her mouth cleared, she is ready to join her partner in a duet. They begin by alerting one another with the low, chuckling *ha ha ha* that to some listeners resembles subdued laughter. Then both may voice long series of *wac wac wac* or sometimes *haw haw haw* notes that introduce the full duet. The male shouts his hollow-sounding *wá-co*, while his mate accompanies him with her *cá-o*. This duet, audible afar, may continue for from two or three to ten minutes before the birds fall silent. The male's *wá-co* is uttered with a double movement of his bill; the female's *cá-o* with a single opening and closing of her mouth. The sequence of notes is not always the same. The difference in the voices of the duetists may not be noticed in the voluminous sound they produce when performing close together but is clearly evident when they are well separated. This loud shouting might be interpreted as a paean celebrating the male guaco's victory over the serpent he has subdued. Heard in the distance, in the twilight or on a dark night, it is a sound of inscrutable mystery until one learns its source. The guaco's large eyes suggest nocturnal alertness.

The falcons may duet while perching only a few feet or yards apart, but sometimes they are separated by as much as fifty yards (50 m). Sometimes the female in her nest accompanies her distant spouse in the darkness of night. The cackling *ha ha ha* responsible for the English name does not carry far. The onomatopoeic name guaco (pronounced *waco*) is more appropriate for this staid and mirthless bird, for this is what we most often hear. Rarely, when well separated, they duet while the male still holds his intended gift.

In the last days of March, the female often called in a soft "complaining" voice that we had not previously noticed. Was she trying to tell her partner that her egg was hatching or had hatched? On April 1 we for the first time saw her carry a snake, an exceptionally small one, into the nest in the palm tree. This was the first definite indication that a chick had hatched, after about six weeks of incubation—a more precise determination of the incubation period could not be made in an inaccessible nest. Now the delivery of a snake to the female was not always followed by a duet, with the result that we probably missed some of these events. However, while the young guaco was growing up, the pair sometimes indulged in long duets on occasions when no snake was visible. One of these prolonged performances came after a long, hard shower in mid-afternoon. At its conclusion, the pair perched on high, exposed branches and half spread their wings, vulture fashion, to dry them, although the sky was overcast, without sunshine.

After the nestling's first few days, its mother spent more time resting on palm fronds in front of the nest, guarding, instead of brooding inside. After a few more days, she watched from high in a dead jacaranda tree, whence she had a good view of the nest site in the palm, fifty yards away. By the end of the chick's second week, she was spending much time away from the nest, which she entered to brood as daylight faded, and she left at dawn. After a few more days, she delayed her entry until it was so dark that even her white breast was hardly visible through my binocular, and she departed next morning so early that she was but a dim and shadowy figure. She continued to accompany the young guaco at night until it was about twenty-five days old. Now, instead of remaining in the nest after taking in a snake and probably feeding it to the nestling, she left it there for the young bird to eat alone, and promptly departed.

I was interested in the guacos' interactions with the creatures that frequented their palm tree. To the small birds and the squirrels, they paid not the slightest attention. Once, while the male perched on the rachis of a frond, a squirrel ran along it beneath him, almost over his toes, without making him stir. With the Black Vultures, larger than the guacos, they soon established a *modus vivendi*. They chased the black scavengers from near the nest but did not molest those eating palm fruits in other parts of the spreading crown. After the nestling grew older, the mother took a snake to it in front of a resting vulture. One evening, when the male found six vultures perching in "his" jacaranda tree, he chased three of them for a short distance through the air but paid no attention to the other three. This was the only aerial pursuit that I witnessed.

Likewise, the monkeys and the guacos soon found that they could share the palm tree. A few days after incubation began, loud, almost soprano cries, different from any that I had previously heard from a Laughing Falcon, were traced to the female in the palm. A party of white-faces had invaded the tree to eat the ripe fruits and she protested their presence, as my son saw. When I arrived, she was no longer visible, having evidently reentered her nook, where she remained silent and invisible while, for the next half hour, the monkeys continued to feast in the palm. Toward noon of the following day, similar high-pitched cries, followed by the guaco's *ha ha ha*, evoked a Rufous Piha's sharp comment. Our housemaid, who had watched from the porch, reported that the guaco had sallied from her nest to chase the monkeys, without pecking them. When I looked up, the bird and the mammals were resting peaceably close together. Soon she returned to her nest, while the monkeys remained in the palm. At sunrise on a morning about a fortnight after the nestling hatched, I found a few monkeys eating palm fruits, while the pair of falcons watched from a jacaranda tree, complaining loudly but making no move to chase the primates away from the nest, which the monkeys did not enter. As long as the nestling remained, a guaco might voice a loud alarm note, followed by a quaver, when a monkey approached. I never saw a monkey show interest in the nest.

On two mornings, as the male guaco rested in a jacaranda tree, holding a snake while waiting for his mate to appear, a Tropical Gnatcatcher flew repeatedly back and forth above him, sometimes swooping close over his head. The tiny bird appeared to be catching insects attracted by the carrion but too small for me to detect so far away. Possibly, however, the gnatcatcher was protesting the presence of the guaco, who continued to hold the snake in statuesque immobility. If in fact the flitting mite was "mobbing" the falcon, this was the only interaction I saw between a guaco and another bird, other than the vultures in the palm.

With the insects and other arthropods that probably infested the debris amid the bases of the old palm fronds, and increased as filth accumulated in a nest that was not cleaned, interactions were more obscure. One evening while incubation continued, loud, high-pitched wails, followed by a mournful liquid quaver, drew our attention to the nest as the female sallied from it. We saw no cause for her distress but surmised that an ant or a scorpion had stung her. After a few minutes she returned to her egg. A similar incident occurred after the nestling hatched. On another occasion the mother emerged from her nook and appeared to pluck things, possibly ants, from her legs.

Through most of April, the unseen nestling seemed to thrive. When it was about ten days old, we first heard its infantine voice issuing from the palm. As it grew older, its calls when hungry became louder. At the month's end, however, it was apparent that all was not well. On the morning of April 27, the father brought a snake to the jacaranda tree and called loudly, with no response from his partner. After waiting in silence for a time, he carried the snake to the palm and appeared to eat it while standing in front of the nest—obstructing fronds prevented a clear view. Then he flew away. The following morning, he brought to the jacaranda a very slender snake about two feet long, which, after calling often and loudly without attracting his consort, he carried to a palm frond about two yards from the nest. While for many minutes he stood there holding the serpent, the chick continued to call feebly; but instead of feeding it, he flew away, leaving the snake dangling from a frond. On April 29 he brought another snake to a jacaranda tree and called. When, after an hour, the female failed to appear, he devoured it. On April's last day, he again brought a snake to a jacaranda, called more briefly, and after a shorter delay disappeared into the forest with it. On neither of these two occasions did he approach the silent nest. That his neglectful partner still lived was evident when the two dueted in the afternoon of this day. Thereafter, they abandoned the locality where we had seen or heard them daily during the preceding four months.

Why did the young guaco succumb? Neither the vultures nor the monkeys were responsible for its demise. Its father continued, as many birds do, to bring food for several days after the nestling died, or at least had become too moribund to utter sounds audible to me. However, before this, he stood holding his snakes in front of the nest, waiting for his partner to come and take them from him, without, as far as I saw, ever trying to find the calling nestling in its hidden recess. Possibly, in a more exposed cavity, such as guacos occupy in dicotyledonous trees, he would have found and fed his progeny. Possibly, also, male Laughing Falcons—like males of the Pearl Kites studied by Richard ffrench (1982) in Trinidad, the Sharp-shinned Hawks watched in Puerto Rico by Carlos A. Delannoy and Alexander Cruz (1988), and other raptors—never feed nestlings directly but always through the agency of their mates. However this may be, it is evident that the male guaco's faithfulness was not matched by his intelligence; a more mentally alert bird would have tried to locate his progeny crying for food so near him. In *King Solomon's Ring* Konrad Lorenz (1952: p.51) wrote that "all true birds of prey are, compared with passerines or parrots, extremely stupid creatures." He considered the Golden Eagle to be one of the most stupid among them all, "much more so indeed than any barnyard fowl." Perhaps the snake-eating guaco is not much brighter.

Probably we must blame the mother guaco for the loss of her nestling. She was certainly neglectful during its last days. Possibly she remained aloof because her nest had become so infested with small stinging creatures that it was no longer habitable, and she perforce left her unfledged progeny to succumb to their attacks. If this be true, the insalubrity of the site was, as I had suspected that it might be, ultimately responsible for the nest's failure. In an earlier year, I had watched a pair of Slaty-tailed Trogons trying to excavate a nest cavity amid the debris at the base of this oil palm's crown, only to abandon the undertaking (Chapter 1). I regretted the young guaco's demise, not only because it abruptly terminated a most interesting study but also because it deprived our avian community of another protector from snakes, which nearly everywhere, except in the Arctic, high altitudes, and on remote islands, are a major enemy of nesting birds.

Through the remainder of the year 1991, we occasionally saw or heard the Laughing Falcons in the vicinity, and toward the year's end they became more vocal and visible. On December 26 we saw the male give a snake to his consort for the first time since the failure of their nest. By December 30, the female appeared to be incubating in the same tall palm, in a nest as invisible as her former one. Events followed their familiar course until February 5, 1992, when the female carried a small, thin snake into the palm tree, suggesting that her egg had hatched, again about six weeks after it was laid. Before the month's end, the nestling had apparently succumbed. Since during this nesting the palm bore no fruit to attract Black Vultures, white-faced monkeys, or squirrels, none of these creatures was suspected as the cause of the nestling's demise. A few days later, the guacos began to visit the slightly lower oil palm north of the house, and by the first week of March, the female was incubating there. Through March, April, and early May, the parents continued to bring snakes to this palm, then abandoned it.

In early January of the following year, 1993, the pair again nested in the palm to the north, failed, and for the third time laid in the palm to the south, with no better luck. Toward the end of the year, we nailed a spacious wooden box, partly closed in front, as high up the massive trunk of the south palm as we could reach with our longest ladder but still well below its lofty crown, hoping that the falcons would nest in a cleaner site. Ignoring our proffered gift, in the first week of January, 1994, they again nested among the fronds of the north palm, only to abandon this undertaking before the month's end. None of their six nestings, three in each of our two oil palms, continued longer than the first, when the nestling succumbed about seventy-three days after incubation began. From this it appears improbable that from any of these nests the young bird fledged and promptly flew beyond our ken. Although the guacos remain within hearing, we have not found another nest.

In the four years when the Laughing Falcons nested in the palms, we saw them bring seventy-five snakes, one frog, and one large lizard. Throughout its range, snakes appear to be the preferred food of this falcon. In Nicaragua, Thomas Howell (1957) took a small rodent's skull from a guaco's stomach, the only mention of other than cold-blooded prey that I know.

Holes in trees are the Laughing Falcon's preferred nest sites, but in arid regions where trunks are rarely thick enough to contain cavities adequate to accommodate birds as large as guacos, they may nest in more open situations. In the department of Lambayeque, Peru, Mark Robbins and David Wiedenfeld (1982) found a nest forty feet (12 m) above the ground in a crotch formed by three radiating limbs of a tree and shaded from the midday sunshine by two epiphytic cacti. Like the nests in cavities, this contained no material brought by the birds; the single nestling rested in the bare crotch. In the dry Ancón district of southwestern Ecuador, S. Marchant (1960) discovered one guaco egg in a spacious open nest attributed to the Red-backed Hawk or the Northern Caracara. I have found no record of a larger clutch.

In many ways, the Laughing Falcon is a unique raptor, milder-tempered than others. Female hawks and falcons tend to be substantially larger than males, apparently to enable them to defend nestlings from their fathers, who might devour the young if permitted close approach to the nest (Amadon 1959). The male Laughing Falcon is the same size as or slightly larger than his consort. Frequent duets, apparently unknown in other diurnal raptors, promote a more intimate association of the sexes than is usual in birds of prey. Bolder raptors attack, and can severely lacerate, the person who climbs to their eyrie. The female guaco at my first nest made only one feeble effort to drive the tayra from the high trunk where it killed her nestling, perhaps because she lacked sufficient maneuverability to confront the sharp-toothed weasel. Once I watched a guaco descend to a pasture, apparently to pick up some small item that I did not see well, a few yards from a domestic hen. Neither gave the least attention to the other. When an immature Collared Forest-Falcon suddenly alighted in a tree where a pair of guacos were dueting, without attacking them, they promptly moved to more distant perches to continue their performance. The presence in a sanctuary of modest size of a pair of raptors of most kinds can cause the loss of resident species. A pair of Laughing Falcons is welcome, for they will reduce the number of snakes that plunder so many nests, but these falcons never molest their feathered neighbors.

CHAPTER 4 ❧

When Less Yields More

As I walked along a woodland trail, a startled Great Tinamou rose from the ground ahead of me. The stout gray-brown bird hurtled through the tree trunks with noisy wing beats that were answered by a sharp whistle from somewhere overhead. After the tinamou had disappeared amid the ferny ground cover, I scanned the crowns of the towering trees of the rain forest for a glimpse of the whistle's author. After much searching, my binocular picked out a plain reddish brown bird about the size of an American Robin or a Eurasian Blackbird: the Rufous Piha, a member of the tropical American cotinga family.

Rufous Pihas stay so constantly in the leafy upper levels of tall forests, from southern Mexico to Ecuador, that they are heard much more often than seen. In addition to the *pee-ha* that suggested their name, they utter a loud, shrill, far-carrying *peeer;* a tripartite whistle that sounds like *whee-er-wit;* a short, loud trill; and a longer, more musical trill. Not only the tinamou's whirring wings but almost any sudden sound, such as a peal of thunder, a human shout or sneeze, a handclap, or a dry branch snapping sharply underfoot, may evoke their whistled comment, even at times when the woodland silence is broken only by the cicada's insistent *chirrilin.* Unsocial birds, pihas do not flock, but each male appears to have his own part of the verdant canopy, where he can be heard day after day for months together. Females closely resemble males in plumage, and their notes are similar but weaker. Both sexes use their voices sparingly. They eat fruits and small invertebrates—insects, spiders, scorpions—all of which they pluck from twig or foliage by an outward dart, without alighting, in the usual manner of cotingas.

Rufous Piha

Like many other members of their family, including bellbirds, umbrel-labirds, and calfbirds, Rufous Pihas do not join in cooperating pairs; females attend their nests and young without a partner. The males' loud, reiterated calls in the treetops appear to be for the purpose of announcing possession of territory and attracting females, but little is known of their territorial habits or their courtship. Only after I had been familiar with these birds for many years did I see behavior that I interpreted as courtship.

On January 7, 1988, while I led a nature tour through the forest at Los Cusingos, four of us watched two pihas perching close together on a branch much lower than where one usually sees these birds, except females at their nests. The two followed each other through mid-levels of the forest. One plucked a berry and presented it to the other. Then the same bird caught an insect, beat it against a branch, and gave it to the second piha. Probably the donor was a male and the recipient a female, but we detected no difference between them. The date was early in the year for courtship, but so long after the termination of the known breeding season that it appeared unlikely that a parent was feeding her well-grown progeny. Moreover, the recipient did not act like a young bird of the preceding year receiving food. For over an hour these two pihas continued to move through the forest together, but we witnessed no more feedings. When we last saw them, they were about fifty yards from the point where we had first noticed them.

Well after sunrise on the next six mornings, I found two pihas together in the same part of the forest. On some days they soon vanished in the high canopy, but on others they followed each other through lower trees, at intervals resting close together at no great height, occasionally voicing a soft trill. One morning they perched quietly for twenty minutes, a few inches apart, on an exposed branch above the trail, where each preened itself and at long intervals called softly. Then one flew away, but it soon returned to the other on the same branch. After a week of apparent courtship, I no longer found them together. The males of a number of other cotingas, including the closely related Screaming Piha of South America, gather in vociferous assemblies, called leks, to attract females with developing eggs to a conspicuous, well-known spot for mating. More widely scattered through the forest, Rufous Pihas do not cooperate in this fashion; and aside from the foregoing episode, nothing appears to be known about their courtship.

A Pale-billed Woodpecker was responsible for the discovery of the first recorded nest of the Rufous Piha, on the last morning of May, forty years ago. As my wife and I were emerging into a pasture from a walk through the forest, we stopped to look for the big woodpecker revealing its presence with loud double taps far above. While engaged in the search for the elusive woodpecker, I noticed a piha resting motionless on a low branch, in a posture that did not seem right for a perching bird. Only careful scrutiny through my binocular disclosed that it was sitting on something that might have been a nest. Although it could hardly have failed to notice us, the bird remained immobile for so long that we resumed our walk, leaving it undisturbed. When I returned nearly an hour later, the piha was still resting exactly as we had found her. I continued to watch for another hour until, after increasing signs of restlessness, the bird flew obliquely upward, revealing a nest that amazed me by its slightness.

In subsequent years, I have found six more nests of the piha, five in the same forest where the first was situated, one in the Caribbean rain forest of Costa Rica. In height they ranged from about 17 to 35 feet (5 to 11 m) above the ground, well below the level where pihas spend most of their time, but where they are more sheltered from breezes that might shake eggs from such shallow receptacles. A nest begun at about 40 feet (12 m) was never finished. Each nest was a nearly flat pad about 3 inches (7.5 cm) in diameter by somewhat less than one inch (2.5 cm) thick. Supported between or upon two or more thin horizontal twigs well out from the trunks of small understory trees, or in one instance on a mossy branch about 1.5 inches thick, these were the most meager arboreal nests that I have seen. Some of the wiry tendrils, often coiled, of which they were made clutched a twig or a petiole.

The builder brings these pieces at long intervals, then spends time and energy, slowly and patiently arranging these recalcitrant items—energy that other birds would devote to gathering more materials. One piha worked for forty minutes, pulling up and tucking in projecting ends and loops of tendrils that stubbornly refused to stay where she put them. Never before had I watched a bird try so hard to arrange so little. Despite widely spaced visits with materials, a nest was virtually completed three or four days after the first piece was placed. Reduced to the smallest size compatible with its function of holding a single egg or nestling, it was likewise composed of the irreducible minimum of materials. Canopied above by foliage but often clearly visible from the ground, pihas' nests are poorly concealed but inconspicuous because they are so tiny.

Fortunately for my studies, these nests were so thin that I could learn their contents by looking up through the meshes of the bottom, for I could hardly climb to any of them without shaking out the egg. The lowest nests could also be examined by raising a small mirror attached to a long, slender pole. No nest contained more than one egg, which was smoky gray or grayish brown, heavily blotched and mottled all over with darker brown, which on the thicker end nearly masked the ground color. I picked up both parts of a fallen shell from which the nestling had just escaped and, fitting them together, found that the egg measured about 31 by 22 millimeters.

I wished to learn how an incubating piha avoids knocking out the egg that appears to rest so precariously on her narrow, shallow nest. In mid-August, my son and I alternately watched a nest throughout a day with a sunny morning and an afternoon of the long, hard rain usual at this season. All day the piha left her nest only four times, for long recesses of 33, 3, 72, and 54 minutes. Her three intervening sessions of incubation lasted 112, 54, and 128 minutes. Returning from her last absence at 1:20 P.M., she sat steadily through the remainder of the day, not leaving the nest after the rain stopped around four o'clock in the afternoon, when she could have sought food among trees still dripping beneath a darkly overcast sky. From 5:44 A.M., when the woods had become light enough for foraging, to 5:44

P.M., when daylight was fading beneath the trees, the piha had covered her egg for 77.5 percent of the twelve hours, which is high constancy for a cotinga. Another piha incubated for 80.5 percent of a six-hour morning, with sessions of 73, 57, and 147 minutes and recesses of 22, 11, and 34 minutes.

Returning from an outing, the piha usually fluttered down from higher trees to a branch near her nest, where she paused to look carefully around, turning her head slowly from side to side. Then she might advance to a point nearer the nest to continue her scrutiny, or she might go directly to it. Gently she hopped onto her nest, to alight with her feet on either side of the egg. Spreading her abdominal feathers until her bare brood patch appeared in their midst, she settled on her egg. The fluffy feathers of her flanks stood up prominently above the edges of her wings, and other downy feathers overlapped the sides of the nest, almost hiding it. She sat rather upright, often looking around from side to side. When alarmed or suspicious, she stretched up her neck and held her upraised head nearly motionless, appearing strained and alert. Reassured, she contracted her neck to assume a more relaxed posture.

Although alert to sounds and movements in the surrounding forest, this and other pihas incubating an egg or brooding a nestling were fearless of humans. I could walk beneath the lowest of the nests without causing the bird's departure. One piha, having built her nest about twenty feet above a forest path, remained on her egg while a party of a dozen people stood looking up at her, talking the while, then walked directly beneath her. I never found it necessary to conceal myself in a blind while I sat for hours watching a piha's nest.

The parent's reluctance to leave made it difficult to learn when her eggs hatched. Tapping lightly on the slender trunk of the nest tree or gently shaking the foliage of a sapling close beside it did not make her budge. I feared that if I used more drastic means to drive her from the nest, she might leave abruptly and throw out the egg, which I could see through the bottom only when she was absent. Accordingly, to examine the nest I had to wait, often for a long while, until the piha flew off spontaneously, or else I had to return repeatedly.

While the piha was at or near the nest, all her movements were slow and careful, as indeed they needed to be for the safety of her egg. I never saw an incubating piha turn the egg beneath her with her bill, as many birds do. In view of the slightness of the nest, this omission seemed prudent. At intervals she slid her abdomen over the nest from side to side, a movement of slight amplitude, much like that of a broody hen, apparently made to adjust the egg to her brood patch. From time to time she rotated in the nest, to face in a different direction, or she preened her plumage; but through a long, wet afternoon the bird that we watched sat in the same position, her body upright. Rarely, the sitting piha called loudly. After she had been incubating a long while, her sideward movements became more frequent and she turned her head increasingly. Sometimes she would become still again, but often this restlessness presaged her departure. Then she would rise slightly, fold down the fluffy feathers that projected over the edges of her remiges, and give her wings a few preliminary beats before she flew right up from her egg, much as a hummingbird leaves her nest. Usually she rose obliquely through the forest, but sometimes she chose a downward course. Sometimes a piha about to fly from her nest seems to shake the egg from between her abdominal feathers, or to disengage toes that have become caught in the tendrils.

Repeatedly, after the female had vanished into the foliage of the treetops, I heard a shrill whistle, sometimes followed by a trill, which I ascribed to her. Often it was answered by another whistle. This occurred at two nests, and suggested that the female might maintain contact with the male in whose territory she nested. However, nothing that I saw during more than seventy hours of sustained watching during building, incubation, and rearing the young at six nests, plus many short visits, suggested that a second parent took an interest in nesting.

At two nests found before the egg was laid, I was able to learn how long it took to hatch. At one, the incubation period could not have been less than 24 days and 20 hours nor more than 25 days and 23 hours. At the other nest it was between 25 days and 18 hours and 26 days and 18 hours. Twenty-five or 26 days is an amazingly long incubation period for a passerine bird about the size of an American Robin, whose eggs hatch in 12 or 13 days; but the periods of other cotingas are as long as for the piha, or longer. Probably the poor insulation provided by the piha's thin, unlined nest is at least in part responsible for the slow embryonic development, but doubtless genetic factors are also involved. If pihas' eggs were not so difficult to obtain, it would be interesting to learn how long they would take to hatch if incubated by a finch or tanager in a well-padded nest. One advantage of the piha's loosely made nest is that it dries more promptly after frequent tropical showers than a thicker nest could do.

At one nest I was present when the egg hatched. As I arrived in the middle of the morning, the parent was sitting restlessly, frequently rising up to look beneath herself. Soon, when she stood up, I could see through my binocular that the chick was breaking out of the egg. At 9:30 the parent picked up the empty shell, the parts of which hung together, and dropped it from the nest while she continued to sit. Most passerine birds carry empty shells to a distance or eat them, but this less careful method of disposal appears to be habitual with pihas, for I found the shell directly below another nest in which the egg had just hatched.

After dropping the empty shell from the nest at 9:30, the mother continued to sit, frequently rising up to look at her hatchling beneath her. Finally, at 10:40, she spread her wings and rose from the nest to the treetops. The nestling's light gray down was already dry and stood up prominently on its head and back, too sparse to conceal its pink skin. It tumbled about on its narrow hammock but avoided the edge. After an absence of three-quarters of an hour, its mother descended from the treetops with a small object barely visible in the tip of her bill. Standing beside the nest, she gave the young piha its first meal, two hours after it hatched. Then she stepped onto the nest to brood it.

A few days later, this nestling had vanished. Fortunately, seventeen years earlier, I had studied the care and development of the young at the first nest, where the egg hatched a day or two after I found it. For a passerine of medium size, this nestling received an unusual amount of brooding. Until eleven days old, it was covered almost as constantly as the egg at the later nest was incubated, its mother sometimes sitting over it for more than two hours, once for nearly three. Although when seventeen days old it was fairly well feathered, two days later, on a morning that was at first lightly clouded and then sunny, the nineteen-day-old piha was brooded nearly half the time, including one session that continued for seventy minutes. When the nestling was twenty-five days old, and again on the following day, I found the mother covering it while rain fell in the late afternoon. She was present on the nest at dawn of the twenty-seventh day after the nestling hatched. Although she did not brood during the dark, misty forenoon that followed, she rested close beside the nest for long intervals. Thus, the young bird was covered through its next-to-last night on the nest; for its final night, I lack observations. Its mother was a most attentive parent.

The nestling's meals were widely spaced but substantial. The rate of feeding ranged from three times during the first six hours of daylight when it was one day old to eleven times when it was twenty-seven days old, or from 0.5 to 1.8 times per hour. Each meal consisted of a single item, brought visibly in the parent's bill. For her day-old chick, she plucked large green insects from the foliage, then beat or rubbed them against her perch before she took them to the nest. The nestling received its third meal for the day at 8:32 A.M. Five minutes later, it was given another green insect but delayed so long to swallow this that the mother took it from the nestling and presently ate the prey herself. Then she settled down to brood and remained for two hours and forty-eight minutes, bringing no more food that morning.

When the nestling was five days old, its diet was varied with a large berry and a small scorpion. At eleven days, the young piha was receiving, in addition to insects, spiders of impressive size and large green fruits that were probably the nutritious drupes of a tree of the laurel family. In the following days, fruits became increasingly prominent in its fare. On the last morning that I watched, the twenty-seven-day-old piha received, in six hours, five fruits, four insects, and two unrecognized items. Unlike nestlings of other species, this one rarely seemed eager for its meals; even after it was feathered, it did not greet the parent's arrival by promptly stretching up a gaping mouth with a brightly colored lining. On the contrary, it often delayed a good fraction of a minute, and sometimes for several minutes, before opening its bill. On the day before the nestling flew, its mother rested beside the nest, holding a small, unidentified object, for forty-nine minutes before the youngster took it. Probably the nestling accepted its meals so sluggishly because it was always so well fed. Moreover, in the absence of competing nest mates, a quick response was not needed to assure a meal. Whatever the reason, the young piha's silent, restrained acceptance of food did not draw attention to itself, as clamorous hungry nestlings often do.

The parent kept the nest clean by consistently swallowing the nestling's droppings until the young bird was over three weeks old. On its last full day in the nest, I twice saw it void its excreta over the side, just after it was fed. On each occasion, the parent dived after the dropping, caught it in the air, and carried it away.

As already mentioned, the newly hatched piha was pink with sparse gray down on its head and back, the only parts that I could see well from the ground. When it was five days old, I saw it flap its stubby wings a few times. Its feathering was so slow, for a passerine bird, that when eleven days old it was still largely naked. Six days later, it was fairly well covered with plumage. When nineteen days old, it pushed its fore parts out in front of its brooding mother and vigorously beat its wings. Twice the active preening of the restless young bird seemed to cause the parent's departure. When I or some smaller animal walked beneath the nest, it stretched up its neck and stood motionless in this posture, just as the adult did when alarmed. Once, as the youngster stood so, its mother alighted beside it with a big green fruit in her bill. Slowly the young bird sank down to the resting posture, then opened its mouth to receive the food.

On its next-to-last day in the nest, the young piha was restless, moving around, preening much, often flapping its wings, and from time to time walking out on a supporting twig for an inch or two beyond the nest, only to return promptly. When a parent called, the youngster replied with a similar trilled whistle, higher in pitch. Now it stood rather than lay in the nest. At sunrise on the following morning, I found it standing in this fashion. By noon it had flown, aged twenty-eight or possibly twenty-nine days. Although much smaller than an adult, it resembled one in plumage.

In the Caribbean lowlands of Costa Rica, another parent piha behaved much the same as the foregoing one in the valley of El General on the Pacific slope. In five morning hours she fed her downy nestling, a few days old, only four times. The only item that I recognized in her bill was a cicada, which escaped as she passed it to her nestling but was caught in the air by her swift outward dart and swallowed by her offspring. Neither by shouting nor by clapping my hands could I make the parent budge from her nest twenty feet above my head. By such steadfast sitting, a piha avoids brushing her egg from the nest, as alarmed pigeons often do when they burst from their broader but shallow structures.

The Rufous Piha takes an amazingly long while to rear her single nestling. Allowing five days for building, an interval of six days between the virtual completion of the nest and laying the egg, twenty-five or twenty-six days for incubation, and twenty-eight days for the nestling period, at least sixty-four days elapse from beginning the nest to the fledgling's departure. This is nearly twice as long as the piha's neighbor, the Garden Thrush, or Clay-colored Robin, a bird of about the same size, takes to raise a brood of two or three, with her mate's help but in a much more substantial nest, in a plantation or dooryard rather than in the forest. In a long breeding season—in El General this extends from late February into September—a piha has time to produce two or possibly three broods. A piha starting a nest in late July was accompanied by a stubby-tailed fledgling, apparently her own from an earlier nest in the same season. Although a piha may nest several times in a year, it is probably rare for her to rear more than one fledgling because, as with other birds of tropical rain forest, most nests fail; of the five pihas' nests of which I know the outcome, only the first that I found escaped predation until the young flew.

Rufous Pihas have the curious habit of dismantling their empty nests and scattering the tendrils that compose them. I watched one parent carry in various directions pieces of a nest that evidently had been successful, for near it she fed a fledgling that had apparently left it a few days earlier. Some of the nests that suffered predation were also torn apart, most likely by the parents who had lost their egg or nestling rather than by the predator. Both Lovely Cotingas and Blue Cotingas have been watched tearing apart nests from which their young had just been lost, an act which in this circumstance looked like a gesture of despair. Many birds pull from an old nest materials for a new one, but this is not the way of pihas and cotingas, who drop the pieces to the ground. In Africa, male Village Weavers demolish unused nests to build others more likely to attract females, in the same desirable sites amid the colony, but this can hardly be the motive of the pihas, who have no lack of sites in suitable forest trees and have not been known to use the same tree twice. We can only surmise why pihas and other cotingas dismantle their empty nests (Skutch 1969).

If they escape the perils of their callow immaturity, pihas, like other birds of tropical forests, probably survive well. Accurate censusing of birds that lurk mostly unseen in the high umbrageous canopy of rain forests, where one can walk beneath them repeatedly without detecting a sign of their presence, is exceedingly difficult if not impossible, but in the hundred-acre tract where most of my studies were made, pihas appear to be the most abundant birds of their size or larger.

As frequently happens in small, isolated sanctuaries, we have lost species of birds over the years, but pihas still announce their presence in the treetops. Paradoxically, I attribute their continuing abundance to their low rate of reproduction. Even in this evergreen forest, the time of abundant fruits and insects, early in a rainy season of about nine months' duration, is followed by a leaner period toward the year's end, when fruits edible by birds are much scarcer, and insects seem to be less numerous. If pihas produced many young during the season of plenty, they might so reduce their resources during the ensuing months of scarcity that many would starve, with the result that they would enter the next breeding season with a smaller rather than a larger population. By rearing one nestling at a time, at a leisurely pace, pihas maintain a stable population that they probably could not increase by becoming more fecund (Skutch 1969).

The restrained reproduction of pihas contributes in another way to the maintenance of a thriving population, in balance with its resources. An influential school of thought, led by the late David Lack (1954) of Oxford University, contended that animals of all kinds rear as many young as they can adequately nourish, simply because the more fecund strains, or genotypes, in a population will in time supplant the less prolific. Birds were held to rear broods as large as they could properly attend, even if this led to an excessive number of individuals with resultant high mortality, especially among juveniles. In northern lands where many young may be needed to compensate for losses during severe winters or on migration, parents of large broods work so hard that they lose weight and probably shorten their lives. Moreover, absorbed in the pressing task of finding food for many dependents, they are less careful of their own safety and more readily overtaken by predators.

Now it is increasingly recognized that, not by rearing the largest broods they can manage but by laying fewer eggs, nourishing fewer young, and conserving their energy, birds may live through more breeding seasons and, in the long run, leave more progeny than if they squandered their vital resources on large broods. Sometimes birds with small broods rear more young per nest than neighbors of the same species attempting to rear larger broods that they cannot adequately nourish, with the result that more nestlings succumb, as has been demonstrated of Mountain Bluebirds in Montana and Common Amakihis in Hawaii. Female Rufous Pihas certainly do not overtask themselves building their skimpy nests and feeding one nestling that has a moderate appetite because it develops slowly. Accordingly, they should live long if they can avoid predators. I have never seen a predatory bird, mammal, or reptile capture a piha. These plainly clad birds of the treetops remind me of the many advantages of a restrained rate of reproduction, adjusted to the long-term carrying capacity of an animal's habitat.

CHAPTER 5 ☿

A Melodious Saltator

Often one aspect of a bird we have long studied or briefly seen remains most vivid in memory. I remember some for the beauty of their
plumage, some for their elaborate nests, some for the circumstances of
my first meeting with them, and some for their voices. Among the last-
mentioned are Grayish Saltators, whose delightful songs that I heard long
ago on the Caribbean coast of Honduras remain fresh in mind. My favorite of their large repertoire was *chic ă chicree*, the second syllable short, the
final *ree* prolonged. Frequently two rather nasal notes preluded a more
whistled and musical verse, the whole sounding like *chuc chic whit-o-wheee*.
Sometimes I heard a saltator sing *whic chic-whic whic whic whic whic whic
whic;* but ever and again he reverted to what appeared to be his (and my)
preferred song, *chic ă chicree*. Often these notes suggested a sweetly melancholy mood.

Grayish Saltators on Guatemala's Pacific slope repeated a similar phrase
and prolonged the final note into a full, melodious trill: *weet-o-wa tre-e-
e-e-e.* This beautiful song was often followed incongruously by a rapid
chatter. Songs that I heard in Mexico, in southern Veracruz and on the Pacific slope of Chiapas, were less melodious. A saltator nesting in a bougainvillea bush outside our bedroom window on a Venezuelan farm was
heard by my wife to sing *look now, you're a great big girl.* If this is rapidly
repeated in a soft, feminine voice, it is an excellent paraphrase of the saltator's song. From the female I have heard only a low, somewhat sibilant *whi
whi whi.*

The songful Grayish Saltator is a welcome denizen of a tropical garden.
About eight inches (20 cm) long, both sexes are brownish gray on their

Grayish Saltator

upper parts, wings, and tail, or olivaceous gray in some South American races. A white streak arches above each eye. The white throat is bordered on the sides by black mustachial stripes, without a band across the chest. The breast is pale grayish. The sides and flanks are gray tinged with buff, which merges into cinnamon-buff on the abdomen and under tail coverts. The eyes are brown, the bill and feet black. Grayish Saltators weigh about two ounces (52 to 63 g). Immature birds are more greenish above; their eyebrows are tinged with yellow; and their yellowish green breasts are distinctly streaked. They might be mistaken for young Streaked Saltators.

This finch has a wide but discontinuous distribution. Northern forms, formerly known as *Saltator grandis*, range from the Mexican states of Sinaloa and Tamaulipas to central Costa Rica but are apparently absent from the Pacific slope of Nicaragua. Southern races, the *Saltator coerulescens* group, spread widely over South America from the Caribbean coast to northern Argentina, east of the Andes except in northern Colombia. In altitude the species ranges from coastal lowlands to about 6,000 feet (1,850 m) above sea level in Costa Rica. In pairs or family groups, Grayish Saltators frequent gardens, plantations, thickets, savannas with clumps of bushes, light open woods, and clearings in tall forests. They prefer country with moderate rainfall. In Venezuela this saltator is called *paraulata ajicera*.

Like other saltators, the Grayish is largely vegetarian. In northern Venezuela, I watched a pair stuffing themselves with tender young shoots of a cucurbitaceous vine, giving some to a young Streaked Saltator they had somehow adopted, as big as they and already able to help itself to the same food. In addition to tender leaves, buds, berries, and other fruits, they eat many flowers. Beside Lake Atitlán in the Guatemalan highlands, I watched a pair take the large, fleshy blossoms of a leguminous vine (probably a species of *Clitoria*), and those of a morning glory (Convolvulaceae), crushing them in bills moistened with their sap and swallowing them whole. In Trinidad, ffrench (1973) often saw Grayish Saltators eating leaves and flowers of such garden plants as hibiscus, bougainvillea, and *Clitoria*. Insects, including ants and weevils, round out the saltators' diet. To know that saltators nourish song with flowers should delight poets.

I have found six nests of Grayish Saltators, two in the Caribbean lowlands of Honduras, one in Costa Rica at an altitude of 4,600 feet (1,400 m), and three in northern Venezuela at about 1,400 feet (425 m). The earliest of these nests contained an egg on March 30, in Venezuela. The latest nests, one in Venezuela and one in Honduras, cradled nestlings at the end of July. In height these nests ranged from eight to twelve feet (2.4 to 3.7 m). All were in cultivated plants, including a bougainvillea with densely tangled branches, an orange tree, a *Bauhinia* tree, a kola nut tree, and on the frond of a date palm in a garden. A nest in Honduras was a thick-walled open cup, with a loose foundation of long, richly branched twigs supporting an inner layer of compacted bamboo leaves. The inside dimensions were three inches in diameter by two and a half inches deep (7.6 by 6.4 cm). In Trinidad, nests, well hidden from six to twelve feet (1.8 to 3.6 m) up in leafy bushes or hedges, were of similar size and had a middle layer of broad dead leaves and a lining of fine fibers.

On this island thirty-two nests were recorded from March to October, but most held eggs in May or June (Belcher and Smooker 1937). In Suriname, Haverschmidt (1968) found eggs from January to June. In the tropics the set appears nearly always to consist of two eggs, rarely three in Trinidad; but south of the Tropic of Capricorn in Córdoba, Argentina, three are not unusual (De la Peña 1979). Bright blue or greenish blue, marked with black spots, blotches, and fine wavy scrawls in a wreath around the thicker end, these eggs are outstandingly beautiful. They measure 25.0–29.4 by 18.5–20.0 millimeters. An exceptionally large egg in Trinidad was 30 by 21 millimeters. The few available measurements, from Honduras to Córdoba, do not suggest a significant regional variation in size.

In Honduras, I watched a nest with eggs for three hours of a morning. As in saltators that I have studied more thoroughly because they live here in El General where Grayish Saltators are absent, only the female incubated. She took four sessions of 10 to 56 minutes, with absences of 2 to 49 minutes. She covered her eggs for 60.7 percent of my vigil. Her shortest absence occurred when she jumped from the nest to help her mate chase away another Grayish Saltator who appeared in a nearby tree. As she left her nest, and occasionally while sitting, she called with her low *whi whi whi*. Her partner did not respond to this call but throughout the morning continued to sing profusely in surrounding trees. He did not feed his mate while I watched, but Haverschmidt saw a male give food to his partner before she laid her eggs.

I passed a few hours watching a nest with one nine-day-old nestling and an unhatched egg. Far from shy, the mother returned to her nest only five minutes after I had set up and entered my blind. She alone brooded, and she gave the nestling most of its meals, red berries and pieces of larger fruits. More timid than his consort, the male would approach the nest only while she sat in it. On one occasion he gave to her, in a neighboring bush, food that she took to her nestling. As at the earlier nest, he was irrepressibly songful, continuing to fill the air with his dulcet notes even with his mouth full of food. The mother brooded the nestling through the night until it was twelve days old and well feathered. At this age it jumped from the nest when a boy climbed up to look at it. On the following day it perched on a nearby twig but returned to the nest in the evening. It finally departed at the age of fifteen days, as the Buff-throated Saltator frequently does (Skutch 1954).

CHAPTER 6 🌸

The Tinkling Hummingbird

Amid woods of pines, oaks, alders, and other broad-leaved trees on the Sierra de Tecpán in west-central Guatemala, I spent the whole of the year 1933. Of the seven species of hummingbirds that I found there, the White-eared was the most abundant. Only three and a half inches (9 cm) long, the male is scintillating green. A broad white streak from behind each eye to the side of the neck contrasts with his blackish head. His forehead and chin are violet, at least when viewed from directly in front; from any other angle they are as dark as his head. His straight bill, of moderate length, is red, tipped with black. The more plainly attired female wears less conspicuous whitish head stripes. Her underparts are pale gray. Green-tipped feathers make her throat and sides appear scaly. From near the Mexican border in Arizona, New Mexico, and western Texas, where they occasionally appear, White-ears range over the highlands of Middle America to north-central Nicaragua.

In the zone of oaks and pines on the Sierra de Tecpán, White-ears frequented light woods and open, bushy places, including those overgrown with raijón (*Baccharis vaccinioides*), a shrub of the composite family with small leaves and flower heads. I found these hummingbirds not uncommon about Lake Atitlán at an altitude of 5,000 feet (1,500 m), on the plains around the town of Tecpán, and on the sierra up to about 9,000 feet (2,750 m). I rarely saw one in the bushy clearings among the cypress forests of the mountaintop, and never in the dark forest itself. But on the open alpine meadows of the Sierra Cuchumatanes, at about 11,000 feet (3,350 m), I watched a few White-ears sucking nectar from purple thistles, in company with more abundant Violet-eared and Broad-tailed hummingbirds. During most of the year, when White-ears are mostly silent, I rarely saw them except when I watched flowers that attracted them. Other observers have found White-ears aggressively protective of their flowers, driving away other hummingbirds up to those twice their size (Bent 1940).

At about the end of August, long before the cessation of the rains, I began to hear at long intervals the clear *tink tink tink* of male White-ears. By the first week of September, while the days were still all too frequently fog-dimmed and dreary, they sounded their little bells with some regularity; their clear notes came to me as words of cheer, proclaiming that gray mists would not forever envelop us. As September advanced with increasing mists, they seemed to become discouraged and lapsed into silence once more. With the advent of October, these hummingbirds became vocal again, and I noticed that some of them tinkled from the same shrubs where I had first heard them a month earlier.

As I roamed the bushy mountainsides and open oak woods, I noticed that the male White-ears were not distributed uniformly or randomly over territory suitable for them but had congregated into definite groups, which I called singing assemblies (they are now often designated leks). The largest of these gatherings that I found was composed of seven birds, whose perches were in the pine and oak trees surrounding an irregular open pasture. This assembly was very dispersed, with the two most widely separated members about six hundred feet (200 m) apart, and beyond hearing each other (unless the hummingbirds' ears were sharper than mine); but each participant could probably hear the voices of two or more of his neighbors. Another assembly contained five birds, scattered among tall raijón shrubs that had sprung up in an abandoned pasture, the birds so spaced that each was about ninety to one hundred feet from neighbors. Other assemblies consisted of three or only two White-ears. Sometimes the birds perched as close as sixty feet (20 m) apart. Between these groups of hummingbirds were long stretches of similar habitat where I listened in vain for their reiterated notes.

Scattered here and there, however, were solitary males who remained aloof from the assemblies. One of them was stationed in a raijón beside the road leading up to the house I occupied, where I frequently met him, perched on a dead twig and tinkling persistently. Another, with a weak, plaintive little voice, called from a low perch on a raijón bush in an overgrown pasture, beyond hearing of all others of his kind.

The male White-ears sometimes chose low perches in the midst of a

White-eared Hummingbird

thicket, only two or three feet above the ground; sometimes high, exposed ones, such as the dead twig of a pine tree forty feet (12 m) in the air. One bird, who engaged much of my attention, regularly alternated between a twig less than a yard from the ground in a thicket of raijón bushes and an exposed leafless branch in the top of an alder tree beside the thicket, fully a dozen times as high. At times a strong wind caused a White-ear to descend from his favorite perch, which was lofty and exposed, to some lower, more protected station nearby. Whatever the site he had chosen, the bird was to be found there day after day, week after week, throughout the months of October, November, and December. When I left the hacienda Chichavac at the year's end, a number of White-ears still proclaimed their presence in the same spots where I had first met them in early September.

Perhaps the most typical note of the male White-eared Hummingbird is a low, clear *tink tink tink*, sounding like the chiming of a small silver bell. This was the note that I first heard and prefer to remember. Some individuals toll their tiny bells very rapidly, others more slowly and deliberately. But as I became familiar with more and more White-ears, scattered over miles of mountainside, I was surprised by the variance of their voices. Many individuals consistently uttered notes so different from the usual clear tinkle that I did not recognize them as belonging to White-ears until

I laboriously stalked the birds and watched them calling. These notes were dull and flat, devoid of the clear timbre characteristic of the species, or high and squeaky, or low and melancholy. One White-ear that I often visited repeated rapidly a harsh, metallic click, a buzz almost painful to hear.

Equally unexpected was my discovery that all members of an assembly sang in much the same way but differently from those in other assemblies. If one bird of a group repeated a silvery tinkle, his neighbors would be found to do the same; if I was attracted to an assembly by chirping notes, this was the prevailing tune. I did not notice enough exceptions to this rule to make me doubt its validity. But what is the explanation of this phenomenon? Possibly it was imitation, all members of an assembly copying the song of its founder, or of one with a dominant personality. Or were the differences in voice innate? I never heard the White-ear with the metallic rattle tinkle sweetly, nor the tinkling birds rattle. Since I made this pioneer discovery about the singing assemblies of hummingbirds, evidence has accumulated that they, like many songbirds, (oscines) learn their songs. In Trinidad, David Snow (1968) and R. Haven Wiley (1971) noticed that Little Hermits in the same assembly have similar songs, which differ from those prevalent in other assemblies. Once I found a Beryl-crowned Hummingbird (also called Blue-chested and Charming) singing like the Rufous-tailed Hummingbirds abundant in the vicinity. His verses were quite different from those heard in a neighboring assembly of his own kind. He lived to be at least seven and a half years old (Skutch 1972).

Whether a clear dawn revealed the pastures white with frost or day broke sadly over a world drenched in gray, wind-blown mist, dreary and penetratingly chill, the White-ears always began to sing in the dim light of early dawn, before such late sleepers as Banded-backed Wrens and Black-capped Swallows left their snug dormitories. When the season of song was at its height, neither wind nor rain nor cold, driving cold-mist could utterly quench the spirits or extinguish the voices of these tiny hummers. They sang most vigorously in the early morning, less and less as the day advanced. In the afternoon their singing was rather inconstant; they were less persevering than the Green Violet-ears, one of whom produced almost as much volume of sound as a whole assembly of White-ears and continued his chant more constantly through the day. While singing, the male White-ear tilted upward his coral red, black-tipped bill and turned his head restlessly from side to side. Occasionally he interrupted his tinkling to utter a rapid twitter, which merged into a low buzz of a most peculiar tone. At intervals he vibrated his wings, or fell silent while he slowly stretched them. Finally, becoming hungry, he flew away to sip nectar from flowers, the nearest of which were often distant from the assembly.

The purpose of all this vocal activity by the males was to attract the opposite sex. Their singing coincided roughly with the nesting of the females. Nevertheless, in many hours of watching, I did not witness courtship. White-ears are so small and shy that they are difficult to keep in sight; on the wing their movements are so swift that I could not distinguish male from female or even follow them long with my eyes. I saw three or four of these hummingbirds flying together, pursuing and pursued, so frequently that I was sure each did not remain at his own station when a female appeared, as manakins and other birds in courtship assemblies usually do, but that neighbors invade the space of the male chosen by a female to be the father of her nestlings.

In mid-October, six or seven weeks after the male White-ears had selected their stations and begun to sing in a tentative fashion, I found a female starting her nest. Later I discovered a dozen more, which, with four that I had found in the same locality in November, 1930, brought the total up to seventeen. A few were never completed. All were distant from the singing assemblies of the males, some far away, others slightly beyond hearing of the nearest male—that is, of course, too distant for *me* to hear his voice. With a single exception, all these nests were placed among the slender branches of the raijón bushes so common everywhere on the mountains, at heights of five to twenty feet (1.5 to 6 m) above the ground. The one nest not in a raijón was in the crotch of an ascending branch of a shrubby *Eupatorium.*

The female White-ear built her nest alone, without the assistance or even the encouragement of one of the males that sang so tirelessly beyond sight or hearing. The raijón bush chosen as a site was never far from the oak trees that supplied the down she needed. The leaves of several species, belonging to both the white and black oak groups, are covered on the underside with a dense, woolly cloak composed of rather short, crinkled, tawny hairs. As I watched a hummingbird hovering amid the foliage, I concluded too hastily that she tore the down from unaltered epidermis. But when I tried to detach this material with my fingernails, or even with sharp-pointed forceps, I found that it would take a long time to gather much. If the hummingbird depended upon such down, to accumulate enough for her nest would have been a difficult task. To avoid this, she took advantage of what insects had done.

Upon examining the woolly stuff with a lens, I was convinced that some of it had been loosened by leaf-mining larvae that ate away the underlying tissue. Tiny pellets of excreta, or the shape of a tunnel that a larva had occupied, revealed this clearly enough. But more of the material in the nests was derived from woolly insect galls on the oak leaves. The central core of one of these pea-sized excrescences in which a larva lived was situated on the midrib and densely covered with long, soft hairs. The colors of these hairs varied from pale buff to deep reddish brown. The more abundant darkly colored galls were on the upper sides of the leaves, but I found the pale ones only beneath the foliage. Despite the rarity of the latter, the White-ears preferred their hairs for their nests, which were prevailingly light colored; the birds neglected, or used sparingly, the brownish down.

Thus insects—either indirectly, by laying eggs that stimulated the leaves to grow hairy galls, or directly, by separating the woolly covering from the internal tissues of the leaves and making it easy to remove—supplied the White-ears with nearly all the down for their nests. Spiders provided cobweb to bind the down together and to attach the structures to supporting twigs. Green mosses and grayish lichens were fastened to the exterior, for camouflage or decoration. Some nests were well covered with these plants, but others were so sparingly decorated that much of the down was visible. The interior of the cozy little cup was nearly as broad as deep, and measured about one inch (2.5 cm) in both diameter and depth. The rim was strongly incurved, a feature that helped to retain the eggs when strong November winds whipped the yielding slender raijón branches and threatened to roll the eggs out.

Because the three nests that I found in early stages of construction in late October and early November were abandoned unfinished, I could not learn how long the birds took to build. Others, which I discovered in November by much searching through the raiijón bushes, each contained two tiny pure white eggs, which averaged 12.7 by 8.0 millimeters in length and width. Two of these nests were in low situations favorable for observation, and before them I passed long hours in my little blind, watching the birds incubate their eggs. Although we have a few reports of abnormal sitting in nests by males, the females incubate unaided in all hummingbirds that have been carefully studied. I never saw a male White-ear show the slightest interest in a nest.

Both female White-ears that I watched sat deeply in their nests. When perfectly at rest, the birds were ensconced with their eyes only a trifle above the rim, their sides were wholly inside, and their backs were invisible to a viewer slightly below the nests' level. Their tails and the tips of their longest wing plumes projected beyond the rim at the rear. They were much better protected than were the Rufous-tailed Hummingbirds that I had watched in warm lowlands, sitting in nests so broad and shallow that much of their bodies remained outside.

The way the White-ears entered and left their little cups revealed their lightness and skillful flight. Returning to their eggs after a recess, heavier birds alight upon the nest's rim, or upon a nearby branch, and walk or hop into the cup. The White-ears never alighted on the rim but invariably flew directly into the nest and, as they settled neatly over the eggs, folded their wings around themselves and were immediately at rest. To leave the nest, birds of other families step onto the rim before taking flight, but the hummingbirds departed more directly. Still sitting on the eggs, they spread and vibrated their wings and rose with little apparent effort, as though they were lighter than air and ascended because hidden moorings had been severed. Often they flew upward and backward until they cleared the nest, then quickly reversed and darted forward and away. To turn their eggs, they flew backward from the bowl onto the rim, alighted on the spot that had been beneath the tail while they sat, lowered the bill into the cup, and in an instant flew away. I could not see the eggs or what was done to them in nests above the level of my eyes, but if the hummingbirds did not turn their eggs on these occasions, they apparently never did. While incubating, they did not rise to adjust their eggs beneath themselves, as other birds do, probably because the length of their bills would have made this difficult in such narrow nests.

In their recesses, the hummingbirds visited the yellow florets of the bur-marigolds (*Bidens refracta*) that flourished everywhere in the oak woods. Although each of the tiny flowers of a head yielded only a minute quantity of nectar, they were so numerous that in aggregate they probably supplied a considerable amount. Poising before the composite flower, the bird moved her bill rapidly from floret to floret, an instant in each, and usually probed many in each head. Three minutes among the bur-marigolds sufficed to satisfy her appetite after twenty minutes of motionless sitting in her nest. In the early part of the White-ears' nesting season, these composites were their main source of nectar. Although a single red blossom of *Salvia cinnabarina* probably yielded as much nectar as a whole head of bur-marigolds, and had the advantage that the entire store could be made available by one movement, these mints were not as widespread as the yellow composites and came later into profuse bloom.

In the mornings the White-ears devoted much time to seeking down and cobweb. They deposited the down inside the nest and spread the cobweb over the outside, to which they also attached a few more lichens. Since the nests had been finished before the eggs were laid, these additions to its bulk appeared to be made from force of habit rather than need; they were made chiefly during the hours of the morning when the birds had built most actively. The daily application of fresh cobweb prevented the deterioration of the nests' bindings and attachment to their supports. While gathering fresh materials claimed their attention, the birds spent brief periods on their eggs, often only a minute and sometimes less. In the afternoons, when they brought nothing when returning from their recesses, they often sat continuously for twenty to thirty minutes, rarely slightly longer. During a whole day, the sessions of one White-ear averaged ten minutes, her recesses five minutes. From her first departure in the morning until her final return in the evening, her total time on her eggs was seven hours and forty-seven minutes and she was absent for three hours and fifty-nine minutes. She incubated for two thirds of her active day.

When finally they hatched, the baby hummingbirds looked more like black grubs than nestlings of a feathered creature. Their eyes were covered by tightly closed lids; their bills were rudimentary; and the line of sparse brown fuzz along the center of their backs did little to cover their bareness. They seemed very small and naked to survive the cold, blustery days that recurred all too frequently during November and much of December. Often as I lay in bed at night, listening to the wind roaring through the trees—none too warm beneath two blankets, even with some odd garments spread above them for added protection—I wondered how the hatchling hummingbirds were faring out on the cold mountainside, in tiny nests exposed to the full blast of the night wind. But the downy cups were thick-walled and warm, and their mother fitted into the space above them as snugly as a cork into the mouth of a bottle, preserving the vital spark in her babies by her own wonderful capacity for heat production. The frosty dawn would reveal them healthily alive and eager for breakfast.

During the day the endurance of the naked nestlings was put to the most severe test because they were left exposed while their mother foraged for them. If ever nestlings seemed to need a father to help feed them or to warm them while the mother sought nourishment, it was these tiny hummingbirds; yet no male ever appeared to aid in their care, for this is not the way of male hummingbirds. On cruel days when wind that was half a gale drove chilling mist through the treetops, I sat in my tent to watch the mother attend her naked nestlings. Despite protection by the cloth that surrounded me and served as a windbreak, despite woolen garments such as I would wear on a walk over snowy fields in the north, I was soon thoroughly chilled, hands and feet becoming numb and painful with the cold. While I sat watching the nest, I marveled that such minute creatures, no bigger than a honeybee, could maintain their body temperature above the death point, even during the few minutes when they were left exposed while their parent foraged.

On a dull, blustery morning in mid-November, I passed five cold hours watching a nest with occupants two and three days old. In this interval they were fed only five times, or on the average once per hour. To deliver food, the parent stood on the nest's rim, inserted the tip of her long, slender bill into a nestling's throat, and with convulsive movements regurgitated into it part of the contents of her crop. She brooded her young for two to sixteen minutes at a stretch and never permitted them to remain exposed for more than eight minutes; sometimes for only two or three. Apparently, she wasted no time during her absences. The harsh weather continued, and two days later I found the younger nestling lying dead and shriveled beside its sibling, evidently a victim of cold and starvation. Later, the survivor inexplicably vanished.

I was interested in the sanitation of the White-ears' nests. It is well known that young hummingbirds eject their rather fluid excreta beyond the nest rim, but they can accomplish this only after they become strong enough to rise up. During their first few days they deposit their droppings on the bottom or sides of the nest, whence these are removed by their mother. She grasps particles in the tip of her bill and tosses them out by sideward jerks of her head, or swallows them, thereby keeping her nest decently clean. Later, when the nestlings are older, they manage to deposit their excreta on the nest rim, where the parent permits them to remain. Passerine birds are more careful of sanitation, not merely flicking aside droppings from the bottom of the nest but carrying them away or swallowing them, and cleaning the rim as carefully as the interior. However, passerines have the advantage that their nestlings' excrement is enclosed in gelatinous capsules that facilitate removal.

The White-ear's method of cleaning her nest resembled her way of turning her eggs. Passerines remove droppings after feeding their nestlings. The hummingbird that I watched on the blustery morning was in the habit of settling down to brood after feeding the nestlings or, if she brought no food for them, she flew directly into the nest. But when leaving, she often flew backward to alight on the rim, lowered her bill into the cup to inspect it, and tossed out excreta before she flew away.

To learn how long the mother continued to brood the nestlings by night, I arose before dawn on many a cold morning during November and December and walked across pastures whitened with frost to visit the nests before daybreak. It would have been more convenient to have made these inspections early in the night, but had my light frightened the hummingbird from her nest then, the nestlings would probably have remained exposed until dawn and succumbed. Morning after morning, as the first promise of dawn brightened the eastern horizon, my flashlight beam revealed the mother sleeping over her nestlings, with her head and long bill hidden in her plumage. I stole quietly away without disturbing her. She continued to brood at night even after her nestlings quite filled the nest, and she rested above rather than in it. She was their nocturnal coverlet until they were seventeen or eighteen days old, when they were well feathered and could keep warm without her protection. The occupants of both nests to which I made regular nocturnal visits were brooded equally long.

In lower and warmer regions hummingbirds cease nocturnal brooding much earlier: Rufous-tails when their nestlings are only six or seven days old and still in pinfeathers; Scaly-breasts when young are eight to eleven days old; Long-billed Starthroats at ten days. These parents sleep on the nest with their heads exposed, their forwardly directed bills tilted slightly upward, just as they sleep when perching on a twig. The early cessation of brooding shortens the time when the parent sleeping with her nestlings might be caught by a nocturnal predator that would destroy the whole family. She should survive to rear another brood.

One of the White-ear nestlings, frightened by my approach, fled from the nest at the age of twenty-three days, when it could fly well. Its nest mate lingered three days longer. Another White-ear, who from the first had been alone in its nest, also remained until it was twenty-six days old. In more benign climates, hummingbirds as small as White-ears often fledge when a few days younger. Fledgling White-ears resembled their mothers, but the white streak on the side of the head was tinged with buff. After leaving their downy cradle, they did not return to seek its shelter during the night but roosted amid foliage.

White-eared Hummingbirds were among the few avian species on the Sierra de Tecpán for which I found evidence of a second brood. One female, having raised a single nestling early in the breeding season built a new nest forty feet (12 m) from her first one, during the week after her fledgling flew from it. She had a busy week, feeding her young in the intervals between working at her new structure. As a result of her divided attention, the second nest was not nearly as well made as the first; it was shallower, thinner walled, and carelessly finished. It did not seem ready when the first egg was laid in it, only ten days after the fledgling left the earlier nest.

From my blind, I watched this hummingbird while she incubated her second set of eggs. Her fledgling, now forty days of age, had been out of the nest just two weeks. He was about as big as his mother. His bill appeared to be slightly shorter, and his back was not such a bright green because many of the feathers were still tipped with the brown down of the nestling plumage. Flying well, he spent much time sucking nectar from the red blossoms of salvias, as I could see through the side window of the blind. When not visiting the flowers, he rested low in a small bushy thicket about thirty feet from his mother's second nest. Here she came to feed him during her absences from her eggs. Although he could competently procure nectar, probably he could not yet catch the insects he needed to complete his diet. Once he visited the flowers while his mother collected food for him, then came to the thicket to supplement his meal with what she had to offer. Perching beside him on a low twig, she delivered the food, as always, by regurgitation, which she began with strong convulsive movements of her body. He was well behaved, never while I watched approaching the nest to pester his parent with demands for nourishment while she warmed her eggs, but always waiting patiently for her to come to him in the thicket. While he rested there, he called slowly *tink tink tink,* which resembled the songs of adult males in their assemblies but was much fainter. These precocious attempts to sing led me to conclude that he was a male.

While she incubated her first set of eggs, the mother found much time for bringing additional cobweb and down to the nest, which was so well finished that it did not appear to require further attention. The hastily built second nest was in greater need of additions, but now the bird was too busy with other things to give time to this and brought nothing to the nest during the morning that I passed with her. Now she incubated more constantly, taking only eight recesses in four hours, instead of twenty-three in the same interval of the morning while she incubated her first set of eggs. Even in a seven-minute absence from the nest, she could gather food for herself and her progeny.

Probably because of the inclement weather, these White-ears nested with extremely poor success. The nine completed nests that I found in 1933 contained two eggs each, making a total of eighteen. Three of these nests were somehow destroyed while they still held eggs, and one was abandoned; only nine eggs hatched. Of the nine nestlings, one succumbed to the cold, two were probably taken by predators, and three met unknown fates. Only three young lived to fly. An egg success of only 17 percent is exceptionally low even in predator-ridden tropical rain forests at low altitudes.

I did not remain at Chichavac into January of 1934, but at the time of my arrival in February of the preceding year, the male White-ears had become silent and I found no nests. By this time fields and woodlands had become very dry and flowers scarce. Regardless of the weather, hardy hummingbirds breed when the flowers supplying the nectar that chiefly nourishes them bloom most profusely; in the highlands of western Guatemala this happens early in the dry season, which begins toward year end, when soil that has been drenched through long months of rain still retains moisture, and sunshine increases. The only other birds that I found nesting at the same time as the White-ears were Green Violet-ears, Amethyst-throated Hummingbirds, and Cinnamon-bellied Flowerpiercers, which, like them, subsist upon nectar and tiny insects. Most birds on the Sierra de Tecpán bred in the six or seven weeks between the last of the nocturnal frosts in early April and the onset of heavy rains in mid-May.

CHAPTER 7

The Violet-headed Hummingbird

Above the gorge through which the Río Reventazón rushes down from Costa Rica's central plateau to the Caribbean Sea, steep slopes were covered by farms of coffee, bananas, and pastures. Through the pastures stretched miles of hedges of *Stachytarpheta*, a straggling shrub of the verbena family that grew ten or twelve feet high and so densely that it substituted for barbed-wire fences. Its small purple flowers are displayed in a thin wreath around slender, whiplike spikes up to two feet long. Daily the circle of bloom creeps upward toward the curving naked top of the spike, a few inches above them. When I visited hospitable Silver Spring farm in June and again in September of 1941, the *Stachytarpheta* hedges were blooming profusely, as they do through most of the year, and attracted such a multitude of hummingbirds as I have rarely seen anywhere. Here, at an altitude around 3,000 feet (915 m), lowland and highland hummingbirds mingled.

Most abundant of the hummingbirds that swarmed with bees, butterflies, and hawk moths at the *Stachytarpheta* were Violet-heads, one for every fifteen or twenty feet of hedge. Mature and juvenile birds of both sexes were present, with adult males least numerous. Only three inches (7.5 cm) long, with the crown, forehead, and throat intense violet-blue, each revealed his full splendor only when poised with his short, straight black bill directed toward me. The upper parts were bronzy green, the slightly notched tail more bluish. Behind the throat the underparts were pale gray, green-spotted on the sides. The slightly larger female was bright greenish blue only on her crown. A prominent white spot behind each eye of both sexes was a good recognition mark. In 1843, Bourcier and Mulsant, French ornithologists who had probably never seen a living Violet-ear, described the species *Klais guimeti*, dedicating it to M. Guimet, a chemist of Lyons who invented a peculiar blue dye also known by his name.

Companions of the Violet-heads at the hedges, or rather their competitors for nectar, were Rufous-tailed Hummingbirds; tiny, deep wine-purple Snowcaps with shining white crowns; equally diminutive Green Thorntails with long, wiry outer rectrices; green and violet Crowned Woodnymphs; brownish Little Hermits from neighboring ravines; and curiously attired Brown Violet-ears, vagrants that mysteriously become abundant, then vanish. Mingling with these hummingbirds of low and middle altitudes were Green Violet-ears, who sing and nest high in the mountains.

When I needed a hedge around my house, then recently built on the Pacific side of Costa Rica, I planted *Stachytarpheta*, despite its unkempt, straggling habit of growth, because it attracted so many hummingbirds. I begged cuttings from an old woman who lived in a thatched cabin along the road to San Isidro and set them in June beneath the barbed-wire fence. They rooted and grew so rapidly that by January they flowered. When the first plants had become vigorous enough to provide cuttings, I extended the hedge, and by repetitions of this procedure I soon had several hundred feet of *Stachytarpheta* along three sides of the garden. As was fitting, the first hummingbirds that I noticed visiting these flowers were Violet-heads. Later they were joined by other hummingbirds, mostly different from these across the cordillera on the Caribbean slope: Snowy-breasts in glittering green; Beryl-crowned Hummingbirds; Blue-throated Goldentails; White-necked Jacobins charmingly clad in blue and green; plainly attired Scaly-breasted Hummingbirds; Long-tailed Hermits; and Rufous-tails, who chased the Violet-heads but could not keep them away. From July or August until February, the ornate mites called Adorable Coquettes joined the ever-changing, scintillating throng.

The Violet-headed Hummingbirds' attendance at the *Stachytarpheta* hedge varied from season to season and from year to year. In some years they became rare in March when the drought was most intense, which was inexplicable, because if the season was not too dry this plant flowered when few others did, and its nectar should have been most welcome; yet in years of more extreme drought it, too, was almost bloomless at this period. Probably the majority of the Violet-heads went elsewhere to search for nourishment. By 1948, after a drastic pruning made necessary by its too straggling growth, my *Stachytarpheta* hedge, so languished that it was replaced by a more prosaic privet hedge with resulting drastic diminution in the number of hummingbirds around my dwelling.

The Violet-heads continue to visit a less exuberant species of *Stachytarpheta*, a slender plant less than five feet tall that springs up spontaneously here and there in the lawn and yields nectar in florets the color of the Violet-heads' crown, displayed in ascending wreaths on long, slender spikes not unlike those of the hedge plant. The small, pinkish flowers of the red-and-green-leaved *caña de India* (*Taetsia fruticosa*), which blooms sporadically around our house, draw Violet-heads to us. The white flowers of the liana *Serjania mexicana* at the woodland's edge also offer them nectar. Violet-heads, weighing less than a tenth of an ounce (three grams), prefer flowers that are small, like themselves.

At the *Stachytarpheta* hedges, male Violet-heads often sang in June, especially in the early morning, usually on low perches in or near the hedges, such as they chose for resting between visits to their flowers. They did not appear to be grouped in singing assemblies, although the whole mountainside at Silver Spring might have been regarded as one great assemblage of old and young of both sexes. In September they were less songful.

Like many other male hummingbirds, Violet-heads remain aloof from nests and pass the season of reproduction singing day after day in the same spot, often associating in this activity with others of their species and sex to form a singing assembly. In El General some of these persistent singers perform throughout the year except for a month or two of silence toward the end of the dry season when flowers are least abundant, as do Rufous-tailed Hummingbirds and Little Hermits. Others, including Scaly-breasted Hummingbirds and Band-tailed Barbthroats, perform only in the rainy season. Singing assemblies of Blue-throated Goldentails and Violet-headed Hummingbirds are active mainly in the drier months.

From 1942, my first full year at Los Cusingos, until 1952, a singing assembly of Violet-heads was located in the tops of tall burío (*Heliocarpus*) and other trees beside the pasture near our house. Here the small birds were difficult to watch amid the foliage. After a decade or more of activity, this station was abandoned, probably because the second-growth woods had become too tall and heavy, but other assemblies persisted in more distant parts of the farm.

After months of silence, I sometimes heard Violet-heads sing briefly while the Sun rose brightly into a cloudless sky in October or November,

Violet-headed Hummingbird and Stachytarpheta Flowers

usually the last months of copious rains. Singing increased through December, often a month of sunny mornings with light or occasionally heavy afternoon showers. In January, when showers are fewer and shorter, the Violet-heads were in fullest chorus and continued throughout the day. With clear skies and soil still moist after eight or nine months of almost daily soakings, flowers are then more abundant, especially in the clearings, than at any other time. As the dry season continues and the ground dries, plants languish and bloom sparingly if at all. Even in years when a few light showers have mitigated the drought of February, March is a month of few flowers. Now, after singing profusely through most or, in wetter years, all of February, Violet-heads fell silent, although a few, probably more favorably situated for food, continued bravely to proclaim their presence in March, at least when this month was not too severely dry.

In April, after returning showers had refreshed the earth and revived drooping vegetation, Violet-heads sang freely again. Their renewal of song corresponded approximately with that of Rufous-tailed Hummingbirds, Blue-throated Goldentails, and Little Hermits, all of which likewise had been silenced by the drought, and with the beginning of singing by Scaly-breasted Hummingbirds, wet-season performers that had long been mute. Most of these hummingbirds would continue to chant through many wet months; but for the Goldentails and Violet-heads, the dry-season breeders, the renascence was brief. May is a month of heavy rainfall and occasionally the wettest of the year; before it was many days old, both these kinds of hummingbirds had abandoned their singing assemblies.

Here at Quizarrá at around 2,500 feet (760 m) above sea level, before this part of the valley of El General had been so drastically changed by settlement and agriculture, no bird of any family so advertised its presence by voice, in January and February, as did the Violet-headed Hummingbird. Singing males perched conspicuously (if so diminutive a creature may rightly be so described) on slender dead twigs, from fifteen or twenty to about sixty feet (5 to 20 m) above the ground. Most were in singing assemblies, with only a few remote from others. Their stations were at or just within the edge of primary forest; at the margins of tall second-growth thickets; in scattered trees, preferably dead, in small clearings surrounded by forest; and in the fringe of trees along a river flowing through cleared lands.

Although females often nest along rivulets that flow through extensive tracts of unbroken forest, and males occasionally sing in the tops of trees well within the forest, they prefer forest edges. I was impressed by this on a horseback ride through the forest from the Río Peñas Blancas to beyond the Río Calientillo early in February, 1942. Although the trees along both sides of the rough trail had been felled to a distance of thirty or forty feet (9 or 12 m) to permit the drying sunlight and breezes to reach and desiccate the muddy track, I heard no Violet-headed Hummingbirds except where the way led through wider clearings (far less extensive than today) made for agriculture; but in most of these larger openings the hummingbirds were singing.

Just beyond the Río Calientillo, in a recent clearing already overgrown with a tangle of bushes and vines more than head high, I found a singing assembly unusually favorable for observation. This group consisted of at least four males in full adult plumage. Three were stationed in as many dead trees, remnants of the original forest, which formed the corners of a roughly equilateral triangle of about fifty feet (15 m) on a side. They perched on exposed twiglets, well above the surrounding low growth, at heights of about twenty-five, thirty, and forty-five feet (7.5, 9, and 14 m). The fourth member of the assembly rested habitually about forty feet (12 m) up in a fire-killed tree about one hundred feet (30 m) from one apex of the triangle formed by the posts of his neighbors. At times I heard the voices of Violet-heads coming from more distant parts of the clearing, but I did not succeed in seeing these birds.

Whether he sang alone or in a group, each Violet-head was to be found at his post hour after hour, day after day, through most of the dry season. From early morning, right through the warm hours when the bright dry-season Sun poured down its fervid rays from the zenith until the cool evening shadows stole out from long forested ridges, the glittering little bird continued tirelessly to repeat his spirited, simple chant, interrupting it only long enough to seek nourishment or repel an intruder. By their sustained singing, as well as by the high, exposed perches they preferred, these Violet-heads reminded me of violet-ears (*Colibri* spp.) I had heard in the highlands of Guatemala, Costa Rica, and Ecuador.

The sharp, rapid song has a simple rhythm. Although some individuals sing better than others, none is really musical. While chanting, the hummingbird turns his head constantly from side to side, scarcely opening his bill. From time to time one Violet-head alights near the singing perch of another, who dashes at the intruder. The two streak away almost too swiftly for my eyes to follow them. The pursuit ends without injury to either participant; after a few minutes both return to their usual perches to sing as blithely as ever.

These persistently advertised, traditional assemblies make it easy for females to find fathers for their progeny. However, neither in this one nor at assemblies of other species that I have watched have I learned the whole sequence of events when a female arrives. The sexes of many species can be distinguished only in favorable optical conditions, and not at all when the birds are in rapid flight. The arrival of another hummingbird on or near the perch of a singing male invariably sooner or later leads to a pursuit, which nearly always takes the birds out of sight. Wagner (1954) and others have described and illustrated the elaborate aerial ballets of a male and female of a number of species, yet apparently few have ever witnessed the consummation of these courtship rites.

In the valley of El General, female Violet-heads begin to build their nests in January or February, occasionally in late December, and the latest nestlings in my records fledged in mid-May. Nests are built in the forest, usually above a stream, or at times above a well-shaded mountain torrent flowing between pastures or second-growth woods a short distance from the forest. The thirteen nests that I have seen ranged in height from thirty-nine inches (1 m) above a narrow forest stream to fifteen feet (4.5 m) above the ground in the forest at a distance from a watercourse. Eight of these nests were found between March 5 and 13, 1940, along the Río San Antonio (a headwater of the Río Pacuar, which is a tributary of the Río Térraba) and a narrow affluent of the first that we called *La Quebrada de los Gorriones* (The Hummingbirds' Brook) for the many hummingbirds' nests, all of Violet-heads, that we found along its course.

I was at that time collecting plants for the Museo Nacional de Costa Rica, and these clear mountain streams, flowing in pristine loveliness through a great tract of unspoiled rain forest, traversed my favorite and most productive collecting ground. Day after day I pushed farther upward along their rocky beds, proceeding slowly because of the difficulty of walking along the wild fluvial pathway and because of the number of things to be observed, collected, or enjoyed. Each bend in the stream opened a fresh prospect of enchanting beauty: a pool of fluid crystal mirroring the wide-spreading crowns of stately tree ferns; water slipping smoothly down a long incline of stratified rock; a cliff overgrown with the richest profusion of ferns, aroids, bromeliads, and orchids; or a long, straight reach bordered by tall, slender trunks with boughs interlocking far overhead. Among the verdure along the shores were many plants new to me and some unnamed by botanists. Here I first became acquainted with some notable birds. Here, too, I first saw female Violet-headed Hummingbirds; and of all the discoveries I made along these unforgettable streams, this was the most noteworthy. As told earlier in this chapter, I saw my first males a year later; they were strangely absent here where females were abundant.

The eight occupied nests of Violet-headed Hummingbirds were found incidentally by the lad who carried my plant press and by me, without our specially searching for them, for we were busy gathering botanical specimens and arranging them in folded sheets of newspaper. The nests were situated along about two and a half miles (4 km) of the Río San Antonio and Hummingbirds' Brook, as nearly as I could estimate distances along so rough a pathway. In addition to the eight nests with eggs or nestlings, we noticed about an equal number that were empty, some bearing signs that the young had flown from them, thus providing evidence that the nests holding feathered nestlings, hatched from eggs laid at the beginning of February, were not the earliest. Probably nesting had begun in January, if not in December. A nest with young ready to fly was only four feet (1.2 m) from one in which the female was incubating two eggs. Another nest with feathered young was about forty feet (12 m) from a different nest with two eggs. This was a truly remarkable concentration of hummingbirds' nests. Occupied nests as close together as even the more widely separated of these two pairs are rare; I have only once found two nests of any other species in comparable propinquity. In rain forests, nests of most kinds of hummingbirds are extremely difficult to find; I rarely see more than two or three of any one kind in a year, even of species abundant in the vicinity.

These nests along the forest streams were all on branches projecting over the water and usually pendulous, from about three to twelve feet (0.9–3.7 m) above the current. Of the five nests in other localities, four were attached to pendent vines or epiphytic shrubs growing over a *sotacaballo* tree (*Pithecolobium longifolium*) that leaned far over the wider Río Peñas Blancas, in an inaccessible site ten feet above the water and twenty feet from the shore. The river was here about fifty feet (15 m) wide, flowing impetuously over a channel strewn with great boulders. The single nest found at a distance from a waterway was attached to a spray of the climbing fern *Salpichlaena volubilis* that dangled beneath a palm frond in the midst of the forest, fifteen feet (4.6 m) above the ground. These hummingbirds showed a definite preference for hanging supports for their nests. The advantage of such a site seemed obvious: even a slender snake could not approach the nest in the night without making it sway enough to waken the incubating or brooding bird in time to fly away.

The lowest of the four nests above the Río Peñas Blancas in front of my house was discovered early in the morning of February 18, 1946, when so recently begun that it was only a tuft of moss and cobweb about an inch in diameter. It was attractively situated amid the glossy foliage of a dangling branch of *Satyria longifolia,* an epiphytic shrub of the heath family; one of the plant's short petioles helped to support the nest above the sparkling current of the broad, rocky stream, low and murmurous at this season. The hummingbird continued to build while I sat on a boulder in the channel only four yards away, but to disturb her less, I thought it preferable to watch from a greater distance and chose a mossy rock by the shore. It was 7:18 when I settled down and began to count her visits to the nest. In quick succession she brought ten billfuls, mostly cobweb and a little moss, then two more billfuls at longer intervals, before she stayed away for many minutes. Soon after 8:00 she brought twelve billfuls as quickly as she could gather them, then disappeared. Between 8:18 and 9:18 she brought only three more contributions, although in the preceding hour (7:18 to 8:18) she had made twenty-four visits to the nest. Her brief periods of concentrated building were separated by long intervals of neglect, during which she might make a few sporadic visits to her nest.

The following morning I watched again, counting the times the Violet-head brought materials to her nest in five-minute intervals. The number varied from zero to seven, with an average of 1.4. From 6:50 to 7:40 she came twenty-five times; from 8:12 to 9:50, seventeen times. Now, in addition to cobweb, she brought silky seed plumes for the lining. On both mornings she worked in silence. No male of her kind ever appeared. By February 21 she was still bringing materials to a structure that appeared to be almost completed. It had been built in four or five working days. No egg had appeared in it by March 3, and by March 11 it had vanished.

The Violet-headed Hummingbird's nest is a tiny, thick-walled cup, composed largely of green moss and lined with seed down that is usually buff in color. An exceptionally high nest appeared to have been built on top of another of the same kind. All the nests that I have seen were beyond (human) hearing of males singing in their assemblies, but at least three of them were only a short flight away from an assembly.

In one nest the eggs were laid with an interval of two days, the second before 7:30 A.M. Each of ten accessible nests contained two eggs or nestlings. The minute eggs are ellipsoidal and white. One set was laid in late December or early January, six in February, four in March, and one in April.

I watched the Violet-head incubate at the nest on a spray of climbing fern dangling below a frond of a small palm. In the midst of the forest, this nest was the only one of the thirteen I have seen that was not above running water, but it was close enough to the Río Peñas Blancas, several hundred yards away, for me to hear the river when the wind blew from that quarter. The second egg in this nest had been laid on February 26, 1944; incubation had been in progress for ten days when I began my vigil at noon on March 7. I watched until, at 5:35 P.M., the light in the forest had become too dim to distinguish the hummingbird on her nest. At dawn the following morning I returned and continued to watch until midday.

For so small a bird, the Violet-head sat for long periods. The eleven sessions that I timed ranged from 15 to 77 minutes and averaged 40.6 minutes.

Her twelve recesses varied from 6 to 28 minutes and averaged 15.2 minutes. She spent 72.8 percent of my combined watches on her nest. She sat so steadily, as compared with some other hummingbirds I have studied—the White-ear, for example—because she devoted little time to seeking additional materials for her nest, apparently never leaving her eggs for that purpose. The whole time I watched, she brought only three or four pieces: three I clearly saw in her bill when she returned to resume incubation at 7:18, 7:39, and 8:19 A.M.—just the hours of the morning when the female at the river had built most actively. Her shortest sessions were in the early morning, before nine o'clock, her longest in the late morning and the afternoon.

When leaving the nest, she rose on the wing directly from her eggs, not first hopping upon the rim, as heavier birds do. Sometimes, after rising a short distance above the nest, she darted back and forth and up and down in a most erratic fashion, going only a few inches, or at most about a foot, before she abruptly changed her direction, and she continued this for several seconds before she flew away. Occasionally she returned with the same irregularly oscillating flight. Could she be catching insects invisible to me? Except for the humming of her wings, I heard no sound from her. Not once did she alight on the nest's rim to turn her eggs; if she moved them, it must have been with her feet. No male of her kind appeared. Soon after she laid her eggs, males in the assembly nearest her stopped singing, as they usually do toward the end of the dry season.

Close around the nest were tall shrubs of *Cephaelis elata*, a rubiaceous plant with small white flowers in dense heads between two conspicuous red bracts. At intervals throughout the morning, a male Crowned Wood-nymph visited these flowers, unopposed by the incubating Violet-head. She was equally indifferent to a Little Hermit and a Long-tailed Hermit that less frequently flew close to her nest, never appearing to take the slightest notice of them. From this, the only nest for which I knew the date of laying, an egg disappeared on March 13, sixteen days after the set was completed. The nest was then abandoned.

The two occupied nests only four feet apart in the same bush that overhung Hummingbirds' Brook were the farthest upstream of all that we found. Two hummingbirds' nests so close together was a discovery so unprecedented in my experience that it called for further observations. A well-feathered nestling had flown from one of these nests as we approached, but I caught and returned it beside its nest mate—where, unexpectedly, it was cooperative enough to remain. The day was already far spent when we made this exciting discovery; we were obliged, after watching only long enough to be sure that the neighboring nest with eggs was also attended, to hurry downstream ere the dense blackness of night caught us so deep in the forest and made walking along the rocky streambed too perilous to be contemplated. But next morning I retraced my course over the long, rough way and learned more about the relations of these two hummingbirds who were such surprisingly close neighbors.

At other nests along this stream I had already found that if I sat quietly on a rock, at no great distance and without concealment, the female would soon return to attend her eggs or nestlings. So I settled myself on a rounded stone that commanded a good view of the two nests in the same small bush. The well-feathered nestlings were bright, alert creatures. They frequently preened their green plumage and from time to time beat their wings into a haze while they clung to the bottom of their nest. When an adult of their kind flew within sight, they seemed to be aware of her approach at once and were all attention, uttering clear droplets of sound in anticipation of a meal. Apparently, they were unable to distinguish their mother from her neighbor, for they called in the same fashion at the approach of either. The incubating hummingbird paid no attention to the other's offspring. She was somewhat afraid of the nestlings' mother; when the latter approached, she would dart from her eggs. Or sometimes she would continue to incubate while the mother fed the nestlings liberally by regurgitation, only to flee as the other departed. Yet the hummingbird with nestlings was not aggressive toward her neighbor with eggs.

As at the nest in the climbing fern that I watched some years later, when approaching their nests each of these hummingbirds would alternately dart and hover, shooting for a short distance to this side and that, irregularly back and forth, and at the end of each abrupt shift in position she would hang momentarily on wings beating too rapidly to be seen. The short, abrupt, erratic darts, the sharp and sudden changes of direction, reminded me strongly of the behavior of a White-necked Jacobin catching gnats above a river, or of a hover fly. Possibly the Violet-heads were indeed snatching from the air a few last minute morsels invisible to me. After darting from one side of the nest to the other, the hummingbird would suddenly drop into it or alight on the rim to feed the nestlings.

These two hummingbirds, like others of their kind that I had watched downstream, sometimes came to hover close above me before going to their nests; or, after feeding the nestlings and before darting away, one approached to have a nearer view of the strange monster spying on them. At one of the downstream nests the mother, apparently without noticing me, arrived suddenly and started to feed her nestlings. Then, her attention attracted by the abrupt raising of my binocular to my eyes, she immediately left the nest and came to hover close before me. Satisfied by this inspection that I was not dangerous, she promptly returned to her nest to resume feeding. Over the years hummingbirds of several species have similarly scrutinized me at arm's length, prompted by simple curiosity or concern for the safety of their nests and offspring. (These examinations suggest that hummingbirds may be nearsighted, which would not be surprising if one considers the smallness of their nests and of the insects they pluck from vegetation or catch in the air.)

I continued to watch the two neighboring nests with that uncomfortable feeling I sometimes have in the woods of being watched by unseen eyes. Of a sudden, a long black snake mottled with yellow slid down an oblique ledge of the fern-shaded streamside cliff rising on my right. It moved rapidly without a pause until it came to rest on a rock in midstream, almost beneath the two nestlings. There it lay motionless with its foreparts raised high, to all appearances gazing up at the two young hummingbirds, as though trying to discover how they might be reached. Knowing from repeated past experiences the mica's hunger for nestlings, I found a stick and killed it.

My only comparable example of occupied hummingbirds' nests close together is that of two nests of Little Hermits only twelve feet apart, attached by cobweb beneath the leaf-tips of low, spiny palms in the forest undergrowth. In many hours of watching while the two females incubated and attended nestlings, I never saw one pay the least attention to her close neighbor. Each behaved as though the other did not exist. These observations accord ill with the belief that hummingbirds are highly pugnacious and intolerant of one another. Perhaps some of the dashing pursuits that we witness among members of this family should be ascribed to playfulness.

On the morning of May 17, 1942, I had the good fortune to watch the spontaneous departure of the fledgling Violet-heads from the nest attached to vines dangling above the Río Peñas Blancas. When I arrived at half past ten they were restless, preening and moving about in their narrow nest, flapping their wings into misty circles while clinging with their feet to its rim. The big white spots behind each shiny eye made the youngsters appear keen-sighted and alert. Presently an Ochre-bellied Flycatcher, whose snug mossy nest hung from a slender dangling root above the opposite shore, flew into the vine that supported the hummingbirds' nest. Although the small olive-green bird was harmless, her close approach alarmed the young hummingbirds. One promptly rose from the nest and easily flew across the river to vanish amid the foliage.

Instead of fleeing when the flycatcher approached, the other fledgling crouched down in the nest and for a few minutes rested motionless there. Soon becoming restless again, it preened, then stood on the rim and clung tightly with its toes while it beat its wings vigorously and rose up as though it would break away from its downy mooring. Then it settled back into the nest once more. When a large black wasp flitted among the foliage close beside it, the fledgling opened its bill as though to defend itself. When the insect hovered nearer, the young bird flapped its wings, ready to dart away if prudence demanded a retreat. Presently the parent came to feed this fledgling who stayed at home, giving no indication that she noticed the departure of the other. After a few minutes she returned and fed this same youngster once more, with nectar sipped from the long, slender flower tubes, red tipped with white, of the epiphytic heath that supported her nest.

About half an hour after the departure of its sibling, the second young hummingbird spontaneously rose from the nest to alight on a slender twig of the heath, about a foot higher. After a brief rest here, it beat its wings again and slowly rose another foot into the air, to a perch less than a yard above the nest, where it rested and preened for a while. Then it flew upward again, until it passed from view amid the close-set boughs of the so-tacaballo tree in whose shade it was reared. These fledglings, like all others I have seen, closely resembled their mother.

The mossy nest had preserved its shape well during a month of exposure to drenching rains. It did not burst asunder and flatten out, as nests of Rufous-tailed Hummingbirds and other species occasionally do. A premature fall from the nest would have deposited the young Violet-heads in rushing water from which escape would have been difficult.

CHAPTER 8 &

The Long-tailed Hermit Hummingbird

Most of the birds I have studied did not study me. At most they kept a wary eye upon a big, potentially dangerous animal spying on them or their nests. Hummingbirds and a few others were different; they carefully scrutinized their watcher. A number of kinds have hovered at arm's length or closer around me, fanning my face with their wings, when they found me in the thicket or forest undergrowth where they dwelt. One was a Violet-headed Hummingbird, as described in the preceding chapter, but most have been hermits of various species. Sometimes, while I watched a Long-tailed Hermit suck nectar from flowers, it interrupted its meal to hover close around me, then returned to the flowers. Such curiosity suggests intelligence.

Many years ago, while I sat at my microscope in a screened room at the Lancetilla Experiment Station in Honduras, examining the tissues of a banana plant, a Long-tailed Hermit visited me. After probing the pink flowers of a coral vine (*Antigonon leptopus*) and big red hibiscus blossoms beside the building, it hovered in front of the small opening in the metal screen through which the microscope received light. For a few moments it scrutinized me and the microscope, then floated in through the opening for a closer inspection. It poised a few inches above my head, where I could watch its long central tail feathers open and close like scissors as it regulated its position. Its curiosity satisfied, it tried to leave the room by a route higher than that through which it had entered, only to find its exit blocked by the close-meshed wire screen. It flew from side to side of the room, trying to leave at various points, but each time gently coming to rest when it encountered an obstacle. After several such frustrations, it panicked and darted wildly around the room, twice dashing against the screen so violently that I feared it had injured itself. Hurriedly I lowered some awnings that would prevent its looking out through the screen, and while I was so engaged it vanished, probably by the gap through which it had entered.

While the Long-tailed Hermits inspected me, I scrutinized them. They were about six inches (15 cm) long. Above they were bronzy green, the feathers fringed with buff, most broadly on the upper tail coverts. Above and behind each eye was a streak of buffy white, bordered below by a broad black band over the lores, cheeks, and ears. The chin and throat were brownish buff, with a broad median stripe of pale buff. The remaining underparts were dull grayish buff, becoming whitish on the abdomen. The long, narrow central tail feathers were white with broader black bases; the lateral rectrices black with buffy tips. The upper mandible of the long, conspicuously downcurved bill was largely black, the lower mandible yellowish. The sexes are so alike that I never could tell whether a bird I watched while it inspected me was male or female, unless it was nesting.

This easily identified hummingbird ranges through the more humid lowlands from southern Mexico to Bolivia, central Brazil, and the Guianas. In Costa Rica it is rarely found as high as 3,300 feet, (1,000 m) above sea level. Primarily an inhabitant of the undergrowth of rain forests, it enters neighboring thickets, plantations, and gardens in search of flowers rich in nectar. This and other hummingbirds are called hermits not because they are especially solitary but because of their modest, often brownish attire. Although females are nearly always alone, the more social males gather in assemblies where they call to attract them.

One most often notices a Long-tailed Hermit while it hovers before a blossom on wings beating too rapidly to be seen. Among its favorites are the long, tubular flowers of wild plantains (*Heliconia*), of which many species grow throughout its range, and those of the related banana (*Musa sapientum*) of Old World origin. To reach with its downcurved bill nectar of the upcurved yellow tubes of *Heliconia irrasa*, the hermit assumes a peculiar position. It hovers facing outward from the floral axis, beside rather than above the yellow, red-margined floral bract, and with its body slightly tilted toward the bract that half-encloses the flowers, inserts its bill very briefly into one. Long, narrow-tubed corollas of shrubs of the acanthus family also attract the hermit, including the red flowers of *Razisea spicata*, the lavender flowers of *Poikilacanthus macranthus*, and the diversely colored flowers of *Aphelandra* species. But the hermit does not disdain small flowers, such as those of *Stachytarpheta* in hedges near forest. The Long-tails' flowers are not concentrated in a defensible territory but often scattered along a route as much as half a mile (1 km) long, which the bird traverses at intervals through the day, sipping nectar as it becomes available. Insects gleaned from foliage, twigs, and trunks and spiders from their webs balance the birds' diet.

One sunny morning in March, I watched a big owl butterfly (*Caligo*) alight upon the large, dull red inflorescence bud of a banana plant. Resting there with its head upward, it pushed its slender proboscis into the white staminate flowers clustered beneath a wide upstanding bract. While imbibing the banana nectar, the butterfly held its broad wings folded together above its back, displaying their finely vermiculated undersides marked with a big, black, yellow-rimmed eyespot on each hind wing and a much smaller eyespot on each fore wing. Only rarely did the butterfly partly open its wings, permitting a momentary glimpse of the rich purple and yellow of their upper surfaces.

While the *Caligo* was present, little, stingless, pollen-gathering meloponine bees often approached but rarely alighted upon the flowers. Twice a Long-tailed Hermit that was flying from banana plant to banana plant approached the inflorescence where the butterfly was enjoying a long feast of nectar, but before it touched a flower, a slight movement of the insect's wings sent the bird away, probably frightened by those staring eyespots. After a brief absence, the hummingbird returned, visited a number of other inflorescences, then flew toward the butterfly from directly behind, seeing only the edges of its folded wings; from this aspect the eyespots were invisible. This time the *Caligo* flew away before the hermit touched it. Possibly, after drinking nectar for a half-hour, it left because it was satiated, not because the hermit approached. After the butterfly's withdrawal, the hummingbird poised gracefully beside the dangling inflorescence, thrusting its bill upward into the serried white flowers.

The Long-tailed Hermit (with the Green Hermit where it occurs) has a virtual monopoly of the nectar richly secreted by the great scarlet passionflower (*Passiflora vitifolia*). A collar around the base of the flower prevents access to the floral nectaries by birds with shorter bills, while it forces long-billed visitors to hold their bills vertically, with their crowns touching the anthers or stigmas raised above the corolla on a long stalk. Shorter-billed Little Hermits often visit these flowers but confine their attention to nectar secreted by glands on the bracts and to small insects attracted by it. They do not, like their larger relatives, get their dark heads dusted with pollen to be carried to the stigmas of other passionflowers. Although the vine that bears these flamboyant blossoms climbs far up into trees of light woodland and forest edges, the flowers are displayed near the ground on special long, nearly leafless, whiplike shoots, which appears to be an adaptation to secure the services of the low-ranging Long-tailed Hermit as a pollinator; hummingbird and passionflower are co-adapted. When, as rarely happens, the scarlet blossoms are displayed forty or fifty feet (12 or 15 m) up at the woodland's edge, the hermit does not hesitate to ascend much higher than one ordinarily sees the bird. From one group of passionflowers a Long-tailed Hermit was chased away by a big Violet Sabrewing that took possession of them (Skutch 1980).

Like a number of other forest hummingbirds, the Long-tailed Hermit often bathes in a still reach of a sylvan stream, half immersing itself in the limpid water by dipping down in hovering flight. After one or more immersions, it perches on a neighboring twig and shakes the water from its plumage, including its long tail, which it twitches from side to side so rapidly that it becomes a blur of white and black, almost as invisible as the hummingbird's wings while it hovers.

When excited or alarmed, the Long-tailed Hermit utters a rapid twitter that hardly distinguishes it from other hummingbirds. Through much of the year, the males sing in the dimly lighted undergrowth of heavy woodland. Each perches within a yard or two of the ground, where his brown form would be difficult to distinguish from the brown fallen leaves if he did not incessantly wave his white-tipped tail up and down, rhythmically, as though beating time to his notes. Although the courtship songs of some hummingbirds enchant the attentive listener with unexpectedly varied movements and miniature melodies, that of our hermit is extremely simple. A squeaky note or two, incessantly reiterated, appears to be the limit of his vocal power. Usually a number of males perch within hearing of one another, cooperating to attract the females for whom they will compete. I have found these gatherings of monotonously squeaking hummingbirds from Honduras to Panama. In our forest in El General, I have discovered none of them, although I have found a number of nests. Apparently, females breeding here must fly a considerable distance to the males who fecundate their eggs. In British Guiana (now Guyana) T. A. W. Davis (1958), who called this species the Buff-browed Hermit, noticed thirty-two assemblies, most of them from July to November. A large gathering might spread over an area two hundred and fifty yards (230 m) long and contain over one hundred hermits. One assembly in British Guiana was active in the same place for at least twelve years.

At La Selva, the reserve of the Organization for Tropical Studies in the Sarapiquí lowlands of northeastern Costa Rica, F. Gary Stiles and Larry L. Wolf (1979) studied the mating behavior of Long-tailed Hermits for four years. They found singing assemblies, which they called leks, in dense thickets along streams, about one for every two hundred and fifty acres (100 hectares) of undisturbed rain forest. Each assembly consisted of from five or six to twenty or twenty-five males. Around his song perches each male claimed a territory, which was larger the more open the surrounding vegetation and which never provided enough flowers to satisfy his needs. It was only a mating station.

As at the assemblies of other hummingbirds, singing was the males' chief means of advertising their availability to females and of keeping in contact with competitors, whom they could hear but rarely see amid the dense vegetation. In a small assembly a single song type was heard, but a large gathering had as many as four. The birds that sang alike were not randomly scattered through the assembly but segregated in different areas. In any group the same song persisted from year to year, learned by new members, as in White-eared Hummingbirds and Little Hermits.

The hermits apparently did not sleep on their territories. They flew from their roosts to the lek in earliest dawn. For a few minutes before they began to sing, their flight calls were audible in the still-dark understory. Most of the residents occupied high, exposed song perches at this time. Singing began at about 5:15 or 5:20 A.M. during the short days of December and January or February and at 5:05 in the longer days of May to July, or a few minutes later on dark, cloudy dawns. The most intense and synchronous singing of the whole day was heard during the ten or fifteen minutes after one or two individuals started the dawn chorus, which decreased in volume as daylight became bright enough to reveal the colors of the paint spots on the backs and plastic tags on the legs of the singing birds. Now began a period of intense activity in which territorial interactions and pursuits rose to a maximum, while singing continued and the lek became chaotic with songs, chatters, squeals, chase notes, and bill-pops. This uproar continued until, around six o'clock, daylight was bright enough for profitable foraging and most of the hermits dispersed to seek breakfast, for which so much strenuous activity had undoubtedly developed hearty appetites.

After their return from breakfast, the hummingbirds started another period of high vocal activity, which declined through the morning to a nadir around midday, when the birds sought their lunch and the assemblies were inactive. Returning in early or mid-afternoon, the hermits sang much until daylight waned in the forest, around five o'clock in the evening. Throughout the day, each resident had alternated periods of singing and interacting with neighbors, usually lasting ten to thirty minutes, with absences of a few minutes to an hour or more.

Supplementing the songs, various displays—mostly by a territory holder and a visitor, who was usually a neighboring male—enlivened the day. In the float display, the active bird flew slowly back and forth over a distance of three to six inches (7.5 to 15 cm) in front of a perching bird, turning his body from side to side. Always facing the perching bird, he opened widely his uptilted bill to reveal the bright orange interior of his mouth. With his gape similarly displayed, the resting bird kept his bill pointed toward the moving performer. Usually the resident male floated open-mouthed in front of the intruder, but the latter, especially when a member of the same assembly, might take the active role.

In the gape and bill-pop, the displaying male hovered a few inches from the perching hermit, facing him, and with elevated bill darted in a shallow arc toward the spectator. At the top of the arc he snapped his bill open and downward, flashing the colorful inside of his mouth in the other's face while he made a sound not unlike a sharp, explosive kiss. This startling display was usually given by a resident male to an intruder, but sometimes their roles were reversed.

The perch-exchange display was usually begun by a resident bird, who hovered in front of a visitor as in a gape and bill-pop act before he circled around to descend from behind toward the visitor. The latter flew away in time for the other to alight on the same spot. The displaced bird now supplanted the other in the same manner, in a sequence that might be rapidly repeated ten times and was occasionally combined with the gape and bill-pop display.

At times a visitor of either sex arrived to perch a few inches from the resident. With wide-open, uptilted bills, they turned their heads toward and away from one another, while they wagged fully spread tails strongly up and down and often, too, from side to side. Drooped, fluttering wings and fluffed feathers that intensified the striped facial pattern all helped make the side-by-side display more spectacular.

These displays were given in no fixed order. Often they ended with resident and intruder hovering face to face six inches to nearly a foot (15 to 25 cm) apart while they ascended together a yard or so (1 m), rising and sinking in the air. Finally, the resident chased his visitor rapidly back and forth through the lek or beyond view.

How shall we interpret these elaborate exercises in which two male hummingbirds participate? Authors who have described them have called them "aggressive," but no obvious aggression, such as pecking or fighting, is mentioned in their accounts. Possibly the displays help to reveal dominance and establish a social hierarchy, but if this is true, the assertion of dominance is subtle. Possibly, also, males display together to keep in practice for the rare occasions when a female arrives for coition. Female hummingbirds are not reported to watch two or more males performing vigorously together and be stimulated by the spectacle, as occurs among manakins, especially in the genus *Chiroxiphia*. The male hummingbirds' interactions often terminate in a chase, from which they soon return to their stations without the least indication that they have fought. A courtship assembly is maintained by a subtle balance between cooperation and competition; its participants cooperate to attract females for whom they compete. It might be compared to a contest between two athletic teams, which cooperate to arrange the game and follow the rules while they compete for victory. In a courtship assembly as in a soccer match, unbridled aggression would be disruptive.

In several hundred hours of watching, Stiles and Wolf witnessed only six probable copulations and two homosexual mountings. The former might occur when a female, after performing with a male much as he would do with a visiting male, stays on his display perch and invites him to mount her. If she flees, he may follow. On one occasion a female, after performing with a male, took wing and was followed by him for about sixty feet (20 m) before she alighted on a perch where he mounted her. I surmise that in Long-tailed Hermits, as in other hummingbirds, mating is most frequently consummated after a pursuit that takes the pair beyond view of a watcher at a singing assembly.

A Long-tailed Hermit who has sung long without attracting a female may relieve his tension by trying to copulate with a dead leaf about his own size, suspended by a spider web, most often on his territory, occasionally on a territory into which he has intruded, or at a distance from an assembly. No semen was found on these leaves. Similar foliaceous matings have been reported of other hermits, including the Green Hermit.

Male Long-tailed Hermits at La Selva began to occupy their stations and sing in late November or December, when *Heliconia pogonantha,* a principal source of their nectar, started to bloom abundantly. Their courtship activity attained full intensity by January, and continued at a high level through June and July. As adult males abandoned their stations in July and August, young males hatched the same year replaced them and sang actively. Singing was brief and irregular in September, when no hermits held territories. In October and November, when food was scarcest, the assemblies were almost deserted. As the next season of singing began, young hermits settled on peripheral territories, from which as they grew older they would work their way to the preferred stations at the center of their assembly. In larger birds whose matings are more easily observed and counted, females prefer the older, more experienced males on central stations.

Nectar-drinking birds tend to be more aggressive than frugivores. Hummingbirds conform to this rule, but not so strongly as some extremely pugnacious honeyeaters of Australia. The reason for the contrast between fruit eaters and nectar drinkers appears to be that the former can usually see at a glance whether a certain fruit is ripe enough to be eaten, whereas to learn whether a flower has been drained of its nectar, it must usually be probed. Nectar drinkers avoid this loss of time and energy by claiming a territory with enough flowers and excluding, to the best of their ability, other nectivores—insects as well as birds. Unlike many other hummingbirds, Long-tailed Hermits do not establish feeding territories that they vigorously defend; their long foraging routes are indefensible. Their display stations have nothing to offer to hummingbirds of other species and need be defended only against other males of their kind that covet these positions. The elaborate displays in which resident males engage with visiting males avert crude fighting, which appears rarely to occur in this species. For all these reasons, these hermits seem to have developed mild tempers. When they try to sip nectar from flowers vigorously defended by territorial hummingbirds, they are easily chased away by territory holders heavier than themselves, like the Red-footed Plumeleteers and White-tipped Sicklebills, or even lighter than themselves, like Blue-chested

Long-tailed Hermit

Hummingbirds and Rufous-tailed Hummingbirds, as Stiles and Wolf observed.

Of the seventeen nests of Long-tailed Hermits that I have seen, all at Los Cusingos, thirteen were in almost identical sites. Each was fastened beneath the drooping tip of a terminal segment of a frond of a small palm, usually a species of *Bactris* that bristled with long, needlelike, black spines. In height these nests ranged from five to eight and a half feet (1.5 to 2.6 m) above the ground, and all were in the deep shade of tall rain forest. Each nest was shaped to fit the tapering, concave end of the palm frond that bore it. It was broadest at the top, hollow to hold the eggs and young, and it tapered downward to a point; roughly it was an inverted hollow cone. The apex of the cone was prolonged as a thin, dangling tail that hung free below the tip of the palm frond.

A nest that I teased apart after the eggs vanished was composed of fine rootlets, delicate branched stems of mosses and liverworts, fibers of various kinds, and similar materials. Most of the nest's components were stiff and wiry, making it fairly rigid and harsh to the touch. Unlike the nests of many hummingbirds, it contained no soft, downy stuff. But in common with most, if not all, hummingbirds' nests, it was bound together by much cobweb, many filaments of which had been carried around the upper surface of the leaf to fasten the structure firmly to it. The nest's general color was brown. The overall length of this nest was eight inches (20 cm), half of which was occupied by the loose tail. In a nest seven inches long, the tail measured nearly five inches (18 and 12.5 cm).

These nests were about two inches (5 cm) in total width at the top. The diameter of the opening in the top varied from $1^3/8$ to $1^1/2$ inches, and the depth of this depression was $3/4$ to 1 inch (3.5 to 3.8 and 1.9 to 2.5 cm). In site, shape, and color, nests of the Long-tailed Hermit closely resemble those of the Little Hermit in the same locality, but they may be distinguished by their obviously larger size. Six Long-tailed Hermits' nests found by Davis in British Guiana were also attached beneath the tips of drooping leaves, usually palm fronds, but with no apparent preference for thorny kinds. These nests were from two to five feet (0.6 to 1.5 m) above the ground in both primary and secondary forest. Unlike the nest that I dissected, they contained silky seed down.

The other four nests that I have seen were in a small banana plantation beside a large tract of rain forest. The broad leaves of banana plants are readily torn from margin to massive midrib into sheets or strips of diverse widths, the strips more numerous and narrower the windier the situation. Three of these nests, apparently all built by the same individual, were fastened to the almost right-angled corners of broad sheets of lamina, which drooped around them and gave excellent shelter from rain and sunshine, especially in the middle hours of sunny days when the leaves wilted. The fourth nest was not attached to a sheet but to a strip of lamina, like nests of the Long-tails' neighbors in the banana plantation, the Bronzy Hermit and the Band-tailed Barbthroat, but the strip was broader than those chosen by these other hummingbirds, about two and a half inches (6.5 cm) wide, giving the Long-tail better protection. Twelve to fifteen feet (3.7 to 4.6 m) above the ground, these nests on banana leaves were higher than those on palm fronds in the forest, and broader expanses of leaves concealed them better. They were composed largely of fine fibers—apparently from the leaf sheaths of banana trunks—rootlets, the fungal filaments often called "vegetable horsehair," and cobweb, without downy material. They had the usual dangling tails, composed of strips apparently torn from decaying banana trunks, dead leaves, and the like. I watched a hermit bring what appeared to be a fibrous rootlet of an epiphyte, longer than herself, and coil it down into the cup, where she sat shaping it with vigorous movements of her body. Thicker-walled than the nests of the two neighboring species, the Long-tails' nests needed better protection from rain because they would hold more water and dry more slowly.

Each of fourteen nests held two eggs or nestlings. In two instances, the second egg was laid in the early morning two days after the first, in one case before 7:30. The pure white eggs are long and narrow. Because they are so fragile, I hesitated to remove them from their narrow nests. Both eggs of a set that I did lift out measured 15.9 by 9.5 millimeters. Six sets were laid in May, two in June, three in July, two in August, two in September, and one in January. These eggs were in the valley of El General, where January, February, and March are usually dry. Here Long-tailed Hermits nest later than in northeastern Costa Rica, where rainfall is more continuous throughout the year and the hermits lay from January to August, mostly from January to March.

Although some of my late nests probably held second or replacement broods, I have only one definite record of a brood following a successful nesting. From a nest in the banana plantation, nestlings flew on September 13 and 14, 1971. By the later date a nest had been started in a banana plant next to that which held the older one, in an exactly similar site. By September 21, this new nest contained its full set of two eggs. While she built and incubated, the mother probably fed her fledged young, whom I could not find, just as the White-eared Hummingbird in the highlands of Guatemala did in similar circumstances. In 1972 a third nest, similarly situated fifty feet (15 m) from the site of the second, held eggs laid at the end of May. The fourth nest on a banana plant, found with two eggs in September, 1980, was attached to a narrow strip instead of a broad sheet of lamina and probably belonged to a different individual.

By skillfully fastening her nest beneath the tip of the arching frond of a forbiddingly armed palm, the Long-tailed Hermit gains a number of advantages. She and the nest in which she sits are invisible from above and even largely screened on the sides by the back and incurved margins of the leaf tip. The green tissue forms a roof above her and keeps her dry in the hardest rain. Her eggs and nestlings seem to be inaccessible to many kinds of nest robbers. To offset these advantages, the hummingbird must sit in what appears to be such an unnatural, strained posture that we marvel that she can maintain it for as long as five minutes without becoming permanently crippled. She invariably incubates and broods with her head inward, toward the leaf surface to which her nest is attached. Since her bill is so long, she can sit with this orientation only by holding it straight upward, and to do so she must throw her head so far backward that it almost rests upon her rump. Her crown is not far from her long tail, which is held obliquely upward and projects far beyond the free rim of the nest. Her body is bent double, her chest turned straight upward—one cannot watch her for long without feeling sorry for her. One wonders why she does not punch a tiny hole in the tissue of leaf in front of her, so that she might stick her bill through it and sit in a more natural posture.

Doubtless the hermit has no need of our sympathy, for she can maintain this seemingly impossible posture for well over an hour, then dart away as though not a muscle or a tendon were strained. An incubating bird I watched through the morning of June 9, 1949, took five sessions ranging from 19 to 95 minutes in length and averaging 44 minutes. The longest session came at the end of the forenoon. An equal number of recesses ranged from 4 to 76 minutes and averaged 25.8 minutes. The longest recess came between two sessions of less than average length. The hermit kept her eggs covered for 63 percent of the six hours. To extract herself from her narrow quarters when she went for an outing, she unfolded her wings while sill sitting on the eggs. Then, beating them rapidly, she rose upward and backward until clear of the nest. Next she hovered a moment facing it, reversed, and darted away. Once, while hovering so, she stuck her bill into the nest, apparently to turn the eggs. It was impossible for her to turn them while she sat, unless she did so with her feet.

At the end of four of her five excursions, the hermit returned with a contribution for her nest in her bill. When she brought a fiber, she first settled in the nest and then stuck it in the wall beside her. But when she came with cobweb, her procedure was quite different; after almost sitting in the nest, she rose on wing and flew slowly around the tip of the supporting leaf, facing it. Once she made two consecutive turns around the leaf tip, in a counterclockwise direction, then settled on her eggs. By this method she stretched cobweb from the sides of her nest around the outside of the leaf. The constant renewal of this attachment, throughout the period of incubation, prevents the nest from breaking away.

Hummingbirds have very rapid metabolism. They excrete frequently, and they could not spend such long sessions on their eggs if it were not possible for them to excrete while sitting. From time to time, the hermit rose up in her nest and shot her liquid excreta well beyond its rim, an act always preceded by a good deal of vigorous wagging of her long, white-tipped tail. Thus she could incubate for long periods yet keep her nest clean. Most birds leave their nest for this purpose.

In the course of the morning, I only once saw a second Long-tailed Hermit. Before sunrise, this hummingbird flew up and hovered all around the nest, almost touching it, while the sitting bird pointed her bill at the intruder. Finally, she left the nest and chased the trespasser out of sight, to return in a minute and resume incubation. (This brief absence was not counted as a recess.) I do not know the relation of the second hermit to the nest's owner; apparently it was just a curious intruder. This interpretation was strengthened as, in the course of the morning, three smaller hummingbirds flew up at different times and inspected the nest much as the second hermit had done, then darted away before I could identify them.

Shortly before I ended my watch at midday, a reddish brown, black-faced weasel dug into a mound of loose earth close by the blind. Presently a frog jumped, or was thrown, out of the mound. The weasel caught it without much of a tussle, left it, then returned for it and carried it into a hole. The hummingbird continued to sit while all this occurred a short distance from her, leaving only when the weasel passed beneath her nest on its way to retrieve the frog.

One nest contained a single egg when found at 7:00 A.M. on August 23, 1950. At 8:20 next morning there were two eggs. At 8:00 on September 10 there was a single nestling, and by 4:50 P.M. on the same day there were two nestlings. The incubation period was 17 or 18 days. At another nest it was at least 17 days.

The nestlings hatch with the dark skin, sparse down, tightly closed eyes, and rudimentary bill typical of newborn hummingbirds. Soon after hatching, each orients itself with its head toward the surface of the leaf to which the nest is attached and with its posterior end outward, which is just the position taken by the incubating and brooding parent, and until it leaves the nest it preserves this orientation rather constantly. I have only exceptionally found nestlings otherwise aligned. One day, when the brooding parent flew from week-old nestlings as I approached, I found both of them lying with their heads toward the edge of the leaf rather than toward its middle; their bodies were parallel to the supporting surface of the leaf. They maintained this exceptional orientation for the next ten minutes. On a few visits I found these nestlings facing the leaf obliquely. But until the last one flew, they were usually found with their heads directly inward.

On June 12, 1949, I spent the first seven and a half hours of the day in view of a nest which held two nestlings in pinfeathers. They received their first meal at 6:38 on this drizzly morning, and when I left at 1:23 P.M. they had been fed eleven times, or at a rate of 0.8 visits with food per nestling per hour. I saw nothing to suggest that more than one parent was in attendance. Flying up through the undergrowth of the forest, she would hover beside the nest beneath a palm frond and utter a single cheep, which nearly always caused the nestlings to stretch their scrawny necks far upward and open their yellow mouths. To feed them, the parent never alighted on the nest's rim; on none of her visits did I see her touch it with her feet or any part of her body. She hovered well out from the nest with her feet folded up and invisible, as when she visited a flower, and reached over the nestlings' backs to insert her long, curved, black bill far down into the mouth and throat of one of them, as though she were about to suck nectar from a corolla tube. But now, instead of drawing nourishment, she forced it upward and outward, feeding her offspring by regurgitation.

When the parent finished feeding a nestling, she drew slightly away from the nest and dropped a little lower. Since her bill was still in the young bird's throat, this movement bent its head far back toward its tail, in what appeared to be a most uncomfortable and even dangerous posture. After removing her bill from the mouth of one nestling, she might hover before the nest, and by means of a sideward twitch of her long tail deftly effect the slight lateral movement of her body which would place it in precisely the position most favorable for feeding the other nestling. On most of her visits to the nest, both youngsters were given food twice or thrice, alternately. Sometimes one was given three portions and the other only two, but usually both received the same attention. In the middle of the morning, the parent flew up and hovered around the nest as though she had come to feed the nestlings, but they did not as usual raise their heads when they heard the hum of her wings, doubtless because they were not hungry. She did not coax them to eat, as many avian parents do, but perched nearby for a short while, then flew away.

The parent never cleaned the nest. To void, the nestlings raised their hindquarters above the nest's rim and shot their liquid excreta into the air, much as their mother had done while she incubated. Their habitual orientation with their heads toward the leaf and their tails outward is evidently an arrangement for keeping the nest clean. Were they to reverse this orientation, it would soon become foul. Once one of the young hummingbirds rose in its nest and rapidly beat its wings with their still rudimentary sprouting pinfeathers.

Unlike most birds that I have watched from a blind, this mother seemed to be curious about the contents of this large brown object that had so suddenly sprung up close by her nest. She repeatedly hovered facing a window, her dark, beady eyes only a few inches from mine. The light streak on her brownish throat was balanced by a liberal deposit of pale yellow pollen on her dark forehead and crown. Her scrutiny of the blind and its occupant completed to her satisfaction, she proceeded to feed her offspring, or settled to rest for a few minutes on a low, slender twig a few yards away.

Years later, I watched a parent Long-tailed Hermit attend two well-feathered nestlings beneath a banana leaf. In the first six hours of a September morning, she brought food to them fourteen times, or at the rate of 2.3 times per hour. On two visits she regurgitated twice to each nestling; on all the rest she fed one twice and the other once, always alternating, never regurgitating to the same nestling twice in succession. The nestling on the left received food twenty-three times; the nestling on the right, twenty-one times. As at the earlier nest, the parent always fed the young while hovering, not touching the nest with her feet.

At the age of about two weeks, the nestlings are well feathered, but they remain in their swinging cradle, still facing the supporting leaf, for another week or more. From a nest beneath a palm frond, the two young departed when 22 and 23 days old, respectively. A nestling that grew up beneath a banana leaf left when between 23 days and 24 days and 9 hours old. At two other nests, the nestling period was at least 22 days. At a nest watched by Davis, the period was at least 23 and possibly as much as 27 days.

It is hard to imagine safer sites for nests than these Long-tailed Hermits choose, yet most suffer hostile visitations. Only four of the thirteen nests of which I know the outcome were successful. All three of the nests in this category beneath banana leaves yielded flying young, but only one under a palm frond escaped premature destruction. If one may generalize from such small samples, smooth banana leaves beside forest are much safer sites for hermits' nests than are thorny palms within the predator-plagued forest. Three nests vanished completely, along with the eggs or nestlings they contained. From two other nests, the eggs inexplicably disappeared while the structures remained intact. From one nest, the nestlings were torn away, leaving the lining to which they had clung pulled up. From another, one nestling vanished but the other remained clinging to the rim, with its body thrown backward into the bowl and blood on its neck. On the following day, it, too, was no longer to be found. Thanks to the banana leaves, 30.8 percent of the thirteen nests were successful, which is not unusually low in tropical rain forest.

What could have taken the lost eggs or nestlings? I doubt that snakes could reach them, and they would not swallow or carry away a nest. A small mammal would probably leave revealing traces of its visit, such as a torn leaf or nest, yet in some cases eggs or nestlings vanished, leaving the nests and their supports uninjured. Swallow-tailed Kites carry away the nests of small birds and remove their contents while soaring, but these wide-winged predators do not descend beneath the forest canopy. I cannot imagine a clumsy toucan reaching a hermit's nest; moreover, they usually remain higher in the forest. This about exhausts the list of known avian predators in this forest except for hawks, especially the small Barred Forest-Falcon that frequents the lower stories, and an occasional owl. Perhaps the forest-falcon is the culprit, but I suspect bats. Here is another of the many mysteries that the tropical forest jealously guards.

CHAPTER 9 ✿

The Long-billed Starthroat Hummingbird

The Long-billed Starthroat is easily recognized by its long, straight, black bill; short, square-tipped tail; glittering metallic blue or blue-green forehead and crown; white streak behind each eye; brilliant reddish purple or magenta gorget with white borders; broad white streak on the lower back; and white tufts on each side of the rump. The male's upper parts are bronze-green; his breast is gray, paling to dull white on the belly; and he is four and a half inches (11.5 cm) long. Females tend to be duller than males, but some are almost as brilliant.

This hummingbird is found from southern Mexico to northeastern Peru, Bolivia, central Brazil, the Guianas, and Trinidad, from lowlands up to 4,000 to 5,000 feet (1,200 to 1,500 m) in various parts of its wide range. Avoiding the interior of closed rain forest, it inhabits light woodlands, shady pastures, plantations, and gardens, in regions of moderate to heavy rainfall. It appears nowhere to be abundant.

Starthroats visit a variety of flowers, favoring those with long, straight corollas. To suck nectar from white banana flowers clustered beneath thick, uplifted, dull red bracts, they hover almost upright, with their bills inclined strongly upward. When the poró trees (*Erythrina berteroana*, of the pea family) in our garden shed their leaves and begin to bloom as the dry season approaches in late November or December, starthroats arrive after a prolonged absence. Their long, straight bills are well adapted for probing the long, sword-shaped scarlet flowers, each consisting of a narrow, tightly folded standard that encloses four short petals, stamens, and pistil. The short, tubular calyx forms a thick collar around the base of the flower. Except for the long-billed Scaly-breasted Hummingbirds that sometimes pierce the collar, and Purple-crowned Fairies that perforate it with short, sharp bills, no other of our local hummingbirds can reach the nectar; and these two species can enjoy it only surreptitiously, when the starthroat who claims a poró tree is not looking.

A second starthroat daring to challenge the resident bird is vigorously assailed. I watched one starthroat dart back and forth a few inches above the head of a second, who was perched. Then it attacked the resting bird from below, seizing its head with its long bill. In self-defense, the resting bird grasped the assailant's bill, and for a few seconds the flying bird hung suspended from the two clasped bills before they separated and darted off in different directions. The poró trees continue to flower abundantly through December and January. When the last flowers fall in early February, the starthroats disappear.

Long-billed Starthroats are solitary, rather silent birds. A weak *tsip, tsip* and squeaky twitters appear to be the best their voices can do. They are not known to form courtship assemblies. Nor do starthroats give spectacular aerial displays, in the manner of many hummingbirds of the north temperate zone and open tropical mountaintops.

In late February and early March of 1968, a Long-billed Starthroat roosted in a dying guava tree on the hilltop behind our house. Its perch was a slender twig at the very top of the tree, with only the sky above, and around the bird a few small leaves that left it visible from all sides. After alighting on its roost, the bird always began to twitch its head rapidly from side to side until, after a few minutes or as much as a quarter of an hour, these movements decreased in amplitude until they ceased, leaving the bird with its bill directed forward and inclined slightly upward. In the darkness of night, I repeatedly found the starthroat in this attitude, its eyes shining brightly in the beam of my flashlight. The high, thin perch appeared to give it maximum security from such terrestrial predators as quadrupeds and snakes, although leaving it exposed to the attacks of owls and carnivorous bats—which were not numerous in this locality. Whether roosting or sitting in a nest, hummingbirds of various species appear always to sleep with forward-pointing bills, instead of turning their heads back to nestle amid the feathers of their shoulders, as many birds do.

Here in the valley of El General in southern Pacific Costa Rica, at nine degrees north latitude and around 2,500 feet (750 m) above sea level, many species of hummingbirds start nesting toward the end of our long rainy season in late November or December, when in sunny clearings shrubs

Long-billed Starthroat and Poró Flowers

and herbs bloom most profusely. They continue to breed until February or early March, when in many years plants languish in the dry soil and nectar-yielding flowers become much less abundant. Among these hummingbirds that choose the *verano* for breeding are Long-billed Starthroats. I found one starthroat incubating a second brood in early March, but nests started in February or later appear rarely to yield young.

In 1972 I published a history of my first Long-billed Starthroat's nest, which I watched carefully from the start of building until the young fledged, and thereafter as long as the parent fed them. Since that date, I have seen seven more nests, all in the valley of El General. The following account combines what I have learned about all of these eight nests, the only ones that appear to have been carefully studied.

Unlike most hummingbirds, which seek some shade or shelter for their nests, starthroats build them in sites no less exposed than that where I found one roosting. Six of my nests were in dead or, in one case, dying trees standing in open places, on branches, an inch or two (2–5 cm) thick. Five were thirty to forty feet (9–12 m) up, the sixth only fifteen feet (4.5 m) above the steep hillside behind our house. The seventh was in a more surprising situation, on electric wires about twenty feet (6 m) above the center of the fairly busy unpaved road by our entrance gate, where cars passed day and night. In the middle of a long stretch between supporting poles, the three vertically separated wires were held apart by an insulator. In the top of this tubular piece the nest was set and half concealed. The eighth nest was attached to similar wires above a busier paved highway, beside a schoolyard that was probably quite noisy at recess time. When our car stopped beneath the nest in the fading light of evening, I could learn about it no more than that it was situated where wires led to a house from the three supporting cables.

At three nests I watched building by a female without a helper, as is usual in hummingbirds. From the bark of trees she gathered lichens, mosses, and liverworts. To detach an encrusting lichen, the builder hovers nearly upright beside a trunk and inserts her bill beneath the selected material, then flies upward, using her bill as a lever to pry the piece off. For years before I could find a starthroat's nest, we watched one of these birds collect cobweb from the wall of our house, to carry it beyond view. Occasionally the hummingbird brings a tuft of seed down to her nest. While she sits in it arranging a new contribution, she bounces up and down, apparently kneading the materials with her feet, while she rotates to face in different directions. When a bird is so engaged, the tufts of white down on her flanks often stand out prominently. With her long bill, the starthroat spreads cobweb over the outside of her nest and the supporting surface, attaching it more securely. In early morning sunshine, one starthroat brought materials to her nest nineteen times in an hour, eleven times in half an hour. A different starthroat came with fifteen contributions in an hour in the middle of the morning. Such concentrated building is exceptional; most visits to the nest are more widely spaced. One starthroat took about eight days to build her nest, another about twelve. The finished structure is a neat open cup that blends well with the dead branch where it is usually situated, appearing to be an excrescence on the rough bark.

From time to time a second starthroat, apparently a male, visits the building female. They fly off together, one seeming to chase the other. I surmise that the male seeks the female to fertilize her eggs, a system very different from that of the many tropical hummingbird species in which males attract females to a courtship assembly at a distance.

On November 6, in a mixed deciduous and evergreen forest at an altitude of about 2,400 feet (730 m) in the Mexican state of Oaxaca, J. Stuart Rowley (1966) found a Long-billed Starthroat's nest on a small outer branch of a *Cecropia* tree, about fifty feet (15 m) above the ground. The female was apparently incubating at this inaccessible site. On November 11 of the same year, he found another nest with two eggs, eight feet (2.5 m) up on a drooping branch of a shrub in the partial shade of a coffee plantation. His photograph of the first nest shows that in site and construction it closely resembled those I found in Costa Rica. The second nest, also illustrated, was so different in situation and construction from all the other nests that I suspect an error in identification.

At my only accessible nest, eight or nine days elapsed between the end of active building and the laying of the first egg on December 8. The hummingbird was absent from her nest on the two nights that intervened before she laid her second egg, early in the morning. An interval of two days between laying is usual in hummingbirds. The two elongate white eggs had very thin, soft shells.

At this nest I watched the starthroat incubate through all of one morning and all of a subsequent afternoon. In twelve hours, I timed fifteen full sessions that ranged from 3 to 137 minutes and averaged 34.3 minutes. Her longest sessions, 137 and 67 minutes, were in the afternoon; the next longest, 53 and 41 minutes, in the forenoon. Her sixteen recesses were 4 to 19 minutes and averaged 10 minutes. She incubated for 77.4 percent of her twelve hours of daytime activity.

I did not see the starthroat move her eggs with her long bill. At intervals she bounced rapidly up and down in the nest, kneading it and possibly turning the eggs with her feet. In the warm afternoon, she usually sat facing away from the Sun. Once, facing west, she leaned far sideways, with her breast feathers puffed out, "sunbathing" in the nest, which I have rarely seen a bird do. From time to time in the morning she brought material, usually cobweb, to her nest, and in late afternoon she came with spiders' silk five times in seven minutes, each time rotating in the nest while she spread it over the outside. To leave the bowl into which she fitted snugly, she flew upward and backward, then reversed to fly away. In this nest, into which I could look with a mirror attached to a long pole, the incubation period was 18½ to 19 days. At an inaccessibly high nest, it was at least 18 days. The empty shells were promptly removed.

When my mirror first revealed the tiny, dark-skinned, short-billed nestlings, they had tightly closed eyes like other newly hatched hummingbirds. When they were about two weeks old, the upper parts, throat, and breast were covered with short tufts of whitish down, more abundant than I have seen on any other hummingbird. This blended well with the light-colored bark where the nest was situated and made them less conspicuous in their exposed cup. Apparently, it also gave some protection from the strong sunshine to which they were exposed for increasingly long intervals while their mother sought food. As I have found with other species of hummingbirds, the tiny, newly hatched creatures were amazingly resistant to sunshine so intense that brief exposure to it would have killed small passerine nestlings. (If naked nestling hummingbirds could not withstand extremes of sunshine, rain, and cold, a single parent could not rear them in climates so diverse as those of wet lowland forests and near the snow caps of equatorial volcanos.)

When the starthroats were nineteen days old, their wing plumes were becoming long. Dull black in color, they contrasted with the whitish down that covered much of their bodies, reminding me of much bigger Brown Boobies at a corresponding stage of development. Often shifting their positions in the nest, they preened much and scratched their heads with a foot raised above a drooped wing, as adult hummingbirds do. Rising in the nest, they vigorously exercised their wings. When twenty-three days old, the nestlings were well covered with brown and whitish plumage. They sometimes preened each other as well as themselves. Two or three days later, they abandoned the nest.

While brooding small nestlings, the parent sometimes bounced up and down, much as she did while building and incubating. Why she did this, I do not know. When a week old, the nearly naked nestlings were brooded only a quarter of the six and a half morning hours that I watched. They were left exposed for intervals as long as twenty-one and sixty-one minutes. The longest sessions of brooding were not in the cool early morning but later, when the sunshine was most intense. While the mother covered the nestlings, they stuck their bills or whole heads out in front of her breast and panted. Nocturnal brooding continued only until the nestlings were ten days old, after which they slept alone, although at an altitude of 2,500 feet (750 m) January nights were often chilly. Such early cessation of nocturnal brooding is usual for hummingbirds, except those at high altitudes where frost forms on cloudless nights.

When the two nestlings were seven days old, their mother came with food eight times in six and a half morning hours. On a single visit she usually regurgitated to each of them from three to five times, alternately, pushing her long bill far down into their throats, thereby delivering the contents of her crop in seven to nine acts of regurgitation. After a generous meal, the nestlings' crammed esophageal pouches protruded grotesquely on one side of the neck. When the young starthroats were nineteen days old, their parent brought food thirteen times in the first six and a half hours of the day. Now she regurgitated to each of them only once or twice on a visit, but she apparently gave them more each time. Parent birds of many kinds that feed by regurgitation space meals much more widely than do those bringing food in their bills.

On January 23, when the nestlings were twenty-five or twenty-six days old, they spontaneously left their nest, which by then had become well flared out by their growing bodies. As often happens, one that had just departed seemed not to be hungry; after accepting a single act of regurgitation it refused to take more. At a nest high in a tree, the single nestling remained only twenty-three or twenty-four days, leaving on January 24 or 25. The solitary nestling on the electric wires remained for the unusually long period of twenty-seven days, departing on February 3.

After leaving the lowest nest where I watched them grow up, the young starthroats remained in neighboring trees, attended by their mother. Eight days after their exit from the nest, they could fly and hover competently. They appeared to pluck from leaves and twigs things too small to be distinguished. Two days later, they hovered beside inflorescences of a poró tree and touched the scarlet flowers with their bills, without inserting them into the tightly closed petals of this important source of starthroats' nectar. Eleven days after quitting the nest, where they had rested so peaceably together, the juveniles became antagonistic to each other. When the parent came to feed them, one struck the other with its body and, after some skirmishing, drove it away. When no meal was in sight, the two might rest calmly a yard apart, preening and stretching their wings, for many minutes; but when their mother arrived to feed them, and they perched expectantly on opposite sides of her, one chased the other away. The parent continued to feed the juveniles until at least mid-February, twenty-three days after they fledged, when they were forty-eight days old and closely resembled adult females.

An adult male, perhaps the father of the juveniles, was often among the trees frequented by the family of three and tried to drive them away. When he assailed a perching juvenile, it clung beneath the twig and pointed its long bill toward the attacker, in an attitude unexpected in a weak-footed hummingbird. The adult promptly retreated. In subsequent days he often darted at a juvenile, who did not move even when the older bird almost struck it. Pursuits among the starthroats were now common. A Snowy-bellied Hummingbird and two Scaly-breasted Hummingbirds also visited these trees, chasing one another and being chased by a starthroat.

Fifteen days after the single fledgling left a high nest in an aguacatillo tree, the mother starthroat started to renovate this nest, but after continuing for a few days, she abandoned the undertaking. A month after the single fledgling departed one of the nests on the electric wires, its mother was again incubating in this nest. It was then early March, rather late for a starthroat to be nesting, but the preceding month had been unusually wet. I did not learn the outcome of this second nesting. Beside Gatún Lake in central Panama, on January 30, 1961, a fledgling flew from and reentered a nest thirty feet (9 m) up at the tip of a dead twig. By April 23, two young were overflowing this same nest, evidently a successful second brood (Willis and Eisenmann 1979).

While building, incubating, or brooding and feeding nestlings, Long-billed Starthroats have a peculiar habit that I have noticed in no other bird. Instead of flying directly away from the nest, they flit from twig to twig around it, resting briefly on each before they fly beyond view. They may do this from four or five to ten or more times before they depart. This behavior was especially prominent at the nest on the electric wires above the unpaved road. Leaving the nest, the starthroat flitted between points on the three wires, on each of which she rested for a few seconds. Sometimes she reversed her direction, but the places where she alighted were increasingly distant from her nest. After as many as ten of these short flights had taken her three or four yards from her point of departure, she flew away. I cannot imagine why the starthroats behaved in this strange manner, which drew attention to their inconspicuous but exposed nests.

CHAPTER 10 &

The Parasitic Striped Cuckoo

Although the Striped Cuckoo ranges from southern Mexico to Ecuador west of the Andes and east of the Andes over most of South America to northern Argentina and southern Brazil, I did not find it here in the valley of El General until a decade after my arrival in 1935, when destruction of the forest barrier opened the way for it. About twelve inches (30 cm) in length, this cuckoo slender-bodied and long-tailed has cinnamon-brown, black-striped upper parts and whitish, brown- or buff-tinged underparts. It has a short, decurved bill and wears a brown, bushy crest. Its most extraordinary feature is its alula, or bastard wing, a tuft of long, stiff black feathers at the bend of the wing. No other bird that I know has such a prominent alula.

I have watched Striped Cuckoos behave in the strangest ways, such as I have seen in no other bird. Standing on the ground or resting on a low perch, they constantly raise and lower the long feathers of the crown. At the same time, they continually extend their alulas and wave them slowly around, sideward or forward, as though sending a semaphore message. They stretch out and close their wings, one at a time, for no apparent reason. Sometimes they extend a wing sideward with its alula prominently erected. As though all this movement were not enough, they shift the body from side to side, much as a broody hen does to adjust her eggs beneath her. Thus, standing or perching, the cuckoo constantly moves, in an apparently purposeless manner, some part of itself—its crest, its long alulas, its entire wings, or its whole body. It seems to suffer from a bad attack of fidgets. The exaggerated, mobile alulas earn for this bird the name Four-winged Cuckoo.

The Striped Cuckoo's diet includes caterpillars, dragonflies, cockroaches, bugs, other insects, and spiders. These birds bound over the ground in pursuit of grasshoppers or hop through thickets searching for other small creatures. At times they run over open fields with back hunched up and head depressed, in a most peculiar attitude. They often dust bathe in a sandy spot.

More often than one sees these retiring birds, one hears their far-carrying, melodious, ventriloquial whistles issuing from a thicket, occasionally in the middle of a dark night. The melancholy minor key of these notes makes them unmistakable, whether they are voiced in pairs or in series of three to six. The second note of a couplet is commonly a half-tone higher than the first. Longer series are accelerated toward the end. These calls may be repeated at regular intervals for so many minutes that some people find them annoying. When the cuckoo sings from the top of a bush, exposed branch, or telephone wire, it may be seen to raise its crest rhythmically between calls. The two-syllable call earns for the bird some of its names: *crespín* in Argentina, *sací* in Brazil, Juan Gil or *saucé* in Venezuela. In Panama, longer calls are responsible for the designations *tres pesos*, or *tres pesos pide*.

As has long been known, the Striped Cuckoo neither builds a nest nor cares for its young but foists its eggs upon birds of other species, nearly always those with well-enclosed nests. The most frequent victims of its parasitic habit are members of the large Neotropical ovenbird family, the Furnariidae, which build bulky nests of tightly interlaced twigs, often entered through a narrow tube. Among the known hosts are seven species of spinetails or castlebuilders (*Synallaxis*); also three species of thornbirds (*Phacellodomus*), whose nests, often pendent from trees, may have two or many chambers. The Chotoy Spinetail's bulky globe of closely interlocked sticks, entered through a long, nearly horizontal tube, receives the Striped Cuckoo's eggs, as does the large stick nest of the Yellow-throated Spinetail, which builds an entrance tube directed almost vertically upward. The burrow in the ground or cavity in a tree where the Buff-fronted Foliage-gleaner nests is not exempt from the parasite's intrusions. In the flycatcher family, the White-headed Marsh-Tyrant's globular nest with its side entrance and the similar structures of species of *Myiozetetes* are invaded; and in another family, the well-covered nests of the Rufous-and-white and the Plain wrens receive the alien eggs. Among finches, the Black-striped Sparrow, which builds a bulky

Striped Cuckoo

domed nest with a wide doorway in the side, is an occasional host of the parasite.

The following are recorded hosts of the Striped Cuckoo:

Chotoy Spinetail, *Schoeniophylax phryganophila*
Buff-browed Spinetail, *Synallaxis superciliosa*
Sooty-fronted Spinetail, *S. frontalis*
Chicli Spinetail, *S. spixi*
Pale-breasted Spinetail, *S. albescens*
Plain-crowned Spinetail, *S. gujanensis*
Stripe-breasted Spinetail, *S. cinnamomea*
Rufous-breasted Spinetail, *S. erythrothorax*
Yellow-throated Spinetail, *Certhiaxis cinnamomea*
Short-billed Canastero, *Asthenes baeri*
Red-eyed Thornbird, *Phacellodomus erythrophthalmus*
Rufous-fronted Thornbird, *P. rufifrons*

Greater Thornbird, *P. ruber*
Buff-fronted Foliage-gleaner, *Philydor rufus*
White-headed Marsh-Tyrant, *Arundinicola leucocephala*
Flycatchers, *Myiozetetes* spp.
Tody-Flycatchers, *Todirostrum* spp.
Plain Wren, *Thryothorus modestus*
Rufous-and-white Wren, *T. rufalbus*
Black-striped Sparrow, *Arremonops conirestris*

(Belcher and Smooker 1936, ffrench 1973, Friedmann 1933, Haverschmidt 1968, Kiff and Williams 1978, Loetscher 1952, Morton and Farabaugh 1979, Narosky et al. 1983, Ridgely 1976, Sick 1984, Wetmore 1968).

Striped Cuckoos' eggs vary in color from white and bluish white to bluish green. They measure from 20 to 22.8 by 16.2 to 17 millimeters and weigh from 3.1 to 3.7 grams. They are only slightly larger and heavier than the eggs of the cuckoos' much smaller hosts; one of these, the Plain-crowned Spinetail, lays eggs that measure 20.4 by 14.4 millimeters and weigh 2.5 grams. Yet the female cuckoo weighs 47 grams and the spinetail only 18 grams. The host's egg is 14 percent of the bird's weight; the parasite's only 8 percent. The spinetail's egg hatches in eighteen days, the cuckoo's in fifteen, which gives the cuckoo nestling a great advantage over those of the host. Two of the parasite's eggs are sometimes found in a nest.

Among the more heavily parasitized species is the Yellow-throated Spinetail, in mangroves, marshes, and swamps in Suriname, where Haverschmidt found the alien eggs in fourteen of twenty-one nests. The cuckoos' eggs were laid in every month except May and November. In Trinidad, breeding was recorded in March and from May to October, but frequent singing from December to April suggested that on this island, as in Suriname, Striped Cuckoos lay their eggs in other birds' nests throughout the year.

It seemed so improbable that Striped Cuckoos could pass through narrow entrance tubes made for much smaller birds that naturalists conjectured that the parasite tore a hole in a nest's wall to steal in and lay its egg. As spinetails promptly repaired holes that I made in the sides of their nest chambers (the only way to examine the contents without tearing apart their laboriously made edifices), they might do the same with gaps made by cuckoos. The problem was solved when Hugh C. Land showed a motion picture of a slender-bodied cuckoo pushing into the narrow passage that led into a Rufous-breasted Spinetails' tightly enclosed structure and later emerging without difficulty (Wetmore 1968). This was in Guatemala, apparently the northernmost point where a Striped Cuckoo has been discovered parasitizing a nest.

The hatchling Striped Cuckoo is devoid of down and the interior of its mouth is yellow, like that of nestling wrens, flycatchers, spinetails, and probably other ovenbirds that foster it. The young cuckoo does not, like cowbirds, often grow up beside the progeny of its hosts; nor can it eject them, as European, or Common, Cuckoos do from open nests. Its situation resembles that of African honeyguides in the deep nest cavities of barbets and woodpeckers, and it employs the same means to eliminate competition for food. As in certain honeyguides, the tips of the young cuckoo's upper and lower mandibles terminate in sharp hooks, with which it worries and bites its nest mates until they perish. Although Striped Cuckoos sometimes lay two eggs in a nest, it is unlikely that two such savage nestlings could grow up together. In nests of ovenbirds and wrens, they would be nourished with small invertebrates with perhaps rarely a berry. Black-striped Sparrows would give them more fruits. In western Panama, a Rufous-and-white Wren gave a number of red berries to a Striped Cuckoo almost fully grown (Loetscher 1952).

Unlike honeyguides, Striped Cuckoos retain the hooks on their bills as long as they remain in the nest. If a person inserts a finger into a Rufous-and-white Wren's nest where a nestling cuckoo rests, it contorts its neck, strikes like a snake, and tries to bite. When the cuckoo leaves its nest at the age of eighteen days (which is about the nestling period of a spinetail) it cannot fly but can run fast. A hand-raised cuckoo from a Rufous-and-white Wren's nest was flightless until twenty-five days old. It continued to accept food from a forceps until the age of thirty-six days, when it showed fear at the approach of its human fosterers and refused what they offered. Thenceforth, it fed chiefly on the ground, over which it moved rapidly. By this time, the yellow lining of its mouth had changed to red.

While still being hand-fed, the fledgling cuckoo uttered short whistled notes much like those of fledged Rufous-and-white Wrens reared in the same aviary, which probably made it more attractive to fostering wrens. Instead of fluttering its whole wings when approached with food, as young birds commonly do, it kept them tightly closed while it spread and waved its black alulas, which, viewed from the front, made it appear smaller, and probably less intimidating, to foster parents smaller than itself. About the time the young cuckoo refused proffered food, it ceased to vibrate its bastard wings in this fashion but displayed them in the manner of adults. Perhaps the primary function of these puzzling alulas, the factor that promoted their evolution, is to encourage timid parents to feed their strange fosterlings (Morton and Farabaugh 1979).

CHAPTER II

A Paradoxical Relationship

Here in this tropical valley live countless thousands of birds of three hundred species. They dwell together in a degree of harmony surprising when one considers their number and diversity of habits. Since a large proportion of them remain paired throughout the year and continuously occupy the area where they nest, disputes for the possession of mates and territories are less frequent and conspicuous than among northern birds, many of which are migratory and must each spring hurriedly find mates and claim their territories anew. Here raptors are not numerous, parasitic cowbirds rare, and peace prevails in the avian community.

But there is one outstanding exception, one perpetual disturber of the harmony among our local birds. It is a small flycatcher with dull brownish upper plumage and a dingy yellow breast streaked with narrow dusky lines—a bird neither beautiful nor distinguished in aspect, that would attract the eye of none but the enthusiastic bird-watcher equipped with a binocular. Toward the end of January or early in the sunny month of February, this plainly clad flycatcher arrives from South America, where it passes the nonbreeding season, and promptly announces its presence by a variety of thin, breezy whistles that suggest a careless, easygoing, vagabond nature. In these airy, carefree utterances, one listens in vain for a trace of the earnestness of the newcomer's neighbor and relative, the yellow-breasted Vermilion-crowned Flycatcher; for the depth of feeling of the brown Garden Thrush; or for the retiring modesty of the Blue-gray Tanager. These notes seem to be the self-revealing expression of a character lighthearted and shallow, bound by no ties. Only the persistence of his repetitions of the long-drawn *pee-e-e-e* and the high-pitched, rapid *pee-de-*

de-de might lead the perspicacious student of avian nature to suspect that behind that voice lurked a vein of stubborn pertinacity unexpected in a character so breezy. Nevertheless, if nature poetry flourished amid the forests and farms of southern Costa Rica, local bards might celebrate the migratory Piratic Flycatcher's voice as a harbinger of spring, like the Cuckoo's call in England, or the songs of the Eastern Bluebird and the American Robin in eastern North America.

Yet, to a certain section of the local bird population, I suspect that the Piratic Flycatcher's airy whistles are the reverse of a cheering message. At this season, I fancy that I hear the yellow-breasted Gray-capped Flycatchers exclaiming to their mates in their thick, earnest voices, and the Vermilion-crowned Flycatchers repeating in their soft, high tones *Confound it! So that pest is back again!*

For in March, the month of gathering clouds and the first light evening showers, the Gray-caps and the Vermilion-crowns, together with a host of other birds of the most diverse kinds and colors, begin to build their nests, that they may bring forth their young in verdant, flowery April and May, when abundant fruits and insects lighten the task of filling hungry nestling mouths. But not so the Piratic Flycatchers; instead of setting about to prepare their nests, they continue to perch idly in the treetops, now and again darting out to snatch up passing insects, and they repeat their thin whistles, as breezy and impudent as ever. Not for this pair the pleasant occupation of choosing, male and female together, the site of the future nest, amid the dark foliage of an orange or lemon tree or at the leafy end of a long bough overhanging the sparkling river, close beside a hive of stinging wasps that will fiercely punish any heavier, less aerial creature that shakes the swinging branch. Not for the female Piratic Flycatcher the light task of building the nest, while her partner perches nearby, dropping a cheery note of encouragement each time she passes with a straw in her bill. These flycatchers have other ends in view; they watch and whistle while others work.

Finally, after a week or two of unhurried labor, the Gray-cap, or her cousin the Vermilion-crown, has completed her nest, a commodious structure of dry straws and weed stems, with a high domed roof to shield the occupants from Sun and rain, and a wide round doorway in the outer side. A few mornings later, she lays the first of her white eggs wreathed with brownish spots, then one or two more on the following days. Now is the time for the Pirates to play their masterstroke of strategy. Not without pur-

Piratic Flycatcher

pose have they waited all these weeks in the tops of neighboring trees, appearing so blithe and innocent, yet watching every move of their intended victims, and quite aware of the precise stage of the nesting operations of the particular Gray-cap or Vermilion-crown they have chosen to despoil of her labor.

One fine morning, after eggs have been laid in the domed nest, one member of the striped pair ventures closer than the owners will tolerate. Then one of the yellow-breasts, as likely as not the male, darts at the intruder, who at once prudently retires. Perhaps the female yellow-breast joins in the aerial chase. The longer and hotter the pursuit, the better for the ends of the Pirates. While one of the pair decoys the owners away, the other enters the unguarded nest, takes a spotted egg in its bill, flies out, and drops it to the ground. They have scored their first point in the unequal contest.

The aggressors retire to catch insects and call in neighboring trees, until, at their convenience, they return for the second round. The yellow-breasted proprietors of the nest, excited and angry now, dart fiercely at them, determined to drive away these impertinent thieves. The chase is ardent; pursuer and pursued twist and double until it is difficult to follow their movements with the eye. But the defense of the yellow-breasts reveals more zeal than strategy; in their spirited sally to drive the invaders from their citadel, they have neglected to maintain a garrison. Again the striped-breasts' opportunity—soon a second egg lies broken on the ground. When the last of the eggs has shared the same fate, the contest ends, as it always does, in favor of the Piratic Flycatchers. Although such battles are spectacular and noisy, with both sides voicing their characteristic cries, none of the contestants suffers injury greater than the loss of a few feathers.

Few birds will lay a second time in a nest that has been pillaged. So the Gray-cap or Vermilion-crown that has lost her nest soon begins, hopeful and industrious as ever, to construct a second domed nest close by, leaving the plundered structure in possession of the invaders. The Pirates carry in a loose handful of small dry leaves—which the builders of these domed nests never themselves take in—as though they felt constrained to make at least a pretense of useful effort. Among this loose litter the female Piratic Flycatcher lays her three grayish brown, mottled eggs and incubates them while her mate whistles in impudent exultation from the nearest treetop. And these thieving birds, once established in their ill-gotten home, guard it with as much zeal, and attend with as much care and affection the eggs and young it shelters, as though they had built it with their own bills. Frequently while she sits over her eggs, the female may be overheard singing to herself a sweet little song that suggests love and contentment.

The season is now well advanced, and the dispossessed yellow-breast labors with more concentrated energy to finish her second nest. Soon it is completed, a new set of eggs deposited in it, and the patient task of incubation begun once again. Occasionally, during an interval when the second nest of its victims remains unguarded, the Piratic Flycatcher will remove an egg from that nest, more from habit than from malice. Rarely, it throws out nestlings. But in general, all goes well with the replacement nest of the

Vermilion-crowned Flycatcher (*left*) and Piratic Flycatcher

yellow-breasts—if snake and weasel and hawk and destructive boys fail to pass its way—so long as the Piratic Flycatchers prosper in their stolen nest nearby. But the eggs and young of the home robbers are preyed upon by the same enemies that take their toll of the offspring of the home builders. If eggs or young are lost, as may happen in from a quarter to half of all the nests occupied by Piratic Flycatchers, these birds will not again entrust their eggs to it. Instead, they demand another domed nest of their victims, the yellow-breasts, and will most likely throw out the new set of eggs that the female yellow-breast is incubating in her second structure nearby, causing that unfortunate bird to build yet a third.

One might suppose that the unhappy pair would move to some more distant spot to construct their later nests, instead of placing these within such easy reach of their persecutors and despoilers. But, as a rule, this is not feasible; were they to go in search of an alternate area suitable for their breeding operations, they might find it already occupied by another pair of their kind, who would resist their intrusion, and who probably also had to contend with a pair of the pestiferous striped-breasts. So the long-suffering Gray-caps and Vermilion-crowns linger upon their own home ground chosen months earlier, and hopefully build nest after nest, until at last, unless they have more than usual bad luck, one is successful, and their bright-eyed fledglings, safely past the most critical stage of their lives, fly from its shelter and clamor incessantly for food in the neighboring trees.

Thus, when a pair of yellow-breasted flycatchers is selected by a pair of Piratic Flycatchers as their victims, they not only lose their first nest but may also lose their subsequent nests. Consequently, *their success depends largely upon the success of their persecutors.* The safety of the second nest occupied by their eggs and nestlings is not contingent upon what happens to this nest alone, but also upon the success of the earlier structure stolen from them by the Pirates, and the risk of loss is doubled. Fortunately, Vermilion-crowned and Gray-capped flycatchers are hardy, abundant species, widespread in tropical America. The Piratic Flycatcher, like the Vermilion-crowned (the wider ranging of its victims), spreads over a vast territory from Mexico to northern Argentina but in most parts of its range is less numerous than the two yellow-breasted species whose nests it occupies. And these, despite the loss of so many nests to the striped thief, are in extensive regions of the American tropics among the more common birds in dooryards, plantations, pastures with scattered trees, and along the shores of rivers and lakes. They avoid heavy closed forests, which are unfavorable for their flycatching.

Here nature has created a situation that offers as profound a moral as any parable sprung from the fecund imagination of Aesop, La Fontaine, or Iriarte. Of the main events in the struggle between the Piratic Flycatcher and its victims I am certain, having witnessed these not fifty yards from my dwelling. And each year, over a vast territory in the warmer parts of America, this little drama of bird life is enacted thousands of times, as it has been, no doubt, during untold centuries stretching beyond the dawn of human history. Here is a relationship between two antagonistic species so old, so firmly established, and so widespread, that it may well be worthy of our serious examination. The reader who is acquainted with none of the chief protagonists—who has never heard the Vermilion-crown call softly *chipsacheery* over and over at dawn and has seen nothing of the devoted industry of the Gray-cap building her domed nest—will have formed no prejudices in favor of one side or the other, and can the more coolly draw conclusions from their strange history.

After long acquaintance with these attractive birds, I have become the partisan of the aggrieved party. Once, while watching the conflict between a pair of Gray-caps and a pair of Piratic Flycatchers for possession of a nest, I longed to be able to drop a word of advice into the ears of the defenders. "Instead of dashing foolishly in pursuit of your slippery assailants," I wanted to tell them, "keep your citadel constantly garrisoned. Take turns warming your eggs; keep them continuously covered, and the pesky little striped-breasts will be unable to harm them."

It would have been sound advice proffered in vain. In the great family of American flycatchers, males are not known to incubate eggs or brood nestlings. For a male flycatcher to sit in the nest would be as extraordinary and unconventional as for a male woodpecker or a male antbird to neglect these duties. Doubtless Gray-caps, conservative as most birds are, would rather continue to risk the loss of their nests than change the immemorial habits of their kind; just as those who have been born and raised on the slopes of an active volcano will linger there, under the constant menace of a disastrous eruption, instead of seeking a safer home in strange parts.

What, then, could the Gray-capped Flycatchers and the Vermilion-crowns do to stop this annually recurrent and oft-repeated outrage? Here is a problem that has sometimes amused me on solitary walks. They might unite against their tormentors and try to destroy them in a war of extermination. But they would probably fail, for the smaller Piratic Flycatchers are swift and agile enough to escape them. Or they might become disciples of the Mahatma Gandhi, wage a passive instead of an active warfare, and refuse to build nests at all, seeing that so many of them are made for the benefit of their enemies. But this Gandhian policy, also, could not be wholly successful; for the two species of yellow-breasted flycatchers, although locally, at least, the chief victims of the striped-breasts, are by no means the only ones.

The pirates occupy a variety of covered or closed nests, including the long woven pouches of oropendolas and other members of the oriole family, the snug globular structures of fibrous and downy materials built in treetops by becards, the retort-shaped nests attached to the tips of slender twigs by Yellow-olive Flycatchers, and they have even been known to take possession of the nest chamber carved by Violaceous Trogons into the heart of a big silvery gray wasps' nest high in a tree. It is probably in such vespiaries that their litter of dead leaves is most helpful, for trogons do not line their nests with soft materials. But I have no record of Piratic Flycatchers occupying an open nest, such as those of thrushes, tanagers, sparrows, and many other songbirds. Hence, were the yellow-breasted flycatchers to declare a strike and refuse to build, the Pirates would be deprived of the most important but by no means the only source of their nests. By such a course, the yellow-breasts would be more likely to accomplish race-suicide than the extermination of their adversaries (Skutch 1960, 1972).

Or, taking the philanthropic—or should I say "philornithic"?—view, the Vermilion-crowns and Gray-caps might conduct classes to teach the less gifted Piratic Flycatchers how to build nests. But the auguries of success of such a generous endeavor are not encouraging. Evolutionists are familiar with Dollo's "law of loss," which points to the improbability that an organ, aborted in the course of evolution, can ever be recovered in its original form. If, in consequence of an altered mode of life or a change of habitat, a need for the lost organ arises, a substitute that is not homologous with it may be developed. Thus, a plant that, in an arid climate, has lost the ability to form leaves may with increasing humidity flatten its stems to increase its capacity for photosynthesis. Such changes require many generations. The rule of loss may apply not only to organs but likewise to instincts, or innate patterns of behavior, such as nest building. It appears unlikely that Piratic Flycatchers could ever recover the ability to make nests such as their ancestors formerly built.

All things considered, it is probable that the best course the victims of the Piratic Flycatchers could take is that which they already follow. Indeed, it is not likely that the philosophic naturalist, in a comfortable armchair or on musing evening walks, can improve upon the ways nature has evolved by millions of interactions between aggressor and victims over an immensely long period. Yet I make bold to suggest a small improvement on the course actually followed by yellow-breasted flycatchers threatened by a pair of Pirates: that instead of making a nest in the vain hope of using it themselves and laying eggs only to have them thrown away, each pair of yellow-breasts, at the outset of the breeding season, build a nest especially for the Pirates, and when it is completed, lay no eggs there but respectfully invite their persecutors to move in and have joy of it. Then, chirping praises of their own philornithy in providing for their handicapped relations the means to perpetuate their kind, they could go ahead and build another for themselves, with better prospects of remaining in possession.

But let them fashion the nest intended for the Piratic Flycatchers with all the care that they bestow upon that destined for their own nestlings; for if the first is flimsily built and collapses in a rainstorm, the tenants will, as I once saw, abandon it, and dispossess the yellow-breasts of their more sturdily built second nest. And let the Gray-caps and Vermilion-crowns wish success to those for whom they have built; although they may not love those clamorous, improvident creatures, they have every reason to wish them good fortune, knowing full well that any mishap that befalls the striped-breasts' nest will be also their own misfortune. For the immediate prosperity of the gifted yellow-breasted flycatchers is closely linked with that of the deficient striped-breasts.

This assessment of a peculiar situation among the birds of tropical America has led to the paradoxical conclusion that the best course certain persecuted species can follow is, if not to love, at least to wish well to another species as a result of whose deficiencies they are grievously annoyed. Nature itself, "red in tooth and claw," teaches in this instance a rule of conduct closely approximating some of Christ's teachings often regarded as fantastically idealistic and inapplicable in this world of conflict and brute force. To love their enemies, figuratively to turn the other cheek, is the course that will bring the yellow-breasted flycatchers the maximum of success in their endeavor to reproduce their kind, with the greatest economy of effort and materials needed to form their eggs. And this is, in effect, the course they actually follow, with cries of wrath and unchristian complaints, no doubt, yet with no great resistance. I have never known a yellow-breasted flycatcher to try to settle accounts with the usurper of its nest by vengefully throwing out the intruder's eggs—an act which, as we have seen, would only redound to its own further loss.

One lesson more may be derived from this strange situation. We commonly assume that the strongest, the most perfectly equipped species will be the most successful in the struggle for existence. But this is by no means universally true. Some organisms are eminently successful by virtue of their very deficiencies. The Piratic Flycatchers, despite their inability to build nests, dominate the obviously better-equipped yellow-breasted flycatchers, which we esteem as the more admirable species. Seeds of a liana and a great tree germinate side by side in the dim light of the forest floor. The light-starved seedling of a dominant rain forest tree grows very slowly; it must form a self-supporting trunk as it increases in stature, and it can never mature and fructify unless one of the giant trees above it falls and leaves in the high canopy a gap in which it can spread ample limbs and enjoy full sunlight. But there will be many competitors for this opening when at length it occurs, and the seedling's chances of ultimate success are exceedingly slender. The vine, which will never be able to hold itself erect, twines slowly upward from limb to limb and from tree to tree, until at last it spreads a tangled maze over the loftiest of them all, and displays its brilliant blossoms over the roof of the forest. Its very lack of a self-supporting stem contributes to its success; the need to form one, to complete itself, causes the failure of the seedling tree.

CHAPTER 12 ✺

The Endangered Horned Guan

On a clear, frosty morning at the beginning of February, I explored a ridge near the summit of the Sierra de Tecpán in western Guatemala. While descending a narrow spur beneath tall broad-leaved trees draped with mosses and other aerial growths, I was arrested by a loud, guttural outcry, almost explosive in its suddenness and power. As I proceeded cautiously down the ridge, the croaking ceased abruptly after several repetitions, and in its stead came a noise like the clacking of castanets. At length, as I moved into a more open space in the forest, I beheld, clear and sharp against the morning sky, the head and neck of a Horned Guan that stood on one of the topmost branches of a tall, gnarled, moss-shrouded tree.

I have seen among birds few appearances so bizarre as that of the slender neck and black head, the small yellow bill opening and closing with a loud clacking, as though the strange fowl tried to intimidate me with this menace. A tuft of black feathers pointing forward over the nostrils partly concealed the bird's upper mandible. Its bright yellow eyes stared fixedly at me with large, dilated pupils. Its bare throat was scarlet, and the whole was surmounted by a tall, slender, truncate spike, covered with bare skin the color of ripe strawberries, arising from the crown and tilting backward at a slight angle. At intervals the guan, as large as a hen turkey, bent forward, stretching out and lowering its neck, and emitted the weird, loud grunts that had drawn my attention to it. Soon it obligingly turned around, showing me that all the upper parts of its heavy body were blackish, while its foreneck and breast were white. A broad, white bar crossed the middle of its long, black tail. I had difficulty naming the color of its legs and toes, which were between salmon and pink.

I settled down on my heels to record, while it was still fresh in mind, the impression made by my first encounter with this strange, rare fowl. While I wrote in my notebook, with fingers too benumbed by the early morning chill to form the letters clearly, the guan vanished without a sound. I did not believe it possible for so large a bird to fly without an audible rustle of wings; but in vain I moved all around the tree, craning my neck for another glimpse of it. Nor did all the noises I could make stir the guan from its hiding place, if indeed it lurked concealed on one of the broad platforms made by the moss that overgrew and joined together several adjacent branches.

Not long after this, while I was carefully pulling the threadlike rhizomes of a filmy-fern from a shaded rock beneath heavy forest and arranging the delicate little fronds between the pages of my notebook, my Indian guide crept around the corner of the outcrop and beckoned me to follow him. Laying down the notebook, I advanced, as silently as the crackling dead leaves permitted, to a narrow clear space a few yards away. There, perching on a horizontal limb almost directly overhead, and not more than forty feet (12 m) up, was a splendid Horned Guan quietly enjoying its noontide repose. Every detail of its odd appearance was clearly visible; through my binocular I could distinguish the fine, dark shaft-streak along the center of each white feather of its foreneck and breast. Apparently quite indifferent to our presence, the bird looked down and seemed to reciprocate the close scrutiny to which it was subjected. When I had gazed upward until my neck ached, waiting to see the guan in action, I decided to arouse it from its lethargy. I clucked, shouted, clapped my hands, but the only effect was to make the bird walk about slowly on the branches.

Since the guan seemed disinclined to demonstrate its mode of flight, I returned to my ferns. When I had put away as many of the filigree fronds as I desired for my collection of plants and was ready to go, I raised my eyes for a farewell glance at the bird. Now at last it had become active. Despite its great size, the guan walked with ease along the slender terminal branches of the tree and plucked the green berries, about the size of gooseberries, which they bore at their tips. When it had eaten all that it wanted, it stood majestically on an exposed part of the bough. Then it spread its

Horned Guan

dark pinions and, without so much as an audible wing beat, glided silently down over the treetops.

The glow that this intimate encounter with so splendid a bird kindled in me was shadowed by a dark misgiving. If the guan had been so confident in my presence, it would probably be equally careless of the approach of a hunter; for it was unlikely that this inhabitant of the most remote mountains had, like crows, learned to recognize firearms and to be wary of them.

And so few individuals of its kind remained! One had only to travel widely over the Guatemalan highlands and see the *milpas,* wheat fields, sheep pastures, and abandoned clearings stretching up and up to the very crests of the ridges, at altitudes of nine and ten thousand feet (2,750–3,000 m), and to notice the ravages of fire extending even above this, to realize how little was left of the heavy primeval forest where alone Horned Guans thrive. Even in their few remaining mountain fastnesses, these largest birds of the heights were mercilessly hunted; for scarcely anyone in Guatemala knew that this peculiar species is the only member of a singular genus, or cared that it was becoming extinct.

Long believed to occur only in the high forested mountains of western Guatemala, where it has been recorded at altitudes of 7,000 to 11,000 feet (2,134 to 3,353 m), the Horned Guan is now known to range across the Mexican border to some of the higher peaks of Chiapas, where, farther north, it has been recorded as low as 5,248 feet (about 1,600 m; Andrle 1967). Although evidently not uncommon in the wilder parts of the Guatemalan highlands in the middle of the last century, it had become rare when I was there in the early 1930s; and doubtless today, with greater ease of travel, growing human population, and more hunters, it has become even rarer. Everywhere these guans prefer species-rich broad-leaved forests to the pine and cypress woodland widespread in Guatemala.

Despite several conflicting reports by local people of Horned Guans' nests, none was found and described by a competent naturalist until fifty years after my memorable meeting with the bird. In the El Triunfo Biosphere Reserve in the Sierra Madre of southwestern Chiapas, from 1982 to 1984, Fernando González-García (1995) spent 842 hours observing at most twenty-three guans he found in the reserve and gathering much new information about their behavior. Naturally, he recorded a greater diversity of vocalizations than I had heard in my brief encounter with the bird on the Sierra de Tecpán. Females with seven or eight different calls had a richer vocabulary than males with only five, including the mooing *hum hum hummm* frequently heard in different contexts. Both sexes clacked their bills in aggressive moods, territorial defense, and when alarmed.

Unlike certain other curassows and guans, which are monogamous, the Horned Guans at El Triunfo practiced successive polygyny. Courtship calling began in early February and continued throughout May. Courtship displays were simple: a male and female usually met in fruiting trees, where they rubbed necks together in silence. After this embrace, the male flew between neighboring trees, "mooing" continuously, sometimes for an hour or more, while the female, without responding, rested, preened, or ate fruits. A male successively courted three or four females, spending three to nine days with each. He fed his temporary consort several times a day. When they were together in a fruiting tree, he plucked fruits and passed them directly to her. At other times, he swallowed green leaves or berries in a tree, attracted her by calling *ah-woo-ah*, and regurgitated the fruits to her, one by one. On one occasion he gave her eight to ten nutritous drupes of the lauraceous tree *Nectandra sinuata,* each of which measured about 1 1/4 by 3/4 inches (30 by 20 mm), and twenty to twenty-five much smaller berries of *Dendropanax populifolius* or *Conostegia vulcanicola.* The courting male called the female to the ground, where he plucked green leaves and passed them to her, or led her to the spot where they dust bathed and gave her grit.

In April, González-García found two nests at the Triunfo Reserve, in trees at heights of seventy-nine feet and fifty-four feet (24 and 17 m). Standing apart from other trees, each nest tree had few branches, laden with bromeliads, orchids, and vines, and served well for the accumulation of litter, of which each nest was largely composed. The nest bowls, twelve by fourteen inches (30 by 36 cm) in diameter, were little more than depressions in the thick litter, formed by the weight of the guans. Apparently, they did little building, but while they incubated they added a few dry leaves of orchids and bromeliads to the loose mass. Unlike certain other species of their family, they brought no green leaves. Each nest received two rough-textured white eggs, measuring 82–85 by 57–60 millimeters.

As usual in polygynous birds, the female guan incubated alone, on most days taking three recesses, one in the morning and one in the evening for foraging, and one at midday or in the early afternoon for foraging and also, on most days, dust bathing. Long sessions on the eggs, averaging 191 minutes, were separated by absences that averaged only 32.9 minutes. Despite different rhythms of coming and going, both females incubated with nearly the same constancy, covering their eggs, respectively, for 84.9 and 84.5 percent of their active days. While sitting, the female guans were alert, stretching up their heads and cocking them to look around when they heard strange sounds. They sunbathed by stretching up one or both wings, and they cooled themselves by vibrating the bare skin of the throat (gular fluttering), occasionally for an hour at a stretch. They preened and scratched themselves, and rarely they caught small insects that passed in reach of the nest. The incubation period was calculated to be 35 to 36.5 days.

Shortly before these eggs hatched, they were replaced with sterile eggs of the more abundant and widespread Crested Guan. The Horned Guan eggs were carried to Mexico City and given to a female common turkey to be hatched. All four eggs yielded chicks who grew up and laid, giving birth to fifteen to twenty young, to participate in a captive breeding program, such as those now widely undertaken to prevent the loss of species threatened with extinction. Since curassows and guans thrive when properly cared for in captivity, such a project should be successful in restocking suitable tracts of broad-leaved mountain forests.

CHAPTER 13 🌸

The Sounds of Wings

Dawn on Barro Colorado Island in January was an exciting time. The narrow clearing where the buildings stood was surrounded on three sides by tall forest; the fourth looked over a wide expanse of Gatún Lake. As the sky brightened, the big Rufous Motmots raised their voices, sounding weird and unearthly in the dimly lighted forest, like someone blowing over the mouth of a large, empty bottle. Soon the much smaller Broad-billed Motmots joined the dawn chorus with their bass *cwaa cwaa*. From the undergrowth came the triple whistles of Black-faced Antthrushes, while off in the treetops Rainbow-billed Toucans croaked like frogs. Most musical of all were the Blue-black Grosbeaks singing at the woodland's edge, and the Southern House-Wren who flew from a cranny in a building where he slept. Away in the treetops black howling monkeys mingled their astounding roars with the avian chorus.

Of all these contrasting sounds, the earliest was the drumming of Crested Guans. These long-tailed birds, as big as hen turkeys, started to drum while the full moon still shone brightly and continued for almost an hour, until the moon paled and daylight increased, when I heard them no more. After sunset of the same day, six guans plucked berries in the crown of a tree at the clearing's edge, where I could see their red throats and the short, irregular white streaks sprinkled over their dark brown underparts. I was delighted by the way these heavy birds walked on slender red legs straight forward along thin branches a hundred feet in the air, balancing themselves like tightrope walkers. They continued to eat until daylight faded, when two drummed as they flew from the tree. I could not see how they made this sound.

Crested Guan

Two evenings later I enjoyed a clear view of the drumming display. From a high treetop beside the clearing a guan emerged, flying as usual until he reached a wide open space, when he beat his wings much more rapidly, making the deep drumming sound; then he planed with set wings for a short distance before he repeated the performance. At the conclusion of the display, he continued with ordinary flight to another tree. On later occasions, I watched guans drumming as they crossed high above the hundred-yard-wide clearing, usually with two bursts of sound separated by a short glide with set wings. These demonstrations were always made in the dim light of dawn or dusk, never in bright sunshine. I watched them in the early 1930s; whether Crested Guans continue to display in the clearing on Barro Colorado Island in central Panama, I do not know.

Although similar sonorous displays have been described for several other species of guans, I have watched them in only two. Unlike the Crested Guan, which is widely spread from southern Mexico to western Ecuador and northern Venezuela, the Black Guan is confined to the highlands of Costa Rica and western Panama, where it is known as the pava negra. Here it lives chiefly in the montane forests, from tree-line down to about 5,000 feet (1,500 m), rarely lower. Its black dorsal plumage is glossed with greenish blue, its underparts are more drab. Contrasting with this sombre attire is the bright blue bare skin around its red eyes and the dull red of its legs and toes.

In 1937 and 1938, I found Black Guans not uncommon at Montaña Azul, below Vara Blanca on the northern slope of Costa Rica's Cordillera Central, where they were the largest resident birds aside from hawks and vultures. I watched them walking gracefully along slender boughs in the treetops, like other guans. In this region still sparsely populated by humans, they were not alarmed when closely watched, but because of their habitual silence they were difficult to detect among lofty branches. They fed largely on the fruits of forest trees. Until mid-March, I always saw Black Guans singly, but after that I noticed pairs. Although they passed the day well hidden in the forest, they preferred to roost in tall trees standing alone beyond its edge. As daylight faded, I sometimes saw a guan emerge from the woodland and fly into the crown of a great tree growing in the pasture below the cottage I then occupied. On several evenings in March, I watched a pair fly across the pasture in the dusk. Without flapping their wings, they glided for long distances on descending courses, like Crested Guans.

Beginning about the middle of March, from time to time I heard a dry rattle, startling in its loudness, which for some days I could not trace to its source. Then, in the dim dawn light of the first morning of April, while I stood waiting for Prong-billed Barbets to leave the cavity in a dead trunk where they slept, I heard the loud, sharp rattle and immediately afterward saw a Black Guan fly into the top of a high tree at the forest's edge. After resting for a few minutes on a lofty branch, the guan started to cross the pasture to the forest on the opposite side. When it was well launched in the air and moving swiftly, it set its wings to glide, and in the midst of the glide it vibrated its spread wings very rapidly but through a small arc, simultaneously producing the surprisingly loud noise that I had already heard. As I saw clearly against the sky almost directly overhead, when the wings were shaken to make the sound, the longer feathers were alternately

Black Guan

separated and knocked together. The sound resembled that of a narrow, flexible strip of wood passed rapidly over an iron grating or held against the spokes of a swiftly revolving wheel, as children delight to do. When the guan arrived at the opposite edge of the pasture, it alighted in a high treetop, whence, after a few moments, it flew down into the ravine beyond, again making the rattling noise while in the air. I heard the rattle a few more times, but less loudly, as the black bird flew into the distance.

I heard this rattle chiefly in the morning and evening twilight, or during hours of the day when the mountainside was shrouded in gray clouds. Much less often the guans rattled when the Sun shone brightly. The difference between this sound and the Crested Guan's drumming corresponds to differences in their outermost wing plumes, which in the Black Guan are nearly naked shafts whereas in the Crested Guan, although attenuated, they have well-developed vanes.

As a family, the guans and their relatives are noisy birds, as everyone familiar with chachalacas will agree. The Crested Guan is one of the most vociferous birds of the forests at low altitudes; when disturbed, it stands on some lofty branch and calls attention to itself by its high-pitched notes until a hunter raises a gun and silences it forever, thereby causing its rapid extermination wherever settlers invade its sylvan home. The Black Guan is so silent that, in many months passed amid forests where it was far from rare, I never knowingly heard a vocal note from it. Paul Slud, however, (1964) heard from this bird grunting noises which, so far as he could tell, "were of vocal origin. They sounded variously like weak grunts, wing drummings, or a pig crunching corn, in the last case accompanied by indrawn grunts which I transcribed as unclear 'bohr's." Carriker (1910) "rarely ever saw the bird on the ground," and I never did; but Slud did so. The Black Guan that he found on the ground was with a young bird one-third grown and capable of fluttering flight. The parent tried to distract Slud's attention from the juvenile by approaching within twenty yards and uttering continuously a squeaky grunt and a more excited, twanging, bull-froglike call.

A Black Guan's nest was a pad or platform of twigs and leaves, situated in a mass of epiphytes fifteen feet (4.5 m) up in a cloud forest tree. In May it held two rough-shelled white eggs (Stiles and Skutch 1989).

The function of guans' flight displays is not obvious. As I saw in the Crested Guan, and more clearly in the Black Guan, they are not always made in front of a watching female. The spatially extended performance of a Black Guan that I observed could hardly be seen from a single point, although it might be heard. Although at least in some species, including the Black Guan, the performance appears to be restricted to the breeding season or its approach, it does not seem to be a courtship display; I did not hear the Black Guan rattle before he was paired. As Jean Delacour and Dean Amadon (1973) suggested, the flight display might serve to strengthen the pair bond or to attract females to mateless males. Although probably not a means of proclaiming ownership of a territory (the treeless areas above which guans often perform are hardly defended as territory by these highly arboreal birds) the displays might help to regulate population density. Although the purpose of the aerial rattling or drumming is not clear, the highly modified wing plumes that produce these sounds would probably not have evolved if they did not contribute something of importance to the success of the species in which they occur.

A similar uncertainty about the function (as well as the means of production) of the well-known drumming of the Ruffed Grouse in northern woods persisted for centuries. Sitting upright on a log with his tail flattened against it, the male grouse beats his wings into invisibility, making a thumping or drumming sound said to be audible for half a mile or more. From prolonged observations and photographs, Arthur A. Allen (in Bent 1932) concluded that the thunderous noise is made simply by striking the air with forward and upward wing beats too rapid for the cinematic camera to register at sixteen exposures per second. Allen believed that these baffling sounds are made to proclaim territory, not to attract females.

From the guans, among the largest arboreal birds of tropical American forests, we turn to some of the smallest, the manakins, the wing sounds of which are definitely associated with courtship and coition. The males of many of the sixty species of manakins—passerine birds confined to continental tropical America and closely adjacent islands—are elegant little birds about four inches (10 cm) long. The females are much more plainly clad in greenish and olive plumage. The Orange-collared Manakin of southern Pacific Costa Rica and adjacent Panama has a black cap, back, wings and tail; orange face, throat, chest, and nape; greenish rump, yellow belly, and bright orange legs and toes.

In more open parts of old forest, light second-growth woods, and thickets, I often find patches of bare ground, a foot or two (30 or 60 cm) in diameter, as clean as though swept with a broom, each with two or more thin, upright saplings at its edge. When I drop a leaf or flower on the bare patch and retire a short distance to watch, I usually do not need to wait long before I see a male Orange-collared Manakin come and remove it. From two to a dozen or more of these courts are scattered through a small area, often far from any similar aggregation. Each belongs to a single adult male, who performs within hearing, if not within view, of his neighbors in a typical courtship assembly or lek.

These manakins have a very limited vocal vocabulary, chiefly a clear *cheeu* and its modifications; but a varied mechanical vocabulary (if I may so designate it) attributed to their modified wing plumes. Loudest of their sounds, and most likely to draw attention to courts screened by dense vegetation, is the staccato *snap,* like the sound of breaking a dry twig. This sharp note is made by a male as he jumps back and forth, a foot or so above his court, between upright stems on opposite sides. As he alights on one, he quickly turns around to retrace his course. When a green female arrives, she and the resident male jump together, crossing each other's paths above

Orange-collared Manakin

the court in a courtship dance, he snapping, she less noisily. Two or three to as many as nine passes may be made before she clings to a stem and invites her dance partner to mount her, or abruptly flies away, to jump with neighboring males until she finds one that she chooses to father her nestlings; her choice is unconstrained. After insemination, she departs to lay two eggs in the tiny open cup that she has attached, vireolike, to a horizontal fork of a tree or shrub, usually a yard or two above the ground, and beyond hearing of males who take no interest in their progeny.

In the midst of a jumping display, a manakin may drop to his bare court, to arise promptly with a loud *grrrt*, apparently also made with his wings. While resting near his court, he raises his wings above his back and beats them into a haze, producing a rolling *snap*, such as can be made by pressing a flexible strip of wood against a rapidly revolving cogwheel. Approaching or leaving his court in an undulatory trajectory, he flies with a deep, intermittent *whirr*. At a distance from his court, his flight is accompanied by a more subdued whirring or rustling sound.

Higher in the same forest where Orange-collared Manakins display near the ground, black Red-capped Manakins gather in assemblies of four or five males. The stages for their amusing antics are branches more or less horizontal and devoid of twigs and foliage for lengths of several feet, or lianas stretched horizontally between trees. In addition to vocal sounds more diverse than those of Orange-collared Manakins, Red-caps call attention to themselves by a large repertory of wing sounds. As he flits rapidly back and forth between his display perch and a nearby bough, the Red-cap makes a loud snap, not unlike that of the Orange-collared Manakin, apparently by striking together the shafts of the enlarged, curved, stiffened secondary feathers of his wings. Perching, he fans his wings into a blur, to the accompaniment of a snapping *whirr*. He raises his wings to beat out a series of resonant *snap*s in somewhat slower tempo, and it is easy to see that the sharp, crackling sounds are synchronized with the wing movements. Flying out from his perch, he circles around and returns with a loud noise such as can be made by holding a piece of stout cloth between both hands and suddenly jerking it taut. As in the case of the Orange-collared Manakin, these acrobatics and vocal and mechanical sounds attract females, who choose freely among the several participants in the assembly, then lay two eggs in a nest distant from the males and never visited by them.

It is difficult to find a family of birds more diverse in every way than the sixty-five species of cotingas, confined to the mainland Neotropics. Stentorian calls of bellbirds are audible at a great distance, but for a whole season I dwelt near a displaying Yellow-billed Cotinga without hearing a single note. What could this shining white bird do to make himself more conspicuous while he displayed by flying in deep catenary loops from one dead branch to another in a high treetop?

Among the more silent members of the family are the lovely male blue cotingas, with a large patch of purple on the throat and another on the abdomen. They often rest conspicuously on high, exposed perches, deeper blue against the azure sky. The only sound I have heard from a Turquoise Cotinga is the low, clear twitter or trill that males make in flight. Whenever a male Lovely Cotinga flew, if only a few feet between branches, I heard a sound between a rapid tinkle and a rattle, less sweetly melodious than the flight sounds of the Turquoise Cotinga and some South American members of the genus. The close association of these sounds with flying and my failure to hear them from resting birds make me agree with David Snow (1982) that they are made by the wings. The different sounds of these two species appear to be related to differences in their wings. The two outermost primary feathers of the Turquoise Cotinga, especially the ninth primary, are much narrower and shorter than adjacent plumes. The primary feathers of the Lovely Cotinga are all broader, and the eighth and ninth have sinuated outer webs.

Although males of the blue cotingas might, on present evidence, be voiceless, this is not true of the females. A mother Lovely Cotinga whose nestling in a high treetop was threatened by an Emerald Toucanet drew my attention to her plight by agonized screams. After her young fell to the ground, she perched above it repeating a clear monosyllable, *ic ic ic.*

At least one family of birds is named for its wing sounds, which are not equally loud in all its species. In our garden on a morning in dry February, a buzzing louder and more insistent than that of our resident hummingbirds made me search until I spied the only Ruby-throated Hummingbird that I have seen in Costa Rica, a male, who had probably flown six hundred miles (1,000 km) across the Gulf of Mexico on his way from the eastern United States or Canada to Central America. Like the Violet-headed Hummingbird and Long-tailed Hermit, woodland hummingbirds that sing persistently in assemblies fly rather quietly. Those of more open country often give spectacular aerial displays to which they call attention by loud sounds made chiefly by air passing swiftly through their wing plumes, which are often modified to make them more sonorous. After the rising Sun had warmed the air on a frosty morning on the high plateau of the Sierra Cuchumatanes in Guatemala, I watched a Broad-tailed Hummingbird swing back and forth, tracing a vertical U forty or fifty feet (12 or 15 m) high and buzzing loudly. At the nadir of his cometary orbit sat a demure female over whom he shot.

This Broad-tailed Hummingbird was at the southern limit of a breeding range that extends to the northwestern United States. Except for some tropical hummingbirds that breed a short way north of the U.S.–Mexican border, all the North American species display by flying high instead of singing in assemblies. These eight hummingbirds zoom through high Us like the Broad-tailed or swing in lower, more open curves, as does the Ruby-throat, flying with a "terrific buzz." The sound of a displaying male

Costa's Hummingbird was described by W. L. Dawson (1923) as "the very shrillest in the bird world . . . fairly terrifying in its intensity . . . like the shriek of a glancing bullet or a bit of shrapnel." This tiny hummingbird demonstrates that great size is not needed to make loud noises.

Pigeons also make loud sounds to call attention to their flight. R. K. Murton (1965) described how a soaring Wood-Pigeon suddenly stalls and claps his wings, apparently to notify other males that his territory is occupied. These British pigeons sometimes direct their wing claps at human intruders, especially those who frighten the birds from their nests. Rock Pigeons leaving their nests on a cliff flap their wings briefly to gain momentum, then punctuate a long horizontal soar with three bursts of wing claps, as Derek Goodwin (1967) described. As in the case of the Ruffed Grouse, to learn just how wing sounds are made is often difficult. Murton believed that the pigeons' claps are made on the downstroke of the wings, like the cracking of a whip, not by striking the wings together. Others have thought that the wings do clash together in the air, like a hand-clap, but whether above or beneath the flying pigeon's body is not clear. Murton compared the wing clapping of Wood-Pigeons to that of Nightjars, directed against humans who intrude into their territories.

The foregoing wing sounds serve special purposes, such as advertising possession of territory, attracting females, repelling intruders, or other ends still unclear. Most wing sounds are incidental to flying, as the ticking of a clock is to telling the time. Large birds commonly flap their wings audibly as they take off and rise into the air, where they may soar silently. Disturbed as it walks over the ground in rain forest, a Great Tinamou shoots away between the trunks with loudly whistling wings that evoke a sharp comment from a Rufous Piha in the treetops. Clacking bills and air whistling through modified tail feathers, as in snipes, add to the diversity of nonvocal sounds made by birds for special purposes. With so many means, vocal and nonvocal, of expressing their emotions or communicating with others, birds can make sounds appropriate for all occasions.

CHAPTER 14 &

Three Flycatching Kites

In January, when in most years El General's long rainy season has ended, the swifts and swallows that circle, flycatching, through sunny skies are joined by much larger birds. American Swallow-tailed Kites have returned from South America to nest in the valley of El General. In bright sunshine they soar above the treetops, catching the eye by pure white bodies, upheld by widespreading black wings. They twist and turn in movements regulated by deeply forked black tails. They stay so constantly high above us that we rarely notice their black mantles. Figures of surpassing grace and beauty, they trace wide, irregular circles against the bright blue sky. Riding ascending currents of warm air and rarely flapping their wings, they dip close to the treetops or soar up high into the blue; they vanish behind the crest of a forested ridge, soon to reappear at another point.

One wonders what these kites are searching for as they course so tirelessly through the air. Looking closely through a good binocular, one may from time to time see a small foot shoot out beneath the snowy body, with a movement almost too swift for human eyes to follow. Sometimes both feet seem to dart out together, but it is difficult to be certain of this. The soaring bird seems to be striking at an unseen adversary, boxing with a phantom. Rarely, if it flies low enough, it can be seen to seize an insect in a quickly darting foot. It is puzzling that the kite should capture small flying creatures in this seemingly difficult and inefficient fashion, instead of catching them directly in its bill, as the swallows and swifts may be doing at the same time, until one reflects that this graceful bird is, after all, a hawk, and seizing prey with the talons is the method almost invariably followed by this group of birds. When it has caught an insect, the kite, without ceasing to soar on widespread wings, lifts its feet, lowers its head, and transfers its victim to its mouth. If the insect is large, the kite may repeat this act several times, tearing pieces from the prey instead of swallowing it whole; and a detached wing may be seen floating slowly earthward.

Insects caught high in the air appear to be the mainstay of Swallow-tailed Kites here in Costa Rica, but, when possible, they vary their diet with more substantial items. In the breeding season, as they circle over the treetops, they look sharply for nests of small birds. Only nests accessible while they soar or hover seem to tempt them; at least, I have never seen a kite alight, or work its way into the crown of a tree, to plunder a nest. High, exposed nests most often attract them, but they will pillage a low one that they can reach while they fly. At the end of April, 1937, I watched three kites circling low over a pasture in a valley between forested ridges. One after another, they clung to the tips of the branches of a laurel (*Cordia*) tree that was shedding its foliage, exposing a high nest in which a pair of Garden Thrushes, or Clay-colored Robins, were feeding unfeathered nestlings. Since the kites did not alight on the tree or try to push in among its boughs but only grasped exposed twigs while continuing to flap their wings to keep themselves in the air, I doubted that they could reach the nest, which was well within the outermost twigs. But after several unsuccessful attempts of momentary duration, one of the kites hovered over the nest longer than before, and, fearing that it would harm the nestlings, I hurried up to drive it away. The kite flew up with a nestling dangling from its bill, but dropped its victim when it saw me. The young thrush fell into weeds, where I could not find it. The three kites retreated down the valley, leaving the thrushes with the survivors of their brood. But next morning, while I was too far away to interfere, they returned to carry off the remaining nestlings.

Although in this instance the kites removed the nestlings from the bulky nest, leaving it in the tree, in other cases they find it more convenient to carry off a small nest along with its occupants, which they extract after they have risen again into the air. Early one afternoon in April of 1945, I sat with visitors on my front porch, watching a pair of Golden-hooded Tanagers feed eight-day-old nestlings in a calabash tree fifty feet (15 m) in front of us. The tanagers' little nest was only six feet (2 m) above the ground in an exposed fork of the main trunk. Suddenly a Swallow-tailed Kite swooped out of the sky and, before we were aware of what was happening, rose again into the air with the nest and two nestlings clutched in its talons. At the moment when the kite seized the nest, a Tropical King-bird darted angrily at the robber but could not save the nestlings. After rising to a good height, the kite soared around holding the nest in its feet, and bent down its head to remove a small object that was doubtless a nest-ling. Then it dropped the nest, which fell slowly earthward.

On another occasion, I was walking through a coffee plantation when I noticed a Swallow-tailed Kite circling low above the tall *Inga* shade trees with a Tropical Kingbird following it closely. Presently the kite flew up with a nest—apparently a kingbird's nest—in its talons. Three kingbirds now pursued the predator hotly, rising above, and appearing to strike, its back. The kite dropped the nest, which fell into a thicket where I could not find it. Kingbirds, who often build their open nests in exposed sites, have as strong an antipathy to Swallow-tailed Kites as Boat-billed Fly-catchers have to toucans. I have watched some spectacular pursuits, when the kingbird, beating its wings steadily, chased the much bigger soaring kite around and around high in the air, usually managing to keep above it. Again and again the kingbird, with an extra burst of speed, would dart down upon the kite, who would swoop earthward in an effort to escape that was not always successful; if the irate flycatcher did not actually strike its enemy's back, it certainly came within a fraction of an inch of doing so. After continuing for some minutes to harry and buffet the kite, the king-bird would fly, twittering shrilly, back to its mate and nest, while the fugi-tive soared silently off over the treetops.

In addition to insects and nestlings, I have seen Swallow-tailed Kites take only an occasional lizard. In Suriname, these kites also appear to sub-sist largely on insects, including Pentatomidae, Fulgoridae, Membracidae, and female leaf-cutting ants (*Atta sexdens*), as F. Haverschmidt (1962) re-corded. Others, however, have watched Swallow-tailed Kites of the north-ern race give their young tree frogs, green tree snakes, and larvae and pupae from wasps' nests, in addition to numerous lizards and nestlings of smaller birds. I have never seen a living kite on the ground, but in the United States, as Arthur C. Bent records in his *Life Histories* (1937), they have been watched carefully searching for grasshoppers amid low herbage. In Trini-dad, ffrench (1973) saw kites skimming over water to drink.

Often several kites soar around together, catching insects. When one bird holds a captured insect in its feet or bill, another kite may pursue it, as though to take the insect from it. This results in some spectacular flying as the fugitive dives and veers aside to avoid the would-be thief, much as it does to escape a kingbird. I have not known a kite to wrest food from another.

A rare case of fruit eating was reported from Colombia by Thomas O. Lemke (1979), who watched groups of three and five kites circling around and diving into the crown of a rubber tree (*Castilla elastica*) sixty-five feet (20 m) tall. From ten to twenty orange-red fruits cluster beneath a thick disk about two inches (5 cm) broad, attached by a short stalk to a slender branch of this tree. Each of these oblong fruits is about half an inch (1.5–2 cm) long and contains a single seed enveloped by juicy pulp. To pluck these fruits the kites flew to the tree, touching the peripheral foliage or disappearing briefly into the crown, grasped a receptacle with one or both feet, and carried it off. Rising into the air, they bent their heads down repeatedly to detach the fruits from the receptacle still grasped in their feet, much as they dismember insects while they soar. Finally, they dropped the empty receptacle and circled around to the tree, from which they could detach two or three receptacles and eat the fruits in one minute. They remained at the tree for about fifteen minutes. These observations were made toward the end of a prolonged, severe dry season when insects and small reptiles were hard to find, probably because they had taken refuge amid the foliage from the desiccating Sun. Another report of fruit eating by kites comes from Brazil, where Helmut Sick (1993) found them eating fruits of murici (*Byrsonima* sp.) and camboatá (*Cupania vernalis*).

Swallow-tailed Kites start building their nests soon after they arrive in Costa Rica in January and continue to breed until April. A pair that I found building in early May apparently did not use their nest, probably because of the lateness of the season. Of the four nests that I have seen, two were on the Pacific slope and two on the Caribbean slope, at altitudes of about 2,000 feet to 5,400 feet (600 to 1,645 m) above sea level. All were at the summits of tall, slender living trees standing at the edge of the forest or in a neighboring clearing; I estimated their heights at from 100 to 125 feet (30 to 38 m). When the nest tree is at the forest's edge, its crown rises free of surrounding trees. The foliage clustering around the nests made them difficult to see from the ground, but they had little or no shade above them. Apparently, to be able to reach and leave their nests through the air, without passing through branches, is more important to the kites than having it screened above. These nests were unfavorably situated for observation, even apart from the eye-strain involved in looking for a long while at a dark object against a brilliant sky.

Swallow-tailed Kite

I watched three pairs engage in the spectacular activity of building their nests. All the twigs they needed for the foundation were broken from the dead ends of high, exposed branches while the kites remained airborne. Soaring slowly over the treetop, or dipping to the side of a lofty exposed crown, a kite grasped a twig in its feet and broke this off by the momentum of its flight, without coming to rest. Apparently, this feat was not without peril to the birds, who needed great skill and judgment to avoid disaster. Clutching too firmly a twig that failed to break might have meant a dislocated leg, or might have pulled the bird from the air and overturned it to become entangled among the branches, with possible injury to the long wings. Often I saw a kite grasp a twig that did not snap off, only to release its hold before it lost the forward momentum of its soaring flight. These birds must have a delicate and discriminating sense of touch in their toes, which seem weak for this work of breaking off twigs.

Often the twiglet that the kite secured proved to be too small and was promptly dropped. When the bird had broken off a suitable twig, which was often branched, the next step was to transfer this to its bill, which it did while soaring slowly and gracefully around above the treetops. To effect the transfer was not always easy, for sometimes a heavy branchlet dangled below the bird's feet, where it was difficult to reach with the bill. Moreover, the kite's weak bill could hardly sustain one of the larger twigs unless it was grasped near its center of gravity, which was found by trial and error. Continuing to soar on outspread wings, the kite passed the stick back and forth between feet and bill until it balanced in the latter. Even after the bird had satisfactorily adjusted the burden in its bill, it often continued to fly in wide circles before gliding to the incipient nest in the treetop with its feet free for alighting. When a bird found its mate on the nest, arranging materials there, it alighted beside the other, who soon slipped off into the air, making way for its partner to deposit the latest contribution. The sexes shared the task of construction rather equally, as far as I could tell.

At one nest, while the builder was trying to transfer from feet to bill the biggest stick that I saw it obtain, this prize slipped from its grasp. The bird shot downward in spectacular pursuit and caught the falling stick in its feet. But the twig dropped again, this time so near the treetops that it fell among the branches before the kite could retrieve it.

The foundation of sticks receives a lining of softer materials, which on the Caribbean slope of Costa Rica, as in Florida and elsewhere, may be long, gray strands of Spanish moss (*Tillandsia usneoides*); in El General, where I have not found this bromeliad, is a beard lichen (probably *Usnea* sp.) of similar appearance. In a fallen nest, I found a great mass of this richly branched gray lichen, pieces of which were as much as two feet (60 cm) long. The lichen had evidently been brought from a considerable distance, for I could find no long growths of it anywhere near the nest site, although I discovered such growths on trees about a thousand feet higher in the mountains and several miles away. A pair that I watched build in this locality three years later brought all their lichens from a point beyond view. Once a kite arrived with a large ball of lichen, but I could not tell whether the bird had found it in this form or, as seemed more probable, had rolled up a long strand into a compact mass for more convenient transportation. This gray ball was shifted back and forth between the kite's bill and feet while the bird soared around the nest tree, before going to the nest. Apparently, the kites soon tire of carrying anything a trifle heavy in their bills. In the most concentrated effort that I witnessed, this pair took five sticks and four billfuls of lichens to their nest between eight and nine o'clock in the morning of January 25.

After adding a piece of material to the nest, the builder may remain sitting there for some time, and if its mate delays too long to bring something else, it calls with high, thin notes, rapidly repeated and ascending in pitch. Probably the absent partner is too distant to hear these calls. Few birds fly so far to fetch materials for their nests. In the late nineteenth century, when Swallow-tailed Kites still summered in the northernmost United States, J. W. Preston (quoted in Bent 1937) told of a pair breeding in Minnesota who brought lichen-covered twigs of larch to their nest from a marsh a mile away. To fetch, one at a time, the two hundred twigs that he counted in the structure, they must have made the same number of round trips, a total of four hundred miles. As many twigs as were in the nest were strewn over the ground below it. The kites also circled much both at the marsh and around their nest. Together they must have flown at least eight hundred miles (1,288 kilometers) while building.

After continuing for a while their spectacular aerial building, the builders may circle around catching insects in their talons, at intervals repeating their slight, high-pitched cries, which always suggest excitement and are surprisingly weak for so large a bird. None of these building kites appeared to pay the slightest attention to the watcher in plain sight so far below them.

I could never learn how many eggs were laid in these high eyries, or just when incubation began. I made certain, however, that both sexes share this task, and both brood the nestlings. At a nest above the Río Pejivalle on the Caribbean slope, I watched one partner incubate for over three hours before its mate arrived to replace it. The newcomer brought a piece of *Tillandsia* that it added to the nest as it settled down to warm the eggs. Ten minutes later, the one who had departed returned with a small piece of the same gray Spanish moss and gave it to the sitting partner. Thus, material may be added to the nest, during the course of incubation, both at a changeover and while the same bird continues to sit.

The nestlings are fed by both parents, at long intervals, as far as I have seen. One morning, when the sky was lightly clouded, food was brought to the nest only twice in two hours. On a sunny morning, food was brought only once in an hour and a half, by a parent that passed it to the other, who all this while had been guarding the nestling(s). Except for a single lizard, I have seen the young receive only insects. I was not eager to make long-continued records of feeding at nests where I could learn neither the number nor the age of the young.

William B. Robertson, Jr., wrote to me that at a nest favorably situated for observation in a pine tree in Florida that he watched for several full days, the parents brought food for two well-grown nestlings at a rate exceptionally high for a raptorial bird, about seven to nine times per hour overall. However, the rate was extremely variable, as in the Plumbeous Kite of which I shall presently tell. On one occasion he watched a single parent, hunting near the nest, arrive with food seven times in fourteen minutes, including such substantial items as tree frogs and green snakes (*Opheodrys aestivus*). These nestlings also received many large insects and lizards (*Anolis carolinensis*) and one or more nestling birds. On several occasions, the dominant nestling appeared to feed its sibling. After leaving the nest, the young spent nearly a week perching in nearby trees, to which the parents continued to bring food at about the same rate as while they were in the nest. When these young kites attempted to fly, the parents repeatedly dived at them, forcing them back to their perches, probably for their safety.

On one of the Ten Thousand Islands off the Gulf Coast of peninsular Florida, Ivan D. Sutton (1955) built a tree blind from which, throughout the nestling periods, he watched a pair of Swallow-tailed Kites at their nest amid the mangrove trees. Although the male parent brooded and delivered food to his brooding consort, he never fed the young directly. When he arrived with an item in her absence, he appeared not to know what to do with it and waited until she returned to take it from him. After the mother began to fly beyond view of the nest to seek food for the nestlings, the father rarely approached it. One of the two nestlings, about a day older than its sibling, received more than its share and grew faster. After a few days the larger one began to harass its emaciated nest mate, who finally succumbed. The survivor tried to eat the corpse but could not dismember it—behavior all very different from that at Robertson's nest, where the dominant nestling appeared to feed the other and both young fledged. Although fratricide, often followed by cannibalism, is widespread among hawks and owls, to find this savage habit in birds that when grown are as social as Swallow-tailed Kites is surprising. Perhaps it is an occasional atavistic reversion in a raptor. The surviving young in Sutton's nest flew from

Three Flycatching Kites : 137

it when thirty-eight or thirty-nine days old, probably a few days sooner than it would have left if it had not been briefly removed for banding.

Swallow-tailed Kites are sociable at all seasons. Often several of them, in addition to the parents, spend much time resting or soaring around near an active nest, without being chased away or seriously threatened by the breeding pair. At one of the nests that I watched, four of these extra birds were present; at another, five; and at yet another, six of them. Long ago I surmised that these extra kites, apparently without nests of their own, might help the breeding pair to build or feed their nestlings, but I could never gather evidence for this. I thought that this failure might be due to the difficulty of watching nests so high above my head and more or less screened by foliage. At his more favorably situated nest, Robertson also failed to detect helpers among the extra kites, sometimes as many as ten, that without opposition frequented the vicinity. Sutton, who enjoyed exceptionally favorable conditions for watching a nest, makes no mention of attendants other than the two parents. Migration does not favor the development of cooperative breeding because (with the notable exception of geese) it disrupts the family bonds that promote this behavior; but occasionally a migratory bird feeds nestlings other than its own, of the same or a different species.

Nesting kites drive away trespassing birds of prey of other kinds. While I watched the nest above the Río Pejivalle, a wide-winged raptor, probably a Black-chested Hawk, soared above it. Uttering a high-pitched cry, the incubating kite slipped from the nest, rose above the intruder, and repeatedly dived toward it, making it veer suddenly to avoid being struck. The big hawk soared away over the treetops, while the kite continued to wheel about in the air. Before it returned to the nest, a White Hawk drifted down toward it, to be harried by the parent just as the first hawk had been. The kite treated the trespassing raptors much as a Tropical Kingbird treats a passing kite, and the hawks avoided the kite much as kites try to escape being struck by an irate kingbird. When the air was at last clear of raptorial intruders, the kite returned to its eggs. In either case the greater maneuverability of the aggressor, kite or kingbird, gives it a great advantage over its larger and more powerful target.

Once I watched a pair of Swallow-tailed Kites worry a Red-tailed Hawk that rested atop a tall charred trunk in the highlands. They soared in circles above the hawk, swooping repeatedly to pass a few inches above its head. As a kite swept so close above it, the hawk thrust its bill suddenly upward, without succeeding in touching its tormentor. This occurred in late July, when the kites appeared no longer to be nesting. On other occasions, I have watched kites treat raptors of various kinds in this fashion.

The kites' nest that I watched in 1961 was situated at the top of a mastate or milk tree (*Brosimum utile*) about 125 feet high, standing in a recently made pasture near the forest. The massive columnar trunk, which rose about eighty feet (24 m) to the lowest branches, had been scarred by fire and weakened by decay that resulted from the wound. Revisiting this nest at the end of April, I found that the trunk had snapped off well above the ground, apparently in a storm a few days earlier. Amid the shattered boughs and withering leaves of the crown was the corpse of a parent, swarming with fire ants. Probably it had been whipped down by the falling boughs before it could fly clear of them. A few yards away were the remains of a nestling, whose expanding feathers were still ensheathed at their bases. These were the only kites I have known to meet disaster. Mostly they seem to soar well out of harm's way.

In the light of the setting Sun at the end of May, a loose flock of about twenty Swallow-tailed Kites arrived from the west, circled around, and one by one settled at the summit of a mastate tree emergent above the canopy of the forest on a hilltop. Most vanished among the abundant foliage, but three remained at the very top, as though preparing to roost there through the night. As the kites nest at the summits of the tallest trees, so they sleep in such lofty situations. In Brazil, Sick found kites roosting in leafless trees.

Arriving in the valley of El General in January, in some years as early as the first week, Swallow-tailed Kites remain with us for about six months, during which they appear to raise only a single brood. They depart for South America in July or August, thereby avoiding our rainiest months toward the year's end, when overcast skies and copious downpours would greatly curtail their time for effective soaring on thermal updrafts while they catch insects. Soon after sunrise on July 7, 1971, I watched a flock of nineteen kites gyrating above the hillside behind our house, voicing their usual high-pitched cries, their white plumage gleaming in the bright rays. When ascending air currents had lifted them high enough, they glided southward until they vanished over the roof of the forest. Like other diurnal raptors, Swallow-tails migrate by day to save energy by making maximum use of thermal updrafts. Populations in Argentina and southern Brazil migrate northward as the austral winter approaches.

Swallow-tailed Kites are among the very few birds that arrive from South America to nest in Costa Rica, others being the Piratic Flycatcher and Yellow-green Vireo; the great majority of our migrants come from the north and do not breed here. I would more heartily welcome the return to our skies of these beautiful raptors if they refrained from plundering the nests of our resident birds.

THE PLUMBEOUS KITE

I passed most of August and September of 1939 in the vicinity of Puyo, a military post and agricultural colony situated on the small river of the same name, a tributary of the Río Pastaza, in the province of Napo-Pastaza, Ecuador. Here, at an altitude of about 3,000 feet (900 m), the eastern foothills of the Andes—so high and rugged just a little nearer the backbone of the range—had dwindled away to a succession of low, rounded, forest-clad hills that continued, seemingly as endless as the billowy surface of a storm-tossed sea, as far as the eye could reach toward the vast Amazonian plain in the east. The excessive wetness of the climate was attested by the exuberance of the epiphytic growths that burdened the trees in the surrounding forests and by the swampy character of pastures even on steep slopes. Pressing close around the narrow clearings, the forest stretched on and on for distances hard to imagine; I needed to be very careful not to lose my way in it. The fauna and flora were composed predominantly of lowland species, but among both birds and plants I encountered highland forms whose presence at so low an elevation was a surprise and was apparently caused by the humidity.

To my great disappointment, the breeding season of the majority of the birds seemed to have ended before my arrival. I had hoped to study the nesting of some typically Amazonian species. Since so few of these were to be found breeding, my discovery, on August 25, of a nest of the far-ranging Plumbeous Kite assumed an importance it might otherwise not have had; and for nearly a month the kite family claimed much of my attention.

These small raptors were about fourteen inches (36 cm) long. The head, neck, and underparts were pale gray, the back, rump, and wing coverts medium gray. When spread, the dark wings displayed a large patch of rufous-chestnut on the outer half of each of them. Their pointed tips extended beyond the straight terminal margin of the tail, which was black crossed by three narrow white bars. The feet were orange-yellow. The eyes were yellow, not red as in all the illustrations and published descriptions of this kite that I have seen. Possibly these breeding kites were not fully mature. I could not distinguish their sexes.

The kites' nest was situated about ninety feet (27 m) above the ground, far out on a horizontal branch at the top of a tall, slender, leafless tree growing beside a rivulet at the edge of a small clearing that bordered the Río Puyo. This elevated site made the structure quite inaccessible to me; but fortunately the back of a high, sharp ridge, rising between the rivulet and the river into which it fell, afforded an excellent view not only of the nest but also of its occupant. The bulky, shallow saucer of coarse sticks, so conspicuous amid the naked boughs, cradled a single small nestling, clad in white down, which I could see clearly as it tumbled around in its lofty eyrie.

By September 12 the nestling was much bigger, well clad in expanded feathers, and appeared almost ready to fly. It now stood upright on the nest—often upon the rim—moved around actively, preened much, and at intervals spread its wings and flapped them vigorously without rising into the air, apparently because it kept a firm hold on the nest with its toes.

It was after the nestling reached this stage of development that I devoted most time to the kites. Between September 12 and 17 I watched the nest for twenty-two hours, in all sorts of weather. When it rained, I found shelter beneath a big cabin of palm-thatch and split bamboo, perched high above the ground upon massive palm trunks, which stood on the back of the ridge between the rivulet and the Río Puyo and commanded an excellent view of the nest. Here a man who had been a lawyer in Königsberg, Germany, lived with his wife and children; the political upheavals in Europe had driven them into the wilderness.

Both parent kites brought food to the nest. The family subsisted largely if not exclusively upon insects; I never saw them eat anything else. During the hours that I watched them, I found no evidence that they shared the Swallow-tailed Kites' unfortunate habit of pulling young birds from exposed nests. This might have been because few other birds were nesting at this time, but I like to think it was otherwise. Although nearly all insectivorous birds seize their prey with their bills, Plumbeous Kites, like Swallow-tails, follow the raptors' usual method of grasping it with their feet, however tiny it may be. My pair of kites caught most of their food while soaring effortlessly on widely spread wings on ascending currents of air in sunny weather. After a capture, the kite would bend its head beneath its body, stretch one foot forward, and transfer the prey to its bill. When the insect was large, the birds appeared to tear it between the feet and the bill and eat it piecemeal, while continuing to soar on set wings.

When atmospheric conditions did not favor soaring, the kites caught a few insects that their keen eyes descried while they perched motionless on an exposed branch high in a tree. Suddenly they aroused themselves, flapped their wings vigorously if the insect flew above them, darted swiftly downward with wings half-folded if it was below, and seized it with a deft movement of one foot, in which they bore it to a convenient perch, there to dismember it between feet and bill and eat it at their leisure, with the little, dainty mouthfuls that befit these graceful birds. Even when fly-catching from a perch, these kites caught most of their insects in the air. More rarely, while perching they spied an insect large enough to tempt them on neighboring foliage, and darted out to snatch it, more in the manner of a cotinga than of a flycatcher. Sometimes they missed their intended prey, flew back to the perch, and tried again to capture it. But as far as I saw while watching the nest, the kites procured much less food by darting from perches than when they could soar. Doubtless, too, volitant insects were more abundant when the air was warm and updrafts encouraged soaring.

The food that the parent kites caught for their own consumption was, as we have seen, eaten in the air when the weather favored soaring but was carried to a perch in a foot when they were "grounded" and forced to hunt from a stationary lookout. Likewise, atmospheric conditions determined how they brought meals to the nestling. Since most food was caught while the parents soared, it was shifted to the bill at a distance from the nest and carried there, one insect at a time. One exceptionally big insect was borne to the nest tree in both feet. Apparently, the kites soon tired of carrying heavy objects in their weak bills and preferred to employ their talons for this purpose.

Even when carried to the nest tree in the feet, the insect was usually moved to the bill before it was brought to the nest. One day when a parent alighted on a branch near the nest with an unusually large insect grasped in a foot, it started to shift the prey to its mouth; but after merely touching the insect with its bill, the bird raised its head and hopped to the nest still holding the offering in a foot. Once I watched a parent detach the wings from an insect while resting on a neighboring bough before delivering the prey to the nestling. On a cloudy or rainy day when the parents, unable to

Plumbeous Kite

soar, appeared to be hungry, they might consume part of one of the few insects they caught before taking the remainder to the nestling. Usually, however, the insect was carried intact to the nest—unless the wings had been pulled off while the parent soared beyond view.

After reaching the nest, the kite rested upon the rim and held the insect beneath a foot, or both feet if it was large, while tearing off small bits with its beak and placing them one by one in the young bird's mouth. Never

Three Flycatching Kites : 143

clamorous at meal time, the nestling waited quietly until it was served and received its food in a well-bred, dignified manner. The character of the food and the dainty way it was delivered and received made feeding the nestling more pleasant to watch than are the meals of hawks that prey upon vertebrates and tear them coarsely. Apparently, the nestling was nourished wholly with insects, of which I definitely recognized only a large dragonfly. A number of the larger insects seemed to be beetles.

On September 16, for the first time, I saw a parent deliver a whole insect to the nestling, who held it beneath a foot while it tore off morsels for itself, just as the adults did when they ate on a perch. The following day the insects were sometimes fed to the nestling bit by bit, sometimes delivered entire. Once, while the young kite was busy with an insect it had received a few minutes earlier, the parent laid the latest one beside it in the nest. If it had wandered along the branch beyond the nest, the nestling would return to receive its meal in the eyrie. When given a whole insect while it perched outside the nest, it carried this back to the eyrie to dismember and eat it. The young kite was now almost ready to fly away.

The rate of feeding the nestling varied greatly from hour to hour and day to day. Most birds that nourish their young with insects or fruits carried in the bill feed with fairly uniform frequency. But at this kites' nest, long intervals when little or no food was brought alternated with periods of—for a hawk—amazingly frequent feeding. The rate of bringing insects to the nest was determined by the state of the atmosphere, whether it was favorable or unfavorable for soaring flight, and whether it encouraged insects to fly. The weather affects the rewards of foraging of many insectivorous birds, especially those that catch their prey in the air; but it was surprising to find that these kites' foraging was so strongly influenced by atmospheric variance.

The kites' dependence upon the weather was revealed by my records made at the nest from day to day. As an indication that the weather favored soaring, I had not only the testimony of the kites themselves but also that of the Yellow-headed Vultures abundant in the region. The weather in the Ecuadorian Oriente was erratic, unlike that of many tropical lands where rain falls at definite seasons and more or less at predictable hours of the day; rain might fall at any time from early morning to late afternoon. This made it easy to watch the kites in different kinds of weather and to record the rate of feeding at the same hours of different days.

On September 12, I began to watch the nest at eight o'clock in the morning and continued until noon. The early morning was cloudy, but about the middle of the forenoon the Sun burned through the clouds, creating air currents that favored soaring. From 8:00 to 9:00 the nestling received no food, but between 9:00 and noon the parents delivered eleven meals, six of these from 10:00 to 11:00. That afternoon, while the Sun shone, the nestling was fed five times between 3:10 and 6:20.

On September 13, when I watched from 6:10 A.M. to 12:00 noon, the weather was very different. The first half of the morning was darkly overcast; during the second half rain fell almost continuously, at times quite hard. The forenoon passed without a ray of sunshine, and I saw no bird of any kind soaring. In six hours, the nestling received only four insects, and before being taken to the nest two of these were partly eaten by the parent, which must have been very hungry. This parent, probably the female, had herself no more than portions of these two insects between 6:39, when she started to guard the nest, and noon, when I departed in the rain, and she probably found little to eat before 6:39. After this hour, the second parent did not appear, while the one thought to be the mother remained continuously in sight, guarding the nest. Both of the insects she caught after 6:39 were captured by darting down from the perch to the foliage below, and both were shared with the nestling. The second of these she ate in part as soon as it was caught, then held the remainder during twenty minutes of immobility, as though uncertain whether to eat what was left or give it to her progeny.

On September 16 I arrived in sight of the nest at 8:15 A.M. when the Sun was breaking through the clouds after a rainy night and darkly overcast early morning. the air was sultry, with a light breeze that soon died away. Through the remainder of the forenoon, intervals favorable for soaring alternated with brief showers during which Yellow-headed Vultures and other soaring birds vanished from the air. In the four hours from 8:15 to 12:15, the nestling received eight insects, brought during the periods of sunshine.

On the following day, September 17, I watched from dawn at 5:45 until 11:00. For about an hour after the rising Sun had dissipated the early morning ground-mist, the sky was clear. But by eight o'clock gathering clouds obscured the Sun and the sky was completely overcast. By eleven, however, the gradually thinning ceiling of clouds permitted the passage of enough rays to cast faint shadows, and soaring birds appeared overhead. In the bright hour following 6:25, when the nestling received its first morsel of breakfast, one of the parents brought it twelve insects, on as many visits to the nest. Seven of these meals were delivered in the eleven minutes from 6:51 to 7:02. Through most of the next two hours (7:02–9:25) the sky was overcast, and this same parent brought food only once more. Meanwhile the other parent, probably the female, rested continuously at the top of the nest tree and gave the nestling only a single insect, which she caught as it flew below her high perch. She did not appear to be hungry, or she might have joined her mate, who had apparently found a spot beyond my view where insects were abundant, and might have proceeded to take advantage of them to fill up the nestling. During the remainder of my vigil, 9:25 to 11:00, the young kite received eleven more insects, bringing the total to twenty-five in the first five hours of the day. With the single exception already mentioned, all were caught beyond my view, where foraging was apparently more productive than in the immediate vicinity.

In twenty-two hours of watching, the hourly rate of feeding, for single hours, ranged from zero to twelve. For three-hour periods, the rate fluctuated from zero to fourteen. The average rate on different days, as determined in watches of four to seven hours, ranged from 0.7 to 5.0 meals per hour. In the whole twenty-two hours, the nestling was fed fifty-three times, or an average of 2.4 times per hour, which for a raptor seemed to be unusually rapid.

It is instructive to compare the kites' rate of feeding with that of a pair of Yellow-bellied Elaenias. These little flycatchers subsist largely upon insects they catch in the air, as kites do, but without soaring because they are too small. Also like the kites, both parents feed the nestlings, and at this particular nest, they hatched only one. From the morning this nestling hatched until it left its nest one afternoon under a drenching rain, I watched it for twenty-two hours, at all times of day and in all kinds of weather. The rate of feeding this elaenia nestling, for single hours, ranged from four to twenty times per hour. The average hourly rate, computed for periods of four to eight hours, ranged from 6.0 to 14.8, increasing with the age of the nestling. Extremes of weather made less difference in ability of these small passerines to catch insects while operating from perches than in the catch rate of the much bigger kites, which depended largely upon weather favorable for soaring.

When I began long-continued watches at the kites' nest, the young bird was already well feathered and no longer required brooding by day. Nevertheless, a parent, probably the mother, guarded it for long intervals while resting high in the nest tree, often on the topmost bough. I admired her ability to rest motionless. On a dark and rainy morning, she perched there almost continuously for over five hours, punctuated by a few brief sallies to seize passing insects and by sitting in the nest for about forty minutes while rain fell hard. Instead of accepting the proffered maternal shelter, her offspring stood beside her under the downpour.

The nestling was guarded chiefly in the early morning, late afternoon, and during inclement weather. In the late morning, when insect catching was profitable, the young bird was seldom watched, at least after it was older. Then the parents were coming frequently with meals, or soaring around in sight of the nest, and could keep it in view. While one parent guarded, the other, if not bringing food, remained continuously absent. On the dark morning of September 13, the second parent, probably the father, did not appear at all during nearly six hours.

One afternoon the guardian of the nest drove away a big Yellow-ridged Toucan that flew past the nest tree. On another occasion, while the supposed female guarded, her partner, arriving with food, found a Yellow-headed Vulture soaring around closer to the nest than he approved and chased it beyond view, then returned to give the nestling the insect that he retained in his bill. Soaring with set wings, the vulture easily kept ahead of the smaller kite, flapping hard.

All through the day, the feathered nestling kite stood up in the nest. After sunset it lay down and I could no longer see it. On the evening of September 12, it rested at 6:05, fifteen minutes before its mother came to brood it. On the morning of September 17, the brooding parent flew from the nest in the gray dawn at 5:53, a quarter-hour before the nestling stood up and became visible.

By September 17, the young kite, already able to tear apart food held beneath a foot, began to sally briefly from the nest, walking out along the supporting bough, then hopping back. The first excursion that I witnessed took it only about a foot (30 cm) beyond the rim, but this was soon followed by a longer journey. Often it vigorously beat its wings, always while it clung to the nest or supporting branch. By September 20, the fledgling was making short flights between boughs of the nest tree. Sometimes it directed its course outward from the tree, as though to fly away, but after one or two wing flaps it returned to the sheltering boughs. While the young bird engaged in these exercises, a parent guarded on the topmost branch, remaining there for nearly an hour.

When the adults brought food, they sometimes fed the fledgling piece-meal, as when it was younger, and at other times delivered the insect whole, for the recipient to dismember for itself. Once, while the young kite, standing on a branch, was engaged in feeding itself with an insect that it had received entire from one of the parents, and doing very well, the other parent arrived with a big, lacy-winged insect. After taking this to the empty nest, the parent flew to the fledgling, who alternately plucked bits from the insect beneath its own foot and received morsels placed in its mouth by the adult.

Next morning, September 21, the fledgling continued to flit through the boughs of its natal tree and to receive food. I last saw it there when I passed at noon, when a parent was giving it an insect, piecemeal. When I returned in the evening, the fledgling had vanished; but a parent rested, from old habit, on the topmost limb of the tree, although now no young kite was present to be guarded. She lingered in the same spot, preening, for the next hour, and flew away just as the Sun sank behind distant craggy Andean summits, at a moment when I had turned away from her to watch a huge black column of vapor rising above the snowy crest of Volcán Sangay, fifty miles to the south. The nest tree remained deserted for the night.

Since I did not know the age of the nestling kite when I first saw it as a downy chick on August 25, I do not know its age when it left the nest tree. It could hardly have been less than four days old when first seen, which would make it at least one month of age when it abandoned the tree. At this time its forehead and brows were whitish, its crown and hind neck finely and closely streaked with gray upon a lighter gray ground. Its back, rump, and wings were dark gray, with a dark rufous patch on the primaries, corresponding to that of the adults. White tips were prominent on the longer wing feathers, and present but less conspicuous on the greater co-verts. The tail was black with white bars on the outer feathers. Black feath-ers surrounded the eyes. All the ventral plumage was so light a gray as to be nearly white, the breast faintly tinged with buff. The feet, like those of the parents, were bright orange.

While I watched these kites, the only notes I heard from them were thin, high-pitched, weak monosyllables, sometimes repeated once or twice, usually when they met at the nest tree after a period of separation. I never saw one of these kites on the ground, but Helmut Sick (1993) re-ported that they seek small reptiles on burnt-over soil.

I could not reach the high nest for examination after the fledgling left. Sir Charles Belcher and G. D. Smooker (1934) described two nests in Trinidad as made of small twigs and lined with leaves and fibrous materials. One held a single egg on March 3 and the other two eggs on April 13. The roundish, unmarked eggs were pale bluish white and measured 40–41.5 by 33–35.5 millimeters.

Widely distributed over South America east of the Andes to Bolivia, northern Argentina, and southern Brazil, and to Ecuador west of the Andes, the Plumbeous Kite is in Middle America only a summer resident. It arrives from the south in February and March and returns southward from July to September. On February 18, 1975, I watched large flocks of Plumbeous and Swallow-tailed kites migrating westward over the Pacific slope of Panama east of the canal. Later, they would probably cross the isthmus and proceed northward on the Caribbean side of Central America and Mexico, where most of these migrants nest. Here in El General I have seen only one solitary Plumbeous Kite, resting on a roadside tree on February 14, 1942. It continued to look down calmly at me while I dismounted from my horse and moved around beneath it, examining it from all sides. It took much waving of arms and clapping of hands to make the wanderer fly and reveal the rufous patch on its wings that confirmed its identity.

THE DOUBLE-TOOTHED KITE

At the top of a tall dead tree standing at the edge of the forest at Los Cusingos sat a Double-toothed Kite leisurely preening itself, conspicuous against the sky. About a yard behind the kite perched a Green Honeycreeper, facing the much larger bird. For the next twenty-five minutes the little honeycreeper remained there, always looking toward the preening hawk. That he stayed to watch the kite was evident from his growing restlessness; he stretched his wings, pivoted from side to side on his perch, and preened a little. Finally, his patience exhausted, he flew away, leaving the kite in the same place, where I found it an hour later. Often a motley crowd of small birds gathers around a resting hawk or owl, mobbing it, or protesting its presence, incidentally teaching young members of the group to be wary of the bird of prey. Apparently, the honeycreeper wanted to mob the kite but failed to attract other birds to join him in a typical mobbing party. The kite's failure to bestir himself and try to catch the little bird that exposed himself to attack revealed that the kite did not habitually prey upon other birds. Mobbing birds sometimes fall victim to the target of their antipathy.

While the kite rested high above me, I scrutinized it with my binocular. About thirteen inches (33 cm) long, it was dark gray above and extensively banded with gray and white below, except on the rufous-tinged chest. Its flanks, under tail coverts, and thighs were white, its square-ended tail broadly banded with gray and black. A black stripe on the center of its white throat was an excellent recognition mark. Its legs were yellow, its eyes orange; its dark bill had a yellow cere at the base; and just behind the strongly hooked tip of the upper mandible were two tiny projections on the cutting edge of each side. Difficult to detect in the field, these "teeth" give the kite its English name as well as its scientific designation *Harpagus bidentatus*. Females have the chest more solidly cinnamon-rufous than do the males.

From southern Mexico to western Ecuador, Bolivia, and southeastern Brazil, at low and middle altitudes, Double-toothed Kites inhabit rain forests, lighter woodland, and adjoining clearings with scattered trees. Although they soar on updrafts, they are much less aerial than Swallow-tailed Kites and are more often seen perching on exposed branches. Largely insectivorous, they vary their diet with lizards that they pursue by hopping along high branches, flapping their wings to balance themselves. On Barre Colorado Island in Gatún Lake, Jon S. Greenlaw (1967) watched kites follow troops of white-faced capuchin monkeys through the trees, resting below the forest canopy while the monkeys foraged above them. When the primates stirred an insect into flight, a kite caught it, carried it to a perch, and held it beneath a foot while it tore off fragments with its bill. Greenlaw cites cases of Double-toothed Kites in other regions using monkeys of different species to make prey available to themselves.

These kites occasionally prey upon other birds. A pair of Black-striped Sparrows hatched two nestlings in a cycad beside my study. My attention drawn by their complaints, I found a kite perching in a calabash tree, whence it could plainly see the nest. I chased the kite back into the forest, but next morning it returned and carried off the nestlings before I could stop it.

On Barro Colorado Island at the end of June, Robert M. Laughlin (1952) found a Double-toothed Kite finishing a nest amid the foliage of a cedro espinosa tree (*Bombacopsis fendleri*) at the forest's edge. The shallow

Double-toothed Kite

saucer, composed externally of twigs, was on the fork of a stout branch seventy-five feet (23 m) above the ground. The day after the kite started to incubate, a pair of Chestnut-mandibled Toucans flew into the tree and one advanced toward the sitting kite. For a time she spread her wings over the nest in a defensive attitude, but, intimidated by the toucan's huge beak, she fled, leaving the intruder to pick up a whitish egg speckled with brown and throw this back into its throat by an upward movement of its head. The male kite repeatedly brought lizards to his consort. He chased from near the nest a big Pale-billed Woodpecker and a troop of capuchin monkeys, who squealed as they fled.

The only nest of the Double-toothed Kite I have seen was found on May 1, 1964, at an altitude of about 3,800 feet (1,158 m) at what is now the

Robert and Katherine Wilson Botanical Garden, a few miles south of San Vito de Java on the Pacific slope of Costa Rica near the Panamanian border. This nest was about seventy feet (21 m) up in the crown of a tall, slender tree at the edge of the forest, beside a coffee plantation. The flat structure, composed of coarse sticks, rested on a stout, mossy, horizontal, lower branch, about four feet (1.2 m) out from the trunk. It was readily visible from the ground but sheltered above by almost the whole height of the tree's leafy crown. Its site contrasted strongly with that of Swallow-tailed Kites' nests, which are exposed above but often screened below. The difference in the situations chosen by these two kites is correlated with their ways of approaching their nests, the Swallow-tails by soaring, the Double-toothed Kites more often by flying.

When I first saw the Double-toothed Kites' nest on May 1, it held two nestlings already well feathered. Both had whitish downy heads. The one that appeared to be older had shed nearly all the natal down from the rest of its plumage, but the younger still bore conspicuous light tufts on its dark wings. Both nestlings had dusky dorsal plumage. In both, the breast was pale cinnamon-rufous, which became lighter posteriorly, fading to whitish on the center of the lower abdomen and the under tail coverts. The breast was marked with prominent dark streaks; the sides of the abdomen with dark bars and spots. The stubby tail feathers were blackish with narrow light tips. The bill and eyes were dark, but the legs and toes were bright yellow as in the adults.

The parent kites seemed to ignore my presence in a clear space between the nest tree and the coffee plantation, so to watch them I sat there unconcealed. On May 3, and again on the following day, I spent the first six hours with them, a total of twelve hours. I made no long watches after midday because of the hard rain that fell almost every afternoon. When I arrived as it grew light at 5:25 on May 3, a parent was brooding one nestling on the nest while the other perched a foot away. After about ten minutes, the first nestling emerged in front of its parent and flapped its wings. At 5:45 the brooding parent flew away as the other parent came with food and stood on the nest to tear the insect into small pieces, which it passed to the young. I could see little of the proceeding because a dense cloud covered the mountain and veiled the nest tree. At 5:51 a parent returned to brood both nestlings, continuing until 6:25, when it flew off through the cloudmist. Thereafter, the young were not brooded through the remainder of my vigil.

Around eight o'clock, sunshine began to penetrate the dense cloud that had rested on the mountaintop since dawn. After their meager breakfast at 5:45, the nestlings received nothing more until 8:24, when an interval of concentrated feeding began. In the next ninety-three minutes, the parents brought food ten times. After 9:57 the meals were more widely spaced, one at 10:30 and one at 10:58, then nothing more until I left at 11:25. In the first six hours of the day, the two nestlings had been fed thirteen times, by both parents. I could not distinguish them to learn whether the father or the mother was the more diligent attendant.

On May 4 the course of events was much the same. When I arrived at 5:25, a parent was on the nest, while the older nestling rested exposed on a nearby branch. After about five minutes, the younger nestling appeared beside the parent on the nest, apparently having emerged from beneath her. At 5:54 the parent flew away. At 6:05 a parent brought a large green insect. Around 7:08 each parent came once with food. Then they remained beyond sight for another hour, while the younger nestling slept on a limb near the nest, its head turned back and buried in its plumage, and the older nestling rested farther off. That morning the interval of concentrated feeding began at 8:10, a little earlier than on the preceding day. In the next 110 minutes, food was brought eight times. Then, after an hour of neglect, three more meals were served between 11:05 and 11:20. In the six hours from 5:25 to 11:35, the parents came with food fourteen times. Taking the two mornings together, twenty-seven meals were brought in twelve hours, which was slightly more than one per nestling per hour.

Each morning one lizard was taken to the nest; all the other items appeared to be insects, some of which seemed to be cicadas and beetles. As far as I could see, only one was brought at a time. Although I could not clearly distinguish everything given to the young kites, I am fairly certain that neither adult birds nor nestlings were included in their fare on these two mornings. The young were fed either on or, more often, beside the nest. The older nestling spent much time perching at a distance from the nest, but when a parent arrived it usually returned for its meal if it were hungry. Occasionally, a parent alighted beside the older nestling where it rested and fed it there, while its sibling remained at the nest, calling. Nearly always, however, the meal was delivered while the parent stood between the two young, feeding them alternately with small bits of the insect, which it held beneath a foot on a branch and tore apart with its bill. The young kites never clamored for their food or tried to push each other aside; like the Plumbeous Kite nestlings I had watched in Ecuador, they took their meals decorously, even daintily, making their repast pleasant to watch. When the nestlings' demands were not urgent, the parent shared their meal. Although a feathered nestling Plumbeous Kite sometimes received whole insects that it tore apart for itself, these Double-toothed Kites, nearly ready to fly away, always had prepared food placed in their mouths by their parents.

Some of the insects that the parents tore apart for their young would have been gulped down whole by one of the larger American flycatchers, considerably smaller than these young kites. One such insect was broken into about thirty-three tiny fragments, each of which was eaten separately by a nestling or parent. Yet, strangely enough, the two lizards, by far the largest items brought to the nest tree on these two mornings, were swallowed whole, probably because they were difficult for the adults to dismember. I watched a nestling gulp down the smaller lizard headfirst, with great effort. The larger lizard seemed to cause some embarrassment to the parent that brought it; the kite flew from branch to branch, instead of taking the meal directly to the nestlings, as when it brought an insect. The lizard finally vanished while parent and young were hidden by the nest. I suspect that the older nestling ate it. For the next hour and a half, this young kite rested on its favorite perch at the outside of the tree's crown, digesting its substantial meal and taking no interest in the next three insects the parents brought and gave to the downier nestling.

I could not watch the adults hunt, as they brought nearly all the meals from the forest, into which they disappeared. Often the kites approached and left the nest silently, but at times they voiced a high, thin *peee weeet* as they arrived or departed. This utterance, weaker than the somewhat similar call of the Eastern Wood-Pewee, might be repeated several times. Sounded as a parent approached the nest tree, it alerted the young for their meals. The latter gave a similar call in a weaker voice.

The parents approached their nest by flapping flight instead of soaring, as Swallow-tailed and Plumbeous kites prefer to do. One morning when the Sun shone brightly almost overhead, a parent circled on set wings a few times, at no great height.

As early as May 3, the older nestling was venturesome, hopping or flying short distances from branch to branch, but never rising much above the level of the nest at the bottom of the tree's crown. It spent much time on an exposed branch at the outside of the crown, whence it could look into the neighboring forest, and from this point it returned to be fed. The young kite with more down also sallied from the nest but did not wander so far. Both preened much and vigorously flapped their wings, usually while they clung to the nest or to a branch with their legs stretched up high but sometimes rising slightly into the air.

On the evening of May 9, I found only one fledgling in the tree, resting quietly beside the nest. Soon it went onto the nest, then flitted from branch to branch. Presently a parent arrived and settled on the side of the nest with out-fluffed plumage, to remain in this posture until I left in the failing light. I was not sure where the fledgling had gone, but at daybreak I found it perching near the nest, behind a thick bough that made it difficult to detect. Apparently, the parent had slept alone on the nest with one of the young birds roosting nearby instead of being brooded. At six o'clock the parent flew away, leaving the fledgling resting where the growing light had revealed it.

When I returned to the nest tree in the afternoon of May 10, no kite was in sight. Around five o'clock a young kite flew into the tree from the forest, rested a while near the nest, then vanished. By nightfall, the parent had not appeared, and as far as I could see, no kite slept in the nest tree.

Four days later, on May 14, I watched a fledgling fly from the forest to the nest tree. It had lost nearly all the nestling down from its body but retained much on its head. After a while, a parent arrived and fed the young bird on a branch near the nest, tearing bits from an insect and placing them in the fledgling's mouth, just as it had done before the young birds could fly. The parent itself ate part of the insect, then flew away. A few minutes later, the fledgling also left. The nest was evidently serving as a rendezvous for parents and young after the latter had begun to fly widely. They were still fed as though they were helpless nestlings, incapable of preparing their food.

CHAPTER 15 &

A Versatile Flycatcher

My first intimate encounter with a Great Kiskadee revealed the aggressive character of this boldly patterned, widespread American flycatcher. At the United Fruit Company's Lancetilla Experimental Garden near Tela in northern Honduras, a Vermilion-crowned Flycatcher built her nest on a thorny frond of a pejibaye palm (*Bactris gasaepes*). When, standing precariously upon superimposed boxes, I looked into this nest with three nestlings, a kiskadee with a higher, inaccessible nest on a nearby telephone pole joined the parent Vermilion-crowns in protesting my intrusion. The larger kiskadee dived at my head, voicing an angry *eeek* when closest above it. Thereafter, when I appeared in the vicinity with the hat I wore on that occasion, a kiskadee flew above me with loud threats and repeated feints of attack. Without that hat, I could pass unthreatened.

One of the largest of the approximately 380 species of American flycatchers, the Great Kiskadee is about nine inches (23 cm) long and weighs about two ounces (52–65 g), rarely more. The sexes are alike. The crown is black, with a central patch of yellow that is concealed unless the bird is excited. A broad white band extends from the forehead above each eye to the hind head. The sides of the head are black. The upper plumage is olive-brown, with rufous margins on wing and tail feathers. The throat and sides of the neck are white, the remaining underparts bright yellow. The eyes are brown, the strong bill, legs, and toes black. Young closely resemble the adults.

The kiskadee is sometimes confused with the Boat-billed Flycatcher, a bird of similar size and color pattern but with a much broader bill, more olive upper parts, and without a conspicuous rufous patch on the closed wing. The voices and nests of these two birds are unmistakably different. The widespread Vermilion-crowned, or Social, Flycatcher closely resembles these two species in plumage but is much smaller, as is the similar Rusty-margined Flycatcher. The color pattern of these flycatchers is widespread in the family.

The Great Kiskadee ranges from southern Sonora, Mexico, and southern Texas through Middle America to northern South America, thence southward over the continent, east of the Andes, to Bolivia and central Argentina. From sea level it extends upward to 5,000 or 6,000 feet (1,500 or 1,800 m) over much of its range, occasionally higher. Inexplicably, this widespread, adaptable bird was long absent from apparently suitable regions, some of which it has recently begun to occupy. In Panama, where it had been abundant in the province of Bocas del Toro in the far west since the early twentieth century, it did not appear in the center of the country, including the Canal Zone, until about 1955. Since then it has become numerous. In the Térraba Valley of Costa Rica, where I have watched birds since 1935, I first saw a kiskadee (at Paso Real) in 1975, and at San Isidro, near the head of the valley, in 1979. I have not met it more recently. Both central Panama and the Térraba Valley have long contained much of the open country that kiskadees prefer. Although these flycatchers are nearly everywhere permanent residents, populations at the extremities of their range, in southern Sonora and central Argentina, are partly migratory. A bird banded in Santiago del Estero, Argentina, reached Santa Catarina, Brazil, eight hundred miles (1,300 km) to the northeast (Sick 1993).

Avoiding the interior of rain forests, kiskadees inhabit open woodland and country with scattered trees, including savannas, plantations, parks, dooryards, and the residential districts of large cities. They prefer the neighborhood of streams and ponds but may be found far from water. They live in pairs or family groups and rarely concentrate in large numbers at rich sources of food.

Of all the American flycatchers known to me, the kiskadee is the most versatile forager, the only one I would characterize as almost omnivorous. The equally big Boat-bill is satisfied with insects and small fruits, but the kiskadee's appetite is boundless. It eats many berries and drupes of palms, and in great banana plantations of the warm lands is so eager for this fruit that I have heard it called the "banana bird." Peppers (*Capsicum*) add piquancy to its diet; cooked rice or bread and milk as well as fruits attract it to feeding boards.

To satisfy its hunger for animal foods, the kiskadee adopts the proce-
dures of a diversity of other birds. Like a typical flycatcher, it captures
moths, beetles, wasps, and many other insects on the wing. From an overhanging bough or projecting rock, it plunges like a kingfisher, but less ex-
pertly, into the water to capture small fishes. Like a heron, it wades in shallow pools to catch the tadpoles that swarm there, wetting its belly and its
whole head because it must immerse it to seize prey with its short bill. Like
the ground-gazing flycatchers of South America, the kiskadee rests on a
branch or service wire, big head cocked sideways, gazing downward until
it spies a grasshopper, lizard, frog, or small snake, perhaps even a mouse,
then dashes down upon the prey. Where such perches are lacking, as on
open grassy plains, the kiskadee ranges in flight like a kestrel, searching for
prey beneath. After seizing an insect or larger victim, the bird beats this
resoundingly against a perch to extinguish its life and make it swallowable;
mice require prolonged treatment before being gulped down. Kiskadees
break shells of snails in the same manner.

Like a Black Vulture, the kiskadee scavenges for stranded fishes and
other offal on the seashore, and it also frequents garbage dumps. W. H.
Hudson (1920) recorded that in spring on the Argentine pampas these
flycatchers follow the plow in company with Hooded Gulls, Guira Cuckoos, cowbirds, and others, hopping awkwardly over the rough upturned
soil to pick up worms and larvae, since they cannot run like more terrestrial
flycatchers. The same writer also saw kiskadees follow rural butchers'
carts, waiting for an opportunity to dash in and carry off any small piece of
meat or fat they were able to detach.

As though all these sources of nourishment were not sufficient to satisfy
a ravenous appetite, the kiskadee devours nestlings and fledglings of
smaller birds, such as Bananaquits and seedeaters. In Honduras the frantic
fluttering and darting of a pair of White-collared Seedeaters drew my attention to a Great Kiskadee perched in their midst. Nearby, I found their
tiny open nest, where a nestling a few days old lay on its side, as though
injured. While I watched, half concealed by a spray of bamboo, the big
flycatcher descended closer to the nest. The parents renewed their attacks,
the male bursting into song and working up to his highest dry trills, as
is the habit of these little black-and-white birds when highly excited.
When the kiskadee alighted beside the nest, the outraged father of the
wounded nestling pounced boldly down upon the big bird and drove it off.
At this point a group of laborers passed by and the kiskadee flew away. Re-

Great Kiskadee and Mica Snake

turning after an interval, I found the parents repeating mournful chirps while they flitted around their empty nest. The plunderer had vanished with his victim.

The Great Kiskadee is as vociferous as it is aggressive. Its most characteristic utterance, frequently repeated, readily suggests human syllables and is responsible for its names: kiskadee where English is spoken; *cristofué* in Venezuela; *bem-te-vi* (I saw you well) in Brazil; and (with an added syllable or two) *bienteveo* or *benteveo* (I see you well) in Argentina. In other Spanish-speaking lands, the bird is called *pecho amarillo* (yellow breast), often with the modifiers *grande* or *bravo*, to distinguish this big bird from a number of similar yellow-breasted flycatchers that are smaller and milder. The old English name for the northernmost race, Derby Flycatcher, is deservedly forgotten.

The call that gives the kiskadee its several names can be variously paraphrased. In Panama I sometimes heard the birds command *speak to me, speak to me* in a rather raucous, imperious tone. The first syllable might be repeated more than once: *speak, speak, speak to me;* or the second and third syllables: *speak to me, to me, to me.* The repetition of the shorter notes, with alternately rising and falling inflection, was the closest approach to a song that I have heard from these birds. Another rendition sounded like *eek ă eee.* When the short middle syllable was omitted, the bird seemed to utter a derisive *hee-heee.*

Like many other flycatchers and certain other birds not highly gifted with melody, the male kiskadee delivers at break of day a dawn song, which I have not heard. According to ffrench (1973), in Trinidad this consists of "three or four double syllables, *kayeer,* followed by a raucous trill, and ending sometimes with a lower-pitched *kweer.*" In Brazil, Mitchell (1957) heard the kiskadee sing at daybreak *bem-te-vi, chee churr,* with variations. In the same country, Sick (1984) also reported a dawn song ending in a churr or trill. When darting at a human or other creature that appears to menace their nest, parent kiskadees voice a shrill, angry *eeek.* Other notes, from harsh screams to clear, almost mellow calls, express the kiskadee's varying moods. While they sit in a nest, building or incubating, soft churrs, or a rambling sequence of low notes, suggest contentment.

Hudson told how a pair of kiskadees, foraging separately, keep in touch. While one watches for a frog beside a pool, or ranges like a harrier over a thistle bed, its partner—the female, let us say—returns to the trees where they are accustomed to meet. Impatient for her consort's return, she calls to him with a very long, clear note that carries far. Several fields away, he hears and responds with a note of equal power. Then, for possibly half an hour, they continue to call back and forth, although the male's loud voice may alert his intended prey. When at last he returns, the partners stand with their yellow bosoms almost in contact, yellow crests elevated, wings beating the branch, while in concert they scream their loudest notes, making a confused, jubilant clamor that rings through the whole plantation. "Their joy at meeting is patent, and their action corresponds to the warm embrace of a loving human couple." Hudson often stood for half an hour, concealed amid trees where a bienteveo was calling her mate, cheered at intervals by the far-off faint response, for the pleasure of witnessing in the end the joyous reunion of the two birds.

Because, as already told, Great Kiskadees have appeared only recently and sporadically in the valley where I have long dwelt, and I have not found them nesting here, I have made no thorough study of their breeding. On the Caribbean slope of Central America, from Guatemala to western Panama, I have over the years found seventeen of their nests, some of which were never completed. Here building begins in February, and nesting continues until July or August. The lowest of these nests was only four feet (1.2 m) up in the thick crotch of a willow tree beside a pond, in the Costa Rican highlands at an altitude of 4,600 feet (1,400 m) above sea level. The highest was forty feet (12 m) above the ground in a dying casuarina tree in a garden in the same locality. Most nests were from ten to thirty feet (3 to 9 m) above the ground. The bulky nest needs an ample support, often in the fork of a large tree.

In the Motagua Valley of Guatemala, I found three nests in small bullshorn acacia trees, inhabited by fiercely stinging ants that would protect eggs and young from climbing predators. In the Sarapiquí lowlands of Costa Rica, a pair of kiskadees placed their nest on a newly built nest of a Tropical Kingbird in the top of a large tank bromeliad attached to the side of a slender trunk in a pasture. In a garden near Almirante, Panama, a pair of kiskadees built on the richly branched inflorescence of an *Archontophoenix* palm. When this spadix died and fell with the nest, the birds made another on a younger spadix of the same palm. One pair of kiskadees supported their nest in an organ-pipe cactus planted close beside an occupied house. Another nest was situated atop a dead stump, twelve feet (3.7 m) high, standing in the open without a leaf to shade it. In Venezuela, a pair of kiskadees built on top of a Rufous-fronted Thornbirds' nest of several rooms of interlaced sticks, hanging from a mango tree above a small pond. Throughout their range, kiskadees often support their nests on the crosstrees of electric or telephone poles, where they are visible from afar. Probably relying on their boldness to deter predators, they are imprudently careless of shade or concealment.

The Great Kiskadee's nest is a large, untidy roofed structure, with a wide doorway in the side. In form it resembles the much smaller nests of the Vermilion-crowned Flycatcher and other species of *Myiozetetes*, and it is very different from the shallow open cup of the Boat-billed Flycatcher. As I have seen repeatedly, and as has been recorded throughout the kiskadees' vast range, both sexes actively build, flying up together with bulging billfuls of materials, and each in turn arranging its own contribution in the growing structure. Hudson reported that bienteveos sometimes take four or five weeks to complete nests, which were probably begun early in the season. At the other extreme, a pair in Honduras finished a nest and laid their first egg in it ten days after an earlier nest was destroyed. After repairs, old nests are sometimes reoccupied. The roughly globular structure is externally so ragged with projecting ends of materials that it is difficult to measure exactly. Often it is a foot (30 cm) or more in diameter. The chamber of a more neatly finished nest was 7 inches from front to back, 4.5 inches from side to side, and 4.5 inches from floor to ceiling (18 by 11.5 by 11.5 cm). The round doorway in the side was 3.5 inches (9 cm) in diameter.

Dry grasses, weed stems, lengths of vines, fibers, wool, or rags, according to what the locality affords, compose the nest's thick walls. Where available, gray, stringy Spanish moss (*Tillandsia usneoides*) is a preferred material, a major component of some nests, long streamers of which dangle below them. In rainy northeastern Costa Rica, I watched a kiskadee pluck two billfuls of the long, reddish, bristlelike leaves of a different species of *Tillandsia* growing on a tree, then carry them into the nest it was lining. Fine grass inflorescences more commonly line the chamber.

In Honduras, kiskadees built into the walls of their structures whole nests of the very abundant White-collared Seedeaters. These tiny cups of fine fibers, rootlets, and cobweb contrasted with the coarser materials gathered by the flycatchers. Probably, in some cases, they devoured the seedeaters' eggs or young before carrying off their nests. Likewise in Argentina, bienteveos exploit nests of smaller birds for building material. However, these big flycatchers are not always bad neighbors. In the Orinoco region of Venezuela, Cherrie (1916) found Great Kiskadees, Vermilion-crowned Flycatchers, and Yellow Orioles nesting simultaneously in the same tree; nests of the oriole and kiskadee were frequently not far apart. Hudson (1920: vol.1:178–79) wrote that "except when breeding the Bienteveo is a peaceful bird, never going out of its way to make gratuitous attacks on individuals of its own or of other species."

In Texas, where Great Kiskadees nest from late March to late June, chiefly in May, they lay two to five eggs, most often four (Bent 1942). In northern Honduras, in April and May, I found three sets of four eggs. A set of three laid in mid-August was abandoned, possibly because the season of reproduction was ending. In Trinidad, where breeding has been recorded in all months except September but mainly from February to May, by far the most usual number of eggs is three, with sets of two only half as frequent. Only one of twenty nests held four eggs (ffrench 1973). In Suriname, Great Kiskadees breed throughout the year, laying two or three eggs (Haverschmidt 1968). In central Argentina, the clutch usually consists of five eggs, less often four (Hudson 1920; Mason 1985). Thus, like many other birds, the kiskadee exhibits the "latitude effect," the size of its broods increasing with degrees north and south of the equator.

Kiskadees' eggs are creamy white or buffy, spotted with shades of brown, chocolate, purple, or lavender, which may be concentrated in a wreath around the thicker end or more uniformly scattered over the whole surface. From end to end of the kiskadee's wide range, its eggs differ little in appearance and size. Fifty eggs, apparently from both Texas and Mexico, averaged 28.5 by 21.0 millimeters; ten from Venezuela, 28.2 by 19.8; twelve from neighboring Trinidad, 28.2 by 20.8; nineteen from central Argentina, 28.9 by 20.6 millimeters (Bent 1942; Cherrie 1916; Belcher and Smooker 1937; Mason 1985). Eggs from Suriname were smaller, 25–27.8 by 19.5 millimeters; the number is not stated (Haverschmidt 1968). Nineteen eggs in Argentina averaged 6.4 grams in weight.

Eggs are laid on either alternate or consecutive days. At a nest in Honduras, two days separated the laying of the first and second eggs, and of the third and fourth. The second and third were deposited on consecutive days. Six days were needed to complete the set of four.

In the Pejivalle Valley of Costa Rica, I spent most of a morning watching a nest where incubation had been in progress for four days. As in other flycatchers, only the female incubated, sitting rather inconstantly for a bird of her size. Her eight sessions in the nest ranged from 18 to 33 minutes and averaged 24.1 minutes. Her nine recesses varied from 8 to 25 minutes, averaging 13.8 minutes. She covered her eggs for 63.6 percent of five and a quarter hours. Thrice her mate escorted her back to the nest. During some of her absences he stood guard in front of it, but not consistently; on some of her recesses he accompanied her instead of remaining to protect the eggs. Once he stood in the doorway to look into the nest. This female sat in silence, but others have hummed a rapid series of soft notes that perhaps conveyed to their partners the message that all was well. Similar "nest songs" are not rare among flycatchers. Because all my nests were either inaccessible or prematurely lost, I did not learn the incubation period, which in Argentina was sixteen days. Both parents feed the young. Surprisingly, I have been unable to find a thorough study of this widespread, familiar bird.

Kiskadees zealously guard their eggs and young. Whenever I approached an occupied nest, they became greatly agitated, crying loudly while they displayed the usually concealed yellow crown patch and vibrating their partly spread wings. As I came nearer, one parent repeatedly swooped down toward me, voicing an angry *eeek,* sometimes coming so close that I raised an arm to shield my head.

One morning in Honduras, I watched a seven-foot (2 m) yellow-and-black mica (*Spilotes pullatus*), a snake that preys insatiably on eggs and nestlings, climb upward through the tangle of vines that embraced the lower half of the trunk of a tall tree. A long stretch of smooth, clean trunk separated the vines from the tree's spreading crown, where about eighty long woven pouches of Montezuma Oropendolas hung like huge gourds. If the snake could have reached them, it might have lurked in the colony until it had devoured all the big birds' eggs and nestlings, as another mica tried to do at a smaller colony of Yellow-rumped Caciques in Panama. Although some snakes are adept at ascending branchless trunks that appear too smooth for them, I was not sure that the mica could scale this one to the colony of oropendolas I had been studying.

Perhaps fortunately for the oropendolas, the mica was not given an opportunity to test its skill as a climber. A pair of kiskadees, whose nest in a lower, nearly leafless tree was about thirty feet (9 m) away, could not tolerate so dangerous an enemy so close to their young. Again and again they shot past the serpent's head, sometimes missing it by barely an inch, and voicing their shrill *eeek* when closest to it. A few such spirited demonstrations halted the snake's ascent; a few more made it turn and twine slowly downward through the vines. As long as the serpent was visible, the kiskadees continued to threaten it, just as other pairs did to me when I visited their nests. The oropendolas, who had so much to lose, paid little attention to the commotion below them, possibly because they felt safe above the long, smooth upper half of the trunk. Only one hen descended to the lower levels to see what it was all about; and two Giant Cowbirds, evidently interested, interrupted their efforts to foist eggs into the oropendolas' pouches and approached dangerously close to the serpent. Despite their bold defense, kiskadees lose many nests to predators, possibly by night when they sleep; but this vigilant pair raised four young, who flew from their nest ten days after their parents drove away the mica.

CHAPTER 16   🧠

The Birdlike Monkeys

Reading Louise H. Emmons' excellent field guide, *Neotropical Rainforest Mammals* (1990) and browsing through John Terborgh's *Five New World Primates* (1983), which I read some years ago, I was impressed by the similarities to birds of the smallest New World primates, the marmosets and tamarins. Their habits resemble those of tropical forest birds about as closely as flightless mammals can behave like birds with wings. Their pelage, more colorful than that of most mammals, is also evocative of birds. These attractive little primates are much more brightly colored than bats, which obviously spring to mind as the mammals most closely comparable to birds.

Weighing about four to twenty-one ounces (100–600 g), the largest of these members of the family Callitrichidae is about the size of a large squirrel. They have long, furry, nonprehensile tails. Their colors range from black to the almost uniform gold of Brazil's golden lion tamarin and the silvery white body and black tail of the silvery marmoset, widespread in South America south of the Amazon. Other species are more variegated. The gold-and-black lion tamarin of Bahia, Brazil, is largely black with a golden crown and forelimbs. The golden-mantled tamarin of eastern Ecuador and Peru has a black head, white muzzle, wide golden band around the torso, golden forelimbs, and grayish hindquarters. The Brazilian bare-faced tamarin shows a similar contrast between the white fore parts and grayish hind parts of the body. The golden-handed or midas tamarin of northeastern Brazil and the Guianas has golden-yellow or orange hands and feet that contrast strongly with its blackish body. These are only a few of the color patterns that these little monkeys wear; although fur is less favorable for displaying colors than are feathers, color patterns among these monkeys approach the variety evident among tropical birds.

Manes, crests, ear tufts, and mustaches embellish the heads of the marmosets and tamarins. The cotton-top tamarin of northeastern Colombia wears a thick, spreading white mane above its naked black face and brown upper parts. Its underparts and feet are whitish. The golden lion tamarin's mane, colored like the rest of its fur, is parted in the middle and drapes around its head. A similarly parted golden mane envelops the head of the gold-and-black lion tamarin, contrasting with its black body. The thick ear tufts of the tufted-ear marmosets stand out strongly against their dark heads and bodies; tufts vary greatly in this widespread Brazilian species. The mottled gray emperor tamarin wears a fantastic, wide-spreading white mustache that curls beneath its chin; its body is grizzled pale gray, its long tail bright rusty orange with a black tip. The sexes of these little primates are alike, as in many of the most beautiful tropical birds. The most probable explanation of the contrasting colors and striking adornments of both the mammals and the birds, which can hardly be cryptic, is mutual sexual selection (Skutch 1992).

Marmosets and tamarins inhabit seasonally inundated or drier forests, gallery forests along streams, second growth, and clumps of trees in savannas. Many of them prefer to forage and rest amid dense tangles of vines, through which they leap with head and body vertical, not horizontal in the manner of squirrels. They live in family groups of two to a dozen or more individuals: a single breeding female, one or more adult males (they may be monogamous or polygynous), two to four adolescents, and babies. Females often bear twins, corresponding to the clutch of two eggs laid by many tropical birds. They may breed once or twice in a year, as the birds do.

It is reported of the black-chested mustached tamarin that mothers carry their babies, but males of most species transport the infants on their backs. As among most birds but few mammals, males help to rear the progeny, doing about as much for them as the mammalian system of reproduction permits. Possibly well-grown young males take turns carrying their siblings, thereby becoming nonbreeding helpers, as in cooperatively breeding birds—an interesting possibility that appears not to have been investigated. Group members frequently groom one another, an activity that corresponds to allopreening by constantly mated birds, especially those that breed cooperatively.

Tamarins and marmosets, adept at concealing themselves behind

Cotton-top Tamarin

trunks and amid dense vine tangles, occupy territories that they defend from neighboring families by vocal confrontations—countercalling that occasionally escalates to fights. One family of each of two species may occupy the same territory. When such a mixed group meets another mixed group at the boundary between their respective domains, members of each species confront their counterparts of the same species, just as happens when mixed-species flocks of birds oppose contiguous flocks. Thus, in southeastern Peru, where emperor and saddle-backed tamarins occupy joint territories, emperors oppose emperors and saddle-backs confront saddle-backs. In other regions, saddle-backs share territories with red-chested mustached tamarins. When families of different species travel together through their joint territory, they do not mingle but forage apart, keeping in contact by calling as they move in the same direction.

The vocalizations of marmosets and tamarins are birdlike whistles in various keys, chirps, twitters, trills, and quavering notes, with some froglike or insectlike sounds, according to the species. Family members often call together.

Like many small birds of tropical forests, these little monkeys subsist largely upon fruits and insects that they gather from foliage, twigs, or bark, often supplemented with the nectar of flowers. Marmosets have front teeth specialized for digging small pits in the bark of trees and lianas to make them exude sap that the marmosets drink, much as sapsuckers do in northern woods. Each group of pygmy marmosets has a few such trees, to which they return daily. Tufted-eared marmosets spend about a third of their day licking up the sap and gum that flow into their hundreds of pits—horizontal slitlike to round holes about $3/8$ to $5/8$ inches wide by $3/4$ to 8 inches long (1–1.5 by 2–20 cm). Tamarins, which lack the forwardly directed teeth of marmosets, steal sap from these pits. Like the sap wells of sapsuckers, the pits undoubtedly attract insects, which the monkeys may add to their fare. It is surprising to find the mouths and teeth of small mammals highly modified to perform the same work that the bills of sapsucking birds seem more naturally fitted to do. It is significant that these monkeys, with a diet so like that of birds, have birdlike claws instead of the broad finger- and toenails of other primates.

Tassel-eared tamarins follow army ant raids, catching the small creatures that the ants stir up rather than eating the ants themselves, much as birds do. The tamarins' relations with the birds of numerous species that regularly accompany these raids should make an interesting study.

These small primates are diurnal, like most birds of the rain forests. At night members of a marmoset or tamarin family sleep together in a tree, preferably one standing apart or rising above others; in a dense tangle of lianas; or in a tree cavity with a narrow doorway.

Three species of titis of the family Cebidae share some of the birdlike habits of callitrichid monkeys, although the titis are larger, weighing up to about $3^1/3$ pounds (1,500 g) and lack the adornments of tamarins and marmosets. At night titis huddle together with interlaced tails on large, sheltered boughs in the forest canopy—much as the black cuckoos called anis and some other kinds of birds sleep pressed together in a row. When the titis awake at dawn, their loud, prolonged, modulated whooping duets ring through the woodland, announcing their presence and reminding one of the dawn chorus of gibbons in forests of the Orient, or of the dawn songs of birds. Later in the day they chirp and twitter like tamarins. Also like tamarins and marmosets, the monogamous male carries his single infant on his back. The dusky titi monkey, widespread in South America, eats many leaves and fruits; the two other titis are more frugivorous. Like other monkeys, they share with birds and some other mammals the important activity of scattering seeds through the woodlands, thereby perpetuating the diversity of species.

Larger than most of the foregoing species, more squirrel-like in form and movements, squirrel monkeys are also more gregarious, wandering farther through the woods in troops of up to a hundred individuals, searching for insects, small ripe fruits such as figs, and nectar. Often they travel with capuchin monkeys. Recently, at Tiskita tourist lodge, overlooking the Pacific Ocean near the mouth of Golfo Dulce in southern Costa Rica, I became acquainted with the Central American squirrel monkey. Its wide separation from relatives in South America suggests that it was brought to southern Central America by humans, long enough ago for this isolated population to become a different species. They were charming little primates, with bright cinnamon-brown backs and limbs, black crowns and muzzles contrasting with white faces, ears, and chests; the more posterior underparts were colored like the back. Each long, slender, loosely hanging, nonprehensile tail terminated in a black tuft. A troop of about twenty waited, with birdlike chirps, on low boughs, whence one by one they dropped to seize, with hands or mouth, pieces of banana from the hands of little girls, then hurried back to their companions.

Marmosets, tamarins, titis, and birds offer an instructive example of the ecological convergence of widely separated lineages. Sharing habitats and foods with many rain forest birds, these monkeys have acquired similar habits and life histories: small families, male participation in caring for the young, territorial exclusiveness with largely vocal confrontations with contiguous conspecific families at territorial boundaries, and, most surprising of all, the modification of the dentition of marmosets that facilitates the digging of sap wells in the bark of trees and lianas, much as certain birds do with their bills.

CHAPTER 17   ✺

Stilt Palms, Birds, and Other Users

Growing up through the wide-spreading boughs of the old mango tree that shades the cabin where I write are two curious stilt palms, locally called *chontas* and known to botanists as *Socratea durissima*. The taller of them rises to about fifty feet (15 m), well above the dark foliage of the mango tree. In the neighboring rain forest, much taller chontas stand straight and slender twice as high, thrusting their spreading crowns into the canopy. Along the Río San Juan in Nicaragua, the Danish botanist Anders Sandoe Oerstead found these stilt palms rising above surrounding forest trees to heights of 100 to 150 feet (30 to 45 m).

These tall palms grow in wet forests from Panama to Nicaragua, from lowlands up to about 2,500 feet (760 m). In our forest, near the upper level of the palm's altitudinal range, they thrive both on the red clay ridges and on the dark alluvial soil of the rocky riverside terraces where the Río Peñas Blancas once flowed. One who, leaving the trail, wanders through tangled undergrowth on rough ground, may first become aware of a stilt palm when he stretches out a hand to steady himself by a prop root, whose sharp spines promptly repulse him. They may lacerate the skin of one who carelessly brushes against them. Spreading widely all around the base of the palm, they uphold it. Peering into the midst of the well-separated roots, one sees that the trunk does not make contact with the ground.

The stilt palm starts to grow from a seed like other palms, with a primary root that strikes downward into the soil and sends out lateral roots. But when the plant is only a foot or two (30 or 60 cm) high, with a few small leaves, roots like thin wires emerge from the less-than-pencil-thick stem and descend to the ground. As the stem elongates and thickens,

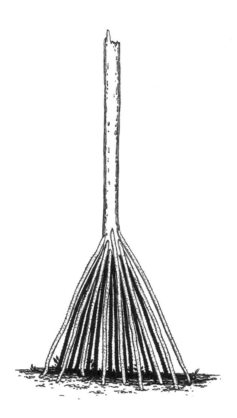

Chonta Palm

it sends forth more roots, always thicker and at greater heights, until on old palms they may spring from the trunk ten feet (3 m) up, to descend obliquely outward to reach and penetrate the ground in a circle around the point where the palm germinated. Meanwhile, the lowest part of the trunk, which never becomes thick, often decays away, leaving the aerial roots as the palm's only connection with the soil. They begin to break out of the trunk chiefly in the early months of the rainy season, which here starts in late March or April and continues into December. A vigorous palm with a trunk of adult thickness may produce from one to eight prop roots in a single season, or in some years none. Forty-five stout roots may uphold an old palm.

As indicated by the specific name *durissima,* the outer layer of the trunk, or cortex, is so hard that I suspected that a root, arising internally, softens this resisting tissue with an enzyme to break through it. I was mistaken. The root presses against the cortex until it bulges outward. Above the highest developed roots the trunk is encircled by a number of these low bulges, each covering the rudiment of a root that may not emerge until a year or more later. Finally, a root splits the longitudinal fibers of the cortex to pass between them, which must require great pressure. As the already thick root grows downward, it is smooth and light brown, with a large root-cap at its tip. A root that I measured daily from its first appearance on a vigorous young palm started to elongate two inches (5 cm) in twenty-four hours but soon doubled its rate of growth, and through much of its downward journey advanced about four inches (10 cm) per day. Breaking out of the trunk on March 18, the root touched the ground and started to grow horizontally over it on April 9, twenty-two days later. It was then sixty-six inches (168 cm) long, having elongated at the average rate of three inches (7.6 cm) per day.

Strong roots are two to three inches (5 to 7.6 cm) thick at the top and taper slightly downward to the ground. They readily penetrate soft woodland soil but tend to grow horizontally over the surface of harder ground, as when the palm grows in a pasture or lawn. The main prop roots anchor themselves and increase their absorbing surface by thinner lateral roots.

Two or three weeks after a root reaches the ground, spines begin to roughen its smooth surface, starting at the top. They break through the root's cortex much as the root itself erupts from the trunk. When mature they are conical, hard, about a quarter-inch (4 or 5 mm) high, and very sharp.

Above the highest roots an old trunk is six to seven inches (15 to 18 cm) thick and tapers slightly upward. Its smooth surface is mottled with shades of gray and brown or green with moss and, is marked with well separated rings where fronds have been attached. Near the top the long straight column abruptly changes its appearance, bulging slightly and becoming green up to the petioles of the fronds. This apparent prolongation of the trunk, four or five feet (1.2 or 1.5 m) long, is not stem but the crown shaft, composed of the thick, tubular, sheathing bases of the leaves, one inside another. If you remove these concentric sheaths, you find them successively more tender, until at the center the youngest fronds, tightly folded, soft and white, are pushing upward by basal growth through all the surrounding tubes, to emerge like long, thin rods at the top—a process which, like the emergence of the prop roots, must require strong pressure. The palm's single vegetative growing point (aside from those of the roots) is at the top of the trunk near the base of the crown shaft, where the leaves are formed.

Not all palms have crown shafts. On those that lack them, dead fronds often drape the trunk; or the fronds break away from persisting bases that raggedly cover the trunk, collecting debris in which epiphytes and even plants that usually grow on the ground flourish. But chontas and other palms with crown shafts shed whole fronds, including their sheathing bases, and remain always clean and tidy. As we shall see, this arrangement is necessary to release the inflorescences that develop inside the tubular sheaths.

These fronds with sheaths that enclose the inflorescences differ greatly in form as well as in size from the chonta's first leaves. After surrounding its thin stem with four successively longer bladeless sheaths, a young chonta produces seedling leaves, each with a tubular sheathing base, short petiole, and ribbed, deeply bifid or V-shaped blade. As the seedling stretches upward in the woodland shade, these two-parted simple leaves are succeeded by compound juvenile leaves. The growing palm bears increasingly large fronds with more leaflets of the same type, each with an entire, nearly straight inner margin and a convex, coarsely toothed outer margin. Juvenile fronds spread out flatly, as in the coconut palm and many others.

An adult leaf resembles a juvenile leaf with many pinnae of a wholly different shape added to its upper side. The first of these accessory leaflets appear on palms ten to twenty feet (3 to 6 m) high (to the top of the crown shaft) and their number increases as the palms grow taller. On fully adult leaves, the leaflets or pinnae are borne in clusters or tufts, each of which contains a single lopsided leaflet of the juvenile type already described, with from one to six strikingly different leaflets inserted beside it. The slenderest of these are thin stalks with wider tips. The broadest are ribbons expanding from a narrow base to about two and a half inches (6 cm) at the apex, and between these extremes are all intermediate widths. The slender pinnae are picturesquely called quaquaversal by botanists. Standing above the broad, flat pinnae, they spread in all directions, imparting to the frond a plumelike grace and greatly increasing its photosynthetic activity.

Large adult leaves consist of a thick sheathing base fifty to fifty-eight inches (127 to 147 cm) long, a stout, terete, slightly grooved petiole five to 12 inches (13 to 30 cm) long, and an expanded frond seven to ten feet (2 to

3 m) long and three to four feet (0.9 to 1.2 m) broad. The largest that I measured had a total length (sheath plus petiole plus blade) of sixteen feet (nearly 5 m). Opposite, subopposite, or alternate, thirty-eight clusters of pinnae were distributed along the stout rachis.

After emerging from the center of the crown shaft, a new frond grows upward until it stands above the older leaves as a long, slender, straight rod, its leaflets tightly folded together fanwise. Sometimes a second, much shorter rod stands beside the first, but this occurs less frequently than in palms that lack a crown shaft, such as the pejibaye (*Bactris gasipaes*) and the African oil palm (*Elaeis guineensis*), which may have two or three tightly folded rods visible at the same time. The interval between the expansion of successive fronds is extremely variable, from twenty-five to sixty days and occasionally more. Thirty-four intervals on four palms averaged 54.7 days. Seven or eight new fronds may expand in twelve months, and since the number of fronds at the end of the year (usually seven to nine, rarely ten) is about the same as at the beginning, it is evident that the life of an expanded frond is about a year or a little more. They regularly fall in the order in which they emerged from the crown shaft, by the splitting of the sheath on the side opposite the attachment of the petiole.

A bulge at the base of the crown shaft reveals that an inflorescence is about to emerge, which cannot happen until it is released by the death and fall of the frond whose sheathing base encloses it. In this locality chontas flower sporadically through much of the year, but chiefly in the midst of the rainy season, from mid-July to late October, often soon after the same palm has dropped the fruits from the preceding year's flowering, or even while the palm bears fruit. The fall of the enclosing sheath exposes a pale, boat-shaped spathe, about twenty-eight inches long by four or five inches broad in the middle (71 by 10–13 cm), with a pointed tip. Within this is a second spathe of similar size and shape. This double envelope stands upright beside the crown shaft, with on its inner side three large bracts of different lengths that partly embrace the full spathes, that against the crown shaft shortest. These five complete or partial coverings of the spadix are thick, tough, flexible even when dry, and glabrous. Few palms have such well enclosed inflorescences; the pejibaye, for example, has only a single spathe.

The two full spathes split open along the whole length of the outer side to permit the escape of the spadix or inflorescence, which is about thirty-five inches (89 cm) long, with about fifteen slender branches. When newly exposed they hang limply, white with the staminate (male) flowers that completely cover them. The behavior of these flowers varies somewhat with the weather. One spadix escaped on a sunny morning followed by an afternoon of hard rain that continued into the night. During the hours of darkness nearly all the male flowers fell; at dawn they lay thickly on the ground beneath the palm. A spadix that escaped on a clear afternoon dropped only about half its staminate flowers during the following night. A few fell during the next day, and nearly all that remained dropped in the second night. Thus, staminate flowers remain attached for from considerably less than twelve hours to over two but less than three full days. Relieved of the weight of the male flowers, the spadix branches rise and spread apart. They now appear much thinner, and rough with the pistillate flowers.

The staminate flowers are twelve millimeters (1/2 inch) broad, with three minute (2 mm long) sepals and three broadly ovate, waxy white petals ten millimeters long by nine or ten millimeters broad, surrounding a tight cluster of thirty-four to fifty-three stamens, which release minute pollen grains covered with tiny spikes, miniatures of those on the prop roots. Smaller than the staminate flower, the pistillate is depressed globular, with the floral envelopes imbricated in two series and a short, broad pistil. Insects come to the flowers as soon as the inner spathe begins to split and continue all through a rainless day to swarm around the dangling spadix, probably attracted by a scent that I could not detect.

The fruits ripen mainly from June to October, about ten months after pollination. Ellipsoidal in shape, they are an inch and a half long by about one inch (38 by 25–28 mm) thick. The thin, brown or brownish olive skin peels off irregularly, exposing the thick, dry, oily white flesh, which to me is almost tasteless. Within this loose covering is a single hard brown seed, irregularly streaked with paler brown, about one inch long by three quarters of an inch thick (25 by 19 mm). A vigorous palm may bear simultaneously four large spadices of ripening fruits.

The conspicuous white pulp attracts birds, especially tanagers. In the chonta beside my study I have seen seven species of this family eating it: Bay-headed, Golden-hooded, Speckled, Blue-gray, Palm, and Scarlet-rumped tanagers and Green Honeycreepers. The tanagers are joined by Buff-throated Saltators, large, mainly frugivorous finches. When brilliant Red-headed Barbets descend from greater altitudes toward the year's end, they add the white palm pulp to their largely frugivorous diet. Gray-headed Chachalacas cling with long toes to the spadices, their long, broad tails conspicuous, to pluck off fragments of the pulp, just as the much smaller tanagers do.

The colorful Fiery-billed Aracari has a different procedure. Plucking a palm fruit in the tip of its great bill, this middle-sized toucan presses the seed out of its white envelope and drops it. Then, holding the empty coat against its perch with a foot, the bird tears off pieces of pulp and mandibulates them, if they are large, for as much as a minute before throwing them back into its throat with an upward toss of its head and swallowing them, the toucan's habitual way of eating. No bird that I have seen eating stilt palm fruits swallows them whole, thereby becoming a potential disperser of the seeds. I surmise that Chestnut-mandibled Toucans, much bigger than the aracaris, swallow entire fruits and, after digesting off the pulp, regurgitate the seeds, sometimes in clearings that they frequently visit. Formerly abundant in our forest, these great-billed birds were long ago exterminated here by poachers, and I have been unable to investigate this. In other localities it is known to eat fruits of the chonta. Among mammals, the spiny pocket mouse eats the chonta's embryos, which appear to be inaccessible to birds that lack the sharp incisors of rodents.

In addition to food for birds, stilt palms offer sites for their nests. When forests are felled to clear land for planting, the tops of these palms are sometimes broken off by falling trees, leaving a stub upheld by its prop roots, which resist the fire set to clear the ground. Or amid the forest, palms may be similarly broken by falling trees or boughs. The interior of such a palm trunk, much softer and less resistant than the cortex, decays away, leaving a hollow tube opening skyward. Woodcreepers sometimes nest in these hollows, which offer excellent concealment but no shelter from rain. In such sites I have found two nests of Tawny-winged Woodcreepers, one of which had an interesting history.

In a clearing, about a hundred feet (30 m) from the forest, the remains of a chonta stood fifteen feet (4.6 m) high, with a hollow center eleven feet (3.6 m) deep, propped five feet (1.5 m) above the ground by its spiny, spreading stilt roots. A pair of Streaked-headed Woodcreepers brought flakes of bark, a lone Tawny-winged Woodcreeper carried in moss, and together they raised the level of the floor about nineteen inches (48 cm) above the dark brown earthy debris in the bottom, evidently the remains of the trunk's central tissue, where many big, shiny brown beetles lived. Alternating layers of moss brought by the Tawny-wing and of bark flakes brought by the Streaked-heads suggested that the two species of wood-creepers worked at different times to shorten the descent from the aperture above the nest; they were not friendly cooperators but competitors for this attractive nest site. The two Streaked-heads feared the Tawny-wing, an aggressive bird. Finally, she chased the pair away and incubated two white eggs. The one that hatched proved to be a young Streaked-head, who was faithfully attended by the Tawny-wing for the nineteen days that it remained in the deep well.

I have twice known terrestrial, rail-like Black-faced Antthrushes to nest in stilt palm trunks. One of these nests was in a well-like hollow, about five inches (12 cm) in diameter, in the top of a stub amid the forest. The two eggs rested thirteen inches (33 cm) below the lowest point of the oblique aperture at the top of the broken-off trunk, on a bed of dead leaves and petioles that the antthrushes had carried in. The second nest was in a surprising situation. A piece broken from the upper part of a tall chonta stood upright below it, held erect by a single loop of a dead frond of a climbing fern. The thin, decaying shell of the segment of trunk was a flexible tube about seven feet (2 m) long and reminded me of a stove pipe. At the bottom, the birds had built on the ground a nest of dead leaves where the two eggs rested. To reach or depart from their eggs, the birds climbed down or up this swaying vertical tube for nearly five feet (1.5 m) from or to a jagged gap in its side, below the open top.

Occasionally, a bird finds the long sheath of a fallen palm frond standing upright, held in this position by the leaf blade draped over a low shrub. In this hollow cylinder, open at the top and not sealed along one side, it may build a nest. The first Bicolored Antbirds' nest reported by an ornithologist was in this unexpected site (Van Tyne 1944).

Pioneers in the forest use stilt palms in their constructions. Flattened out, the hard outer shells of old trunks make a wall; narrow strips of them hold the palm fronds or sugarcane leaves of a thatched roof. Long ago, while I rode horseback through a large tract of forest, the swift approach of a night that threatened to be rainy made me seek shelter. Following narrow side trails, I found a solitary cabin in a new clearing cluttered with charred logs and stumps. The good woman who dwelt there, surrounded by children and pigs, served the unannounced stranger a dish of rice and beans with a boiled egg, and said that he might sleep on the *tabanco*, a shelf of palm slats stretched across the poles that served as rafters. I climbed up a notched trunk, pushed aside a litter of odds and ends, and spread my

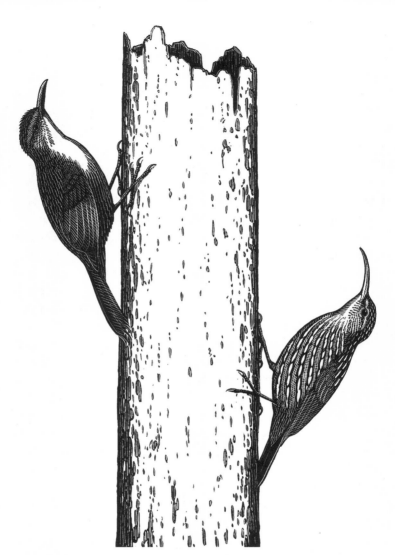

Tawny-winged Woodcreeper (*left*) and Streaked-headed Woodcreeper

ground cloth and blanket over the platform, where I slept soundly enough, despite the shrill squeals of the pigs just outside the walls of upright trunks. Next morning I was rewarded by the brilliant sight of about twenty-five Scarlet Macaws preening themselves in treetops aglow in the rising Sun, along with a few noisy Mealy Parrots.

The soft tissues at the growing point of a palm trunk, where new leaves are formed, are the edible "palm hearts." Suckering palms, like the pejibaye, sprout new stems around the base of the original trunk, producing a succession of harvestable hearts. They can profitably be grown in plantations and canned. Each single-stemmed palm, like the chonta, yields only one heart, to procure which the tree is cut down and will not regenerate. To fell a chonta, the prop roots are severed. The trunk is decapitated, and successive layers of leaf sheaths are pried off until one reaches the soft new leaves at the center of the crown shaft. To destroy a stately palm, perhaps fifty or more feet high and as many years old, for as much food as a cabbage yields in a few months seems vandalism; but this consideration does not save palms from hungry poachers in insufficiently protected forests.

When I came here, my hundred acres (40 hectares) or so of old forest contained many stilt palms and more palmitos (*Euterpe macrospadix*), also single-stemmed palms, which grow almost as tall as the chontas and have flat fronds with many ribbonlike leaflets, slender trunks that rise directly from the ground, and only a few aerial roots clustered tightly around their bases. Palmito hearts are a favorite food of the country people; with fish they make the traditional Easter feast. Over the years neighbors stole nearly all my palmitos, which I could not guard continuously. Happily, many of our stilt palms remain standing; their slightly bitter hearts are edible but less esteemed.

In the exceptionally severe dry season during the early months of 1985, the stilt palms fared badly; many small and middle-sized palms on the dark, rocky soil of the riverside benches succumbed to the drought. Others were reduced to a leaf or two on a shrunken crown shaft but revived after rains returned in April. On the red clay ridges the chontas survived better, but a few up to seventy-five feet (23 m) high dried up. In the same woods, dicotyledonous trees resisted the drought better than the stilt palms, possibly because their wholly subterranean roots are more efficient absorbers of water than are stilt roots.

Aside from humans, the only important enemy of chonta palms that I have noticed is the giant red-winged grasshopper, or chapulín gigante (Tropidacris cristata). The nymphs are boldly marked with vertical black and yellow stripes. Adults are four or five inches (10 or 13 cm) long, with a wingspan of up to ten inches (25 cm). The fore wings are mottled olive-brown, the hind wings largely red with black spots. Although over the years I occasionally noticed these big grasshoppers in El General, they never, to my knowledge, became a pest until 1995, when they devoured the chonta foliage, making the palms look very ragged. They also attacked coconut palms and African oil palms, as well as diverse dicotyledonous trees. The plague continued into the following year.

Finally, we may ask why the chonta trunk stands on such high prop roots, losing direct contact with the ground. The trunks of other trees with prop roots, such as the widespread cecropia or *guarumo,* preserve contact with the soil. But the cecropia is a dicotyledonous tree with a cambium to thicken the slender stem of the seedling, whereas the monocotyledonous palm lacks a cambium. Without waiting to develop a massive base, the thin-stemmed chonta seedling grows more rapidly upward toward the light. Unable to thicken the base of its trunk after it has risen above the undergrowth, the chonta supports itself by adventitious prop roots, springing from the trunk at ever higher levels. These roots so adequately support the trunk, and in most years draw enough water and nutrients from the soil of the rain forest, that the thin seedling stem disappears because it is no longer needed.

CHAPTER 18

Living with Chachalacas

  The field naturalist seeks birds in their native forests, fields, marshes, and deserts, or on the oceans. The householder attracts free birds to the garden or windowsill by daily offering food. Although usually the beneficiaries remain aloof from their benefactors, with patience they may be induced to take food from human hands. Some people who are unable to roam afield, or who live in an apartment without a garden, nevertheless crave association with feathered creatures; keeping a bird or two as pets, they become more intimate with them than the watcher of free birds, or even the operator of a feeding station, can often do. For many a city dweller, the household pet is the only contact with a nonhuman animal—frequently the chief solace of a lonely life.

  The ability of creatures the most diverse to become strongly attached to the person who gently rears them from an early age, or of two animals of different kinds—even hereditary enemies like crows and owls—to become friendly when raised together with sufficient food, is one of the most heartening aspects of nature. It reminds us that beneath all differences in form and habits, living creatures have much in common. The primary nature of all is pacific and friendly, or at least neutral, as we would expect of organisms formed by the cosmic process of harmonization (Skutch 1985). Fierceness, aggressiveness, hostility, and rage are secondary accretions, foisted upon them by evolution in the long, harsh struggle to survive in an overcrowded world. As Aristotle recognized long ago, if animals had no need to compete with and often kill one another for food (and, I would add, living space) all, including humans, would live peacefully together.

  I would not deprive anybody of the satisfying experience of caring devotedly for another living creature, but I strongly urge those who crave the companionship of a nonhuman animal to select one of a kind that has long been domesticated, or at least one that has been captive bred, and to become informed regarding their proper care. The capture of wild birds for the cage-bird trade is both cruel and wasteful and threatens the extinction of not a few species. Large numbers perish miserably in transport, or in the hands of purchasers who do not know how to care for them. Control of this wicked traffic is one of the most distressing problems of conservation.

As a boy in Maryland, I had pigeons as pets, and after acquiring a farm in Costa Rica I raised horses for riding, cows for milk, and chickens for eggs. But Laca and Chacha were the only wild birds that I have ever reared, and I undertook to do so only because the eggs from which they hatched had been abandoned by their mother.

Chacha and Laca were Gray-headed Chachalacas, members of the tropical American curassow family. Although most of the thirty-eight species of curassows and guans live in forests, chachalacas prefer lighter vegetation, including bushy abandoned fields and tangled thickets above which rise scattered trees. From eastern Honduras and Nicaragua through the rainier parts of Costa Rica and Panama to northwestern Colombia, Gray-headed Chachalacas live in flocks of about six to twelve birds in which the sexes cannot be distinguished. About twenty inches (50 cm) long, they are elegantly slender as with graceful ease they walk along high, thin branches, or rest, several together, on such exposed limbs, silhouetted against the sky. Their dark gray heads and upper necks contrast with the olive-brown of most of their plumage. Brown eyes are set amid bare, slate-gray skin. The featherless sides of the throat and the inside of the mouth are red; the short bill, slender legs, and long toes are grayish. When chachalacas spread their wings for a few flaps followed by a long, descending glide, a large patch of chestnut becomes visible on each wing. The expanded, greenish black tail shows that all but the central feathers are broadly tipped with buffy gray. Although chachalacas fly strongly, they prefer to ascend by flying and leaping from branch to branch.

Strangely, Gray-headed Chachalacas lack the stirring, many-voiced chorus of species north and south of them, including the Plain Chachalaca that ranges as far as southern Texas. Nevertheless, they are voluble, with a variety of utterances ranging from soft notes to prolonged squeals and an occasional piercing scream. Resting and preening in sunshine after their

Gray-headed Chachalaca

morning meal, they converse together, mingling harsh notes with soft purrs or rattles that remind one of a domestic hen settling down to brood her chicks.

Nests of Gray-headed Chachalacas are not easy to find. In the many years that I have lived near these birds, I have seen only seven. Most were situated from three to eight feet (0.9–2.4 m) above the ground in vine-draped bushes and small trees, or in tangles of creepers. One was in a large heap of dead branches in a clearing near woodland. Each nest was a broad, shallow saucer made of a variety of coarse materials: sticks, lengths of vine, inflorescences, and leaves, many of which had been plucked and added to the nest while green, and in drying had matted together. The usual set is three large, dull white eggs, with rough, pitted shells, or sprinkled with embossed white flecks that appear to be lime. Often the eggs are heavily stained by contact with the green vegetation on which they lie.

At the nest most favorably situated for study, I watched from a blind for many hours. Only one parent, doubtless the female, came near the nest; but the flock to which she appeared to belong passed through nearby trees. Her absences from incubating her eggs, one in the morning and one in the afternoon, lasted an hour or a little more. The days were warm and, even when the sunshine did not fall directly on her, she panted much, stretching up her head with widely open mouth, the bare red skin of her throat distended and vibrating in what ornithologists call gular flutter, which cools by increasing evaporation from the mouth.

Hatching was rapid. During the female's absence from the nest one afternoon, I heard peeping and tapping sounds in shells in which I detected no fracture. Early the following morning, the mother picked up a piece of empty shell and laid it on the side of the nest. Soon I heard soft peeps, and glimpsed a downy chick in front of her breast. By mid-morning, three chicks had emerged in front of her, their down already dry. Gently she nibbled their heads. Before noon, all three restless chicks were venturing out to move around beside her, panting as she did. Soon she left the nest to eat ripe black berries and unripe red berries of a neighboring bush of *Hamelia patens*. Her throat distended with them, she returned to the nest, mashed one in her bill, and offered it to the chicks, who pecked at it but did not appear to eat. After holding the berries for five minutes, she swallowed them all. A little later, she again filled her throat with these berries, one of which a chick took from her bill.

The chicks were becoming more restless. Around noon one of them climbed to a slender vine about an inch above the nest's rim, perched unsteadily, and in less than a minute returned to the others in the nest. At ten minutes past one, the mother rose from the nest and slowly climbed down through the tangled vegetation to the ground—a mode of departure that I had not previously witnessed. Because she left on the far side of the nest and foliage obstructed my view, I did not see the chicks go. I was sure that their mother did not carry them down in her bill, but they might have clung to her while she descended, a mode of leaving the nest that has been attributed to Plain Chachalacas, perhaps mistakenly. On the ground, the mother walked slowly away, calling softly for chicks that I failed to see amid the tangled growth. They abandoned their nest when less than a day old. No second chachalaca came to assist at the critical moment of their departure (Skutch 1983).

Downy ducklings jump from nests much higher than those of chachalacas. Light and fluffy, they are rarely injured by their fall. Chagrined by my failure, after such patient watching, to learn exactly how the little chachalacas left their nest, I searched for another nest favorably situated for observation. Years passed before another was discovered, six feet up in a nook among five stout ascending branches of a fig tree, in the pasture beside the river, close by tall second-growth woods. Hanging fern fronds draped it all around. The chachalaca had laid her three eggs on leaves and other debris that had accumulated in the depression between the branches, with little or no nest building. During a morning that I watched from a blind set in the edge of the woods, the parent took a recess from incubation that lasted eighty-one minutes, and later a short outing of thirty-five minutes. In the afternoon of the following day, she was absent for three hours. Whenever she left the nest spontaneously, she walked far up an ascending branch, then flew to the high tops of neighboring trees. To return, she walked down the branch. No other chachalaca accompanied her to the nest, but during her recesses she appeared to join others in the fringe of trees along the river.

One morning, when I checked the nest, the eggs were unattended, cold, and wet. The preceding day, a trespasser had cut a long pole to knock down oranges that he peeled and ate, all within a few yards of the nest. This was too much for the shy chachalaca. When, after two rainy nights and the intervening day she had not returned, I placed the thoroughly chilled eggs beneath our broody black hen, Diana. After a week, she hatched all three, on May 6.

The fluffy newly hatched chachalacas were not unlike domestic chicks but their down had more pattern. The top of the head and center of the back and rump were black, with a little dull brown on the sides of the crown. The hind head and sides of the neck were brighter brown, which paled to buff on the lower sides of one chick. The wings and sides of the body were barred with black and buff. The sparse down on the flanks and abdomen was white. The bill was horn colored, with the apical half of the

Gray-headed Chachalaca Chicks

upper mandible black, and at its tip was a prominent white egg tooth that fell before the chicks were a week old. The grayish brown eyes were surrounded by gray bare skin. The legs and feet were pale with whitish claws. The chicks peeped softly like domestic chicks, perched, and tried to climb, hooking their bills over fingers that held them.

I was uncertain how baby chachalacas, normally fed from their mother's bill, would fare with a domestic hen, who picks up food, perhaps mashes it in her bull, then lays it down for her chicks to pick up for themselves. On the day they hatched, the chachalaca chicks would neither pick up food when called to it by their foster mother nor take it from my fingers or a forceps, although rarely they tried to snatch it from the hen's bill. They did not take long to adjust to their unusual situation. By the second day they were picking up their food: commercial poultry mixture, blue berries from a rubiaceous shrub in the garden, cooked rice, and black beans that I gave to Diana, not intending them for the chicks. They ate the beans after she mashed them in her bill and laid them down. They drank, raising their heads to permit the water to run down to their throats. They came to Diana's call and huddled beneath her for warmth, but fled from me to hide in corners of the granary, where we kept them.

In the evening, I placed Diana in a basket, with the chicks beneath her, as we did when we raised domestic chickens. But the day-old chachalacas jumped up on the basket's rim, to perch there with heads turned back and snuggled into the short down of their shoulders as far as possible. Their mother would have brooded them on a perch. After they fell asleep, I tucked them beneath the hen for warmth. Soon the three formed the habit of sleeping pressed together in a row on the basket's rim, above Diana, who sat in brooding posture. They early showed their preference for high places. In the granary was a chicken coop, shaped like an inverted V, and twenty-two inches (56 cm) high. Its apex soon became their favorite perch. Before they could fly, they climbed up and down on the sticks that enclosed the cage, to rest on top, beneath their foster mother. Whenever she vigorously flapped her wings for exercise, they rushed into corners.

When three days old, each chick weighed about one ounce (28 g) before breakfast. At eleven days, they could fly a few feet on a descending course. A day later, they could flutter a few feet upward. At three weeks they could fly for several yards, and their range rapidly increased. They consistently tried to reach the highest perch in sight: the rim of the corn shelling machine in the granary; in the house, they fluttered and climbed to the tops of the highest furniture. Much of the time they now voiced low, soft notes—*teweet, teweet*—different from the chickenlike peeps they had uttered when younger. Occasionally, in a weak voice, they repeated the *white white* contact notes of adult chachalacas.

The growing chicks ate almost everything we offered them, including *masa* (cooked corn, ground for making tortillas), dry oatmeal, cooked rice, bananas, wild berries, hard-boiled egg (especially the yolk), and leaves of the *tuete (Vernonia patens)*, a tall, white-flowered shrub of the composite family that grows in pastures where it is not wanted. They were so eager for these green leaves that they tried to pull pieces from each other's bills, or to tear a strip apart between two of them.

When three weeks old, their weight before eating in the morning averaged nearly two ounces (52 g). Despite their varied diet, they appeared to be growing too slowly in the granary, with no access to the ground. After weighing them, I released them outside, beside some shrubbery, with Diana nearby. Their first clear view of the outside world made them tremble. Soon they recovered their composure and began to eat, plucking green foliage of low plants and swallowing a few soft dead leaves gathered from the ground. Meanwhile, Diana, who for three weeks had enjoyed no opportunity to scratch, was plying her feet vigorously and calling the chicks to the insects and worms that she uncovered in the soft earth.

All day the chicks followed their foster mother through the garden, coming to her call whenever her tireless toes disclosed something edible and she invited them to feed, picking it up and dropping it for them to take. They tried to pull an earthworm apart between them. They squatted in the sunshine, all three in contact. When a hawk flew by, low above the ground where it had apparently spied them, they rushed into the dense hedge on hearing Diana's sharp warning notes. This unhesitating response to the voice of a different species surprised me; but afterward I remembered that birds of many kinds are alerted by the alarm notes of associated species.

At four o'clock in the afternoon, I found Diana already perching under the roof of the tall chickens' shelter behind the house, where she always slept when not broody. The young chachalacas were hiding beneath neighboring shrubbery. After I chased Diana down, she called them and walked around with them. By placing food at the foot of the long, inclined pole up which the chickens climbed, I enticed the family to this point. Diana walked up the pole and the chachalacas followed. After they were settled on a perch, I removed the pole. Broad metal bands around the four posts that supported this shelter prevented prowling quadrupeds from climbing up.

Two young chachalacas huddled beneath Diana's spread left wing. The third could not find room there, and apparently while trying to adjust itself it fell to the ground, injuring a leg. It perched clumsily and could not walk well. Confined to the house, it complained constantly with weak peeps, ate little, and did not improve. Hoping that it would do better outside, I placed it with its foster mother and siblings. All day it shuffled after the others, eating as they did. After the hen had gone early to roost with the two sound chicks, I searched in vain for the crippled one.

Diana and the chicks now went to the roost long before dusk. After being brooded there for a while, the chicks would fly down alone while daylight faded, for a last snack before they slept. Then, without guidance, they returned to Diana on the roost, racing nimbly up the long pole, inclined at an angle of about forty-five degrees, that led to her.

At the beginning of June, Diana disappeared. A trail of black feathers leading toward the forest revealed that she had been caught by a tayra, one of the large black weasels that over the years have stolen many chickens from us and our neighbors. After the loss of their guardian, the chicks, now nearly four weeks old, passed the remainder of the afternoon on the porch and in an adjoining room, calling much and eating little. As evening advanced, their distressed complaints became strong, full chirps that resounded through the house. In the fading light, they ran together up the inclined pole to the perch where they had been brooded beneath Diana's wings. Until it was dark, they continued to repeat loud chirps. Finally, they fell asleep, resting in contact head to tail, appearing small and lonely on the high perch, where I could not reach them to bring them into the house for warmth. Their bodies were still in down, but their wing feathers covered them well.

It seemed time to name the two survivors. The slightly larger chick, apparently a male, was called Chacha; his sister became Laca. Without the hen, they became more strongly attached to the members of our family—Pamela, Edwin, and me. When we emerged from a room, they scampered toward us, feet pattering over the porch. When hungry, they ran to us, peeping. As we approached them, they would squat down and tremble, in what appeared to be a greeting ceremony, or perhaps a submissive gesture, which Laca habitually performed as long as she remained with us. They spent much time lying flat, bodies pressed together and long tails stretched behind, on a box or a chest. Rarely their rest was interrupted by a quarrel, when they flew up against each other and pecked. Soon after these brief flurries, they snuggled side by side. They preened frequently, and anointed their plumage with oil from the gland at the base of the tail.

When the chicks were six weeks old, their bodies were well covered with juvenal plumage, but their heads were downy, the feathers of the crown still ensheathed. Their bills had darkened. Their lengthening tails were bedraggled from lying so much on the floor or the ground. They spent more time outside the house but near it, walking over the lawn, plucking grass or tender leaves. As days passed, their excursions lengthened, sometimes taking them beyond view.

They were playful, chasing each other on foot around and around a bush, then running over the ground to circle a neighboring shrub. One of them apparently tried to play this game with one of the pair of Gray-necked Wood-Rails that frequented the garden, but the long-legged rail did not understand and confronted the chachalaca. Occasionally a chachalaca playfully chased a White-tipped or Gray-chested dove eating corn on the lawn. When tired, the two often rested amid dense foliage and vine tangles instead of in the house. Or, in the sunshine on the grass, they lay on their sides close together, each with one wing stretched out. Rarely one dusted itself, lying in a little hollow in loose soil, kicking with its feet and moving its slightly expanded wings to send a cloud of dust over itself. Then it preened.

Chacha and Laca did not like to be caught. Taken in hand, they struggled to escape; and the holder had to be careful of sharp claws that could draw blood. But the moment they were released, they seemed to forget the episode. As Laca grew older, she became resigned to being held and gently stroked.

The chief problem of their young lives was finding a place to sleep. As night approached, they often whimpered and complained as though perturbed. Sometimes they flew around wildly, up on the house roof and down to the ground, before they went to roost. Or they would climb up to the chickens' shelter only to fly out, doing this repeatedly before they settled down. Thinking that the open-sided shelter was too exposed for them, I boarded up a corner, but they refused to sleep there. They preferred the opposite side, where they roosted pressed together, at the very end of one of the sticks that served as perches, the most exposed site they could find on this construction. From there they might fly to a neighboring orange tree, to pass the night amid its dark, dense foliage, where they were less likely to be caught by one of the rare owls in the vicinity but more accessible to mammals and snakes. Or they might go to the orange tree only to return to the shelter. Sometimes they slept where I could not find them. Their behavior at nightfall was erratic and unpredictable.

In August, when they were three months old, Laca and Chacha were almost full grown. Their legs and tails were long, and all but the central pair of plain juvenal tail feathers had been replaced by adult feathers with broad buffy tips. The central pair still had the pointed ends of the juvenal plumage. After breakfast, one August morning, the two stood facing each other on the lawn, stretched up their necks, raised the feathers of their crowns, and poured forth a weak version of the adults' garbled chatter, which I had first heard a few days earlier. Then they ran over the grass, chasing the doves and each other, up onto the porch and down again, in wide circles.

Late on the afternoon of August 22, Chacha failed to return to the house with Laca. We never knowingly saw him again. We like to think that he joined a party of wild chachalacas that sometimes passed by, but possibly some mishap had befallen him. As night approached, his sister, restless and lonely, took a long time to settle down, jumping from perch to perch in the shelter, flying down and up again, and finally falling asleep in the same exposed spot where the two had so often roosted in closest contact.

After the loss of her brother, Laca became even more closely attached to us. She would follow us through the garden and over the pastures, walking, or flying low over the ground to catch up if she fell behind. When I found a sprout of tuete, I would gather a few of the tenderest leaves and hold them while she plucked and swallowed pieces, with low, soft notes expressing her pleasure in this favorite food. We had to be careful that she did not follow us out to the road where cars passed. While I sat at my table, writing, she rested for hours silently at my feet, often nibbling my socks or the ends of my trouser legs; but the windowsill where Chacha used to rest while I wrote was vacant. Sometimes when I shifted my feet without seeing her under the table, I stepped on her long, thin toes spread widely, flat on the floor. Or when I stood outside, perhaps watching a bird, she waited close to my feet and, unaware of her presence, I moved and trod on her toes. A volley of shrill peeps admonished me for my carelessness; but she suffered no harm and fell silent the moment I released her. When I went to town in shoes different from those I wore at home, she sat for long intervals beside the empty ones.

At meal time Laca perched on the back of Pamela's chair, accepting tidbits that my wife passed to her. Feeding her was easy because she was almost wholly vegetarian and ate almost everything that we ate. She loved cake and other sweet things. Living always in the open, chachalacas have not developed sanitary inhibitions, and it seemed impossible to train Laca to be careful of her droppings, which were frequent. Wherever she went in the house, we had to clean; but we did not grumble about this chore because we loved her.

By September's end, the central tail feathers with rounded tips that replaced the pointed feathers of Laca's juvenal plumage were almost full grown, and she appeared mature. She had begun to lead a double life. So attached to the house and its occupants by day, at night she behaved like a wild chachalaca. Toward evening she would leave us, starting by walking over the ground, plucking green foliage as she went, then rising into trees and flying farther away. Frequently she changed her roost, which probably increased her immunity from nocturnal predators. At first she favored orange or tangerine trees near the house. Later, she flew far up the hillside behind it, where small trees, shrubs, and vines rose above an impenetrable thicket of the climbing fern *Dicranopteris pectinata.* Somewhere amid this exuberant verdure she would vanish, until next morning she came early to the house for breakfast. On an October evening when rain was falling hard, she went to roost in the chickens' shelter for the first time in many nights.

While I brushed my teeth one morning in October, Laca flew into the bathroom through the open window and noticed her image in a mirror. With crown feathers raised and uttering a continuous stream of weak, high-pitched notes, she delivered peck after peck at her double, which of course returned each of them, reflected bill meeting real bill tip to tip. This continued until I stopped her. A month later, her reflection in a mirror excited a different response. Now, no longer appearing antagonistic to her image, she seemed to court it. Instead of pecking, she more gently touched its bill while, with the feathers of her head and hind neck raised, she maintained a continuous flow of soft purrs and near trills, interspersed with low contact notes. This went on for several minutes, until I removed her. On subsequent encounters with a mirror, she paid little attention to her image, apparently having learned that it was not a living bird.

One morning in November, Laca found a dozen hens' eggs spread out on a kitchen table. Moving restlessly over them, she tried to push some of them beneath herself by hooking her bill over them and pulling inward. On another occasion, she tried to cover the top of a blue egg container, covered with little domes shaped to hold eggs. She tore strips from newspapers and tucked them beneath herself, as though trying to start a nest. These activities convinced me that I had not mistaken her sex, as male chachalacas take no part in nesting. She often picked up shiny or colored objects, such as keys, pens, and pencils, which she soon dropped.

Starting in mid-October, Laca tried to join a flock of five or six chachalacas that from time to time passed through the trees near the house. At first she was repelled with pecks. On one occasion, a visiting chachalaca chased her over the ground. One November afternoon, while standing in the window of my study, she heard voices of distant chachalacas and repeated high, soft contact notes. She flew to the mango tree that rises above my roof and called more, then uttered purring notes. Then she flew to the hillside where several chachalacas perched high in dead trees. Soon she returned to me. Three afternoons later she was in a cecropia tree in front of the house, with a second chachalaca, who presently flew toward the river, while she came to me. Early on a December morning, she was in a poró tree (*Erythrina berteroana*) beside the house with several other chachalacas, two of whom put the tips of their bills together; I could not see whether food was passed. Soon the others disappeared and Laca joined me. Early on a January morning, while five chachalacas ate the tiny berries of a wayside miconia tree (*Miconia borealis*), Laca rested in a neighboring tree, without mingling with them. After they flew, one by one, to the hillside, Laca followed them. Through most of the day, she was absent. After a prolonged, hard shower in the afternoon, she returned, very wet, and stayed with us before going to roost.

For weeks, Laca appeared to follow the flock without being accepted. Her irregular absences became more frequent and prolonged. She might stay with us all day, disappear after an early breakfast for the rest of the day, or come only for supper. After a long absence, she would suddenly fly in and squat, trembling, at my feet. Not until January 25 was she absent through a whole day. On the next day she arrived only for breakfast, and thereafter she did not come home at all. Apparently, she had won admission to the flock that she had tried so long to join. I last saw her before sunrise on the final day of January, standing in the gateway behind the house, looking in. I called; but just then the flock of chachalacas passed by, and she followed them up the hillside. The attraction of her own kind had become stronger than that of the companions of her immaturity and the home in which she grew up. The flock she had joined no longer came near the house and she passed from our ken. Although we had expected this result when we undertook to rear her and her siblings from the eggs, when the time came for separation we were sad. She was such an affectionate, even-tempered bird, never showing resentment when we stepped on her toes or held her away from coveted food, never pecking us as our domestic hens sometimes did.

Although my dreams are nearly always forgotten before I wake, a month after Laca's departure I had one so vivid and moving that it was remembered. Laca returned, flew against an obstruction, and knocked out an eyeball. We tried to replace it but could not decide which way was up. While I held her, she tried to kiss me, and I wept. Was this dream an intimation of some accident that had befallen her while she roamed through thickets and light woods with her new companions, or simply a consequence of the loss that we all felt? At least we had the satisfaction of knowing that we had restored to the free life of her kind a bird that without our intervention would not have hatched. Our reward is an enduring memory of one of the most pleasant and encouraging aspects of the living world, the ability of creatures of quite different kinds to develop friendly relations, mutually enhancing each other's lives—a memory that helps dispel the gloom or disgust that sometimes oppresses us when we contemplate nature's harsher aspects.

CHAPTER 19 ✿

The Strenuous Lives of Migratory Birds

Each year, as daily the Sun shines higher in northern skies, billions of birds that have flown southward to escape winter's cold and dearth return to their northern birthplaces. What signals their departure from tropical lands where they have lived for many months is not clear. It cannot be only increasing day length, for this changes little in the equatorial zone where many of these migrants winter, and days grow shorter in the Southern Hemisphere when many migrants, such as Bobolinks and shorebirds, begin their northward journeys. Probably an internal annual rhythm is the primary factor in their movements, modified and kept in step with the changing seasons by external influences.

By the number of species and individuals involved and the lengths of their flights, migration is a much more conspicuous phenomenon in the Northern Hemisphere, where most of the planet's land is situated, than in the Southern. At least, this is true of land birds, if not of marine birds. Species that nest on the narrowing tip of South America, or on Tierra del Fuego, can escape the harsh winters of that region by easy flights over hospitable lands to the tropics. Similarly, Australian birds need not leave that continent or fly far over Torres Strait to reach the forests of New Guinea. Likewise, birds that nest in western North America fly overland to winter in tropical and subtropical western Mexico and northern Central America. The migratory birds of eastern North America and much of northern Eurasia confront much more severe tests of their endurance. These are the land birds that make the longest, most hazardous migrations. In America many fly nonstop across the Gulf of Mexico or wide expanses of the Caribbean Sea; in the Old World the Mediterranean and vast, inhospitable deserts, including the Arabian and the Sahara, lie between the northern breeding areas and winter homes in Africa of innumerable birds. To prepare for such long flights, in part over water or barren lands that provide little or no food, these migrants store fuel in the form of fat, which may increase their weights by 25 to 50 percent.

Many are the perils of these long migrations. Individuals poorly prepared for their journeys may falter over the Gulf of Mexico and drown if no convenient ship offers a rest. Those whose strength fails over the sands of the Sahara are in a no less distressing plight. Contrary winds may blow migrating birds off their course, or inexperienced young may lose their way, perhaps to be detected by bird watchers on the opposite side of the Atlantic, where they are exciting rarities, but more probably to perish at sea. At the staging places, where many birds alight to recuperate after long traverses, they may be decimated by waiting raptors (Lindström 1989). But probably, over the long term, the chief cause of migrants' mortality in spring is unseasonable weather. As birds approach their northern destinations, anticipating burgeoning trees and active insects, they are greeted by a late cold spell with freezing temperatures and snowy landscapes. Aerial insect catchers—swallows, swifts, and flycatchers—are the most distressed if, with their reserves of energy almost exhausted after many hours of travel, they find insects inactive. Barn Swallows crowd into old woodpeckers' holes or any sheltering crannies they can find, layer upon layer. Those at the bottom stay warmest but may be suffocated by the mass of birds above them. If they survive, they often lack strength to push through the corpes that cover them (Weatherhead et al. 1985).

A family of geese, parents with surviving young, remains intact for a year or more, traveling from and to their breeding area together. Among smaller birds, especially passerines, males tend to precede females on the spring migration. Males arriving on the breeding grounds as early as the weather permits can choose the best territories to offer to females, who appear a few days or weeks later. After an absence of half a year or more and a journey of thousands of miles, precise navigation brings experienced migrants to the very same plot of ground they occupied in previous summers, perhaps only to find it preempted by the earlier arrival of another male of their species. Their territorial claims are not settled without strenuous and occasionally fatal fighting. This situation contrasts sharply with that of birds permanently resident in warm lands, where in years of bird study I have rarely seen serious conflicts over territories. With more time to adjust boundaries, perhaps with known neighbors, permanently resident and continuously mated birds have developed milder, more pacific temperaments.

Here in the Térraba Valley of Costa Rica I have never seen fights among permanently settled Yellow-bellied Elaenias, but wandering or migratory Lesser Elaenias are so quarrelsome that I formerly called them "Bellicose Elaenias." Similarly, at high altitudes, Mountain Elaenias, who perform altitudinal if not longer migrations, are exceedingly belligerent birds. On the west coast of North America, Barbara Blanchard (1941) was impressed by the sharp contrast between the behavior of resident and migratory populations of White-crowned Sparrows. In the seven weeks before they started to incubate, White-crowns established in pairs on their territories in California were orderly and law-abiding, whereas White-crowns newly arrived in the Puget Sound region of Washington presented a scene of confusion and unsettledness. Likewise, Mary Erickson (1938) noticed that the longer period available to resident Wrentits for finding a territory or mate reduced the severity of competition among them.

When the females of migratory birds arrive, males that a short while before were contending for territories begin to vie for mates, each striving to attract, by profuse singing and displays, a partner to nest with him. A female's choice appears to be influenced by both the character of the male himself and the quality of the territory he offers. Which more strongly influences her decision is difficult to learn, but often she prefers to become the second consort of a male already mated on a superior territory rather than the only partner of a male with an inferior territory. As a second spouse she may receive little or no help in rearing her brood, but the greater productivity of the chosen territory may enable her to nourish her progeny adequately without their father's assistance.

At high latitudes where the breeding season is brief, everything must be done hurriedly. With—or, among passerine birds—more often without help from her mate, the newly arrived female builds a simple, cup-shaped nest; time does not suffice for construction of the more elaborate nests that permanently resident birds take weeks to finish. Unlike many residents, she does not allow the newly completed nest to remain empty for days. She tends to lay, at daily intervals, larger sets of eggs than do closely related birds resident in the tropics. This "latitude effect," already evident as one approaches the Tropic of Cancer, is ever more pronounced at higher latitudes, where clutches of four to six or more eggs contrast with the two or three laid by many tropical passerines.

It has long been known that monogamous birds indulge in "stolen matings" with the opposite sex. Now DNA fingerprinting (the disclosure of nuptial infidelities by comparing the genetic composition of nestlings with that of the adults who attend them) is revealing that such lapses from strict monogamy are much more frequent than we formerly believed. That females are often unfaithful to temporary partners they have hastily chosen, perhaps more for their territories than for themselves, is not surprising. They may not even know the boundaries of the territories in which they have settled. Permanently resident birds that live in pairs throughout the year, or as long as both survive, are more firmly bonded. I surmise that such birds seek or permit stolen matings less frequently than do birds only seasonally mated. The subject needs further investigation.

With more hours of daylight, larger broods, and abundant insects in spring and summer, migratory birds work much harder to feed their families than do tropical birds with fewer young and shorter days. The crowded occupants of northern nests appear always to be hungry, each trying to stretch up higher than its siblings, mouth widely gaping, to receive the next billful brought by a parent. I was impressed by the contrast of this behavior with that of the single nestling of the Rufous Piha, a resident of Neotropical rain forests. Without a competitor, the young piha responded sluggishly to its mother's arrival with a meal, as though feeling assured of receiving the offering. The piha takes over almost two months, in the skimpiest of nests, to rear her solitary nestling from egg laying to fledging—twice as long as a pair of slightly larger American Robins take to raise a brood of three or four in a much sturdier nest. This is an extreme example of the contrast between tropical residents and northern migrants; the migrants' incubation and nestling periods tend to be shorter than those of related birds in the tropics. At high latitudes summer is short, and birds that breed there must hurry to rear enough young to balance their annual mortality, which is high whether they remain to endure winter's hardships or risk the hazards of long flights to milder regions.

By reducing the number of days that immobile eggs and young are exposed to predation, the northern birds increase the success of their nests. Possibly a smaller diversity of nest-plundering snakes and mammals is another favoring factor. In any region, the success of nests varies greatly with species, habitat, and season, but a compilation of many studies reveals that birds in the north temperate zone enjoy greater success than do those of the humid tropics. Northern birds with open (roofless) nests generally rear to fledging at least one young in 40 to 60 percent of their nests, whereas in humid lowland tropics, the corresponding figures are in the range of 20 to 30 percent. In gardens where efforts are made to exclude predators, the tropical birds do better than in neighboring rain forests, and in Neotropical highlands they nest more successfully than at low altitudes (Skutch 1985). But what birds gain by migrating beyond the tropics to nest is often lost on their long, hazardous journeys.

In August or September, where at middle latitudes summer temperatures prevail and food is still adequate, many Neotropical migrants hurry back to the lands of their ancestors. They visit northern regions just long enough to reproduce, and seem eager to return to their true homes in tropical America, where as species, if not as individuals, they are present most of the year. They avoid the spring migrants' risk of running into unexpected snow storms, but those using the Atlantic flyway may be overtaken by a devastating Caribbean hurricane. In addition to the ancient risks of losing the way and exhaustion on long flights over water or deserts, the autumnal migrants confront new hazards that we have created, especially tall buildings and taller television towers that we have thrust into the skies. On cloudy nights when guiding stars are obscured, lights at the summits of these slender steel towers, supported by wide-spreading cables, attract thousands of disoriented travelers to their doom. Heavy in spring, the mortality is greater in autumn, when the number of nocturnal migrants may be doubled by inexperienced young on their first long journey. Those who have witnessed the distressing tragedy on a stormy night at the height of the fall migration have told how, after crashing into the tower or its supporting cables, injured and dying birds rain down, screaming, to the ground, to be devoured by scavenging mammals or fire ants if they do not promptly recover well enough to fly. Lights that warn aviators of danger lure disoriented birds to disaster—surely a tragic paradox. At the comparatively low, 673-foot WCTV television tower in Leon County, Florida, 42,384 corpses of 189 species were collected in the twenty-five years from October, 1955, through September, 1980 (Stoddard and Norris 1967; Crawford 1981).

Arriving in the area where they winter, returning migrants may find the same plot of ground that they abandoned a few months before unoccupied and awaiting them—experienced migrants alternate annually between two known territories. But the number that return to the tropics in autumn is much greater than the tally of those that departed in spring, and territorial conflicts inevitably occur. Many migrants live alone on defended territories during their sojourn in the south. I have watched Wilson's and Chestnut-sided warblers, newly arrived in Central America, fighting on the ground, and Yellow Warblers chasing one another in territorial disputes. Summer Tanagers may quarrel for days until they have settled on their individual plots. Other migrants join a mixed flock of resident and migratory birds. In the highlands of Guatemala, wintering Townsend's Warblers form the nucleus of such a flock, which is joined by a single migratory Red-faced Warbler. If a second intrudes, the two sing against each other until one abandons the flock.

Compared with the resident birds with which they mingle in their tropical or subtropical winter homes, the migrants lead strenuous, perilous lives. They perform two annual migrations, which may be long, are usually hazardous, and take them through unfamiliar regions; residents remain throughout the year on well-known land. Many migrants must win territories twice a year, one for breeding and one for wintering; residents may retain a single territory as long as they live. Especially at the northern terminus of a long and exhausting flight, acquisition of a breeding territory is urgent and often involves fighting; at the southern end, where they will stay for months without nesting, winning a territory appears to be less urgent but sometimes involves fighting or a prolonged dispute. Resident birds may leisurely adjust territorial boundaries with familiar neighbors in milder ways that rarely attract attention.

Migrants hurriedly build simple nests; with a much longer breeding season, residents may take weeks or months to construct nests that are much more elaborate. Migrants toil through long days to raise large broods; residents work less in shorter days to rear small broods. Many of them breed cooperatively, self-supporting young remaining with their parents for a year or more and helping to feed and protect their younger siblings, thereby lightening the burdens of parents; by dissolving families, migration prevents cooperative breeding. With an accelerated breeding schedule that reduces the time their nests are exposed to predation, migrants nest with greater success in northern lands than do residents in tropical forests. However, the migrants' greater productivity of young is counterbalanced by greater mortality of both adults and young, especially on long migrations. Abandoned by their parents as soon as they can adequately feed themselves, the young of migrants are less prepared to confront the hazards of life than are the young of residents, who learn more from longer association with the adults in habitats they will occupy throughout their lives. Until the approach of their first birthday on their breeding grounds, most migrants appear not to form pairs. These pairs will persist only until breeding is finished, although they may be renewed if both members return to the same territory in the following spring; when only a few months old, a male and a female resident may unite for life.

An interesting consequence of all these differences is that the sexes of brightly colored residents are more often alike than are those of related migratory birds, among which males may be ornate but females of the same species are more often plainly clad. Examples of this difference are numerous among wood-warblers, tanagers, and orioles. In these families both sexes of resident species retain the same colors throughout the year, but the nuptial attire of colorful migratory males is often eclipsed after breeding.

The exacting toil of rearing large families in a brief season appears to shorten the lives of migrants, especially females. Long journeys take their toll. Although Neotropical migrants survive better than do their summer neighbors that remain through harsh winters, they do not live as long as do birds of comparable size that reside permanently in the tropics. A compilation by Russell Greenberg (1980) contains fourteen studies of long-distance migrants, mostly American flycatchers and wood-warblers, with annual survival rates of 60 percent or more, whereas none of nineteen studies of temperate zone residents and partial migrants, of both the New World and the Old, revealed survival rates of that magnitude.

Birds permanently resident in the tropics survive much better than do birds only wintering there. In a two-year study of birds in the Semengo Forest Reserve in equatorial Sarawak on the island of Borneo, M. P. L. Fogden (1972) found annual survival rates of adults of thirty-four species ranging from 50 to 100 percent, but only four were less than 75 percent. On the island of Trinidad with a South American avifauna, the annual survival rate of tiny White-bearded Manakins was 89 percent, and a number of other birds were long-lived (Snow and Lill 1974).

As the slow retreat of the ice that had covered much of the temperate zone of North America made increasing areas habitable by birds about eighteen thousand years ago, some took advantage of the opportunity to extend their breeding areas northward; others failed to do so. The families of Neotropical land birds are very unequally represented among the pioneers. The five largest avian families confined to the New World are the flycatchers with about 384 species, the hummingbirds with 330, the antbirds with 250, the tanagers with 230, and the ovenbirds with 214. Of the flycatchers, twenty-one species became, in whole or part, northern migrants; of the tanagers, four; and of the hummingbirds, also four. However, the much smaller wood-warbler family, with only 110 species, contains forty northern migrants. Of the ninety species of icterids—orioles, blackbirds, and their kin—ten are in this category, as are eight of the forty-three species of vireos and their allies. A few smaller families contain Neotropical migrants.

Why have the great ovenbird and antbird families failed to colonize lands recently (on the geological time scale) available in the north temperate zone? Why has none of them become a Neotropical migrant? The nesting habits of ovenbirds appear to be responsible for their sedentary lives. None breeds in an unroofed nest such as most long-distance migrants occupy. Ovenbirds construct and maintain elaborate closed nests that take weeks or months to complete; they dig burrows, often long before they will lay in them; or they seek sheltered nooks for their broods. Moreover, many of them sleep in nests and lead their fledglings back to them. This lifestyle is incompatible with long annual migrations. Only a few ovenbirds that breed high in the Andes or in the far south of South America seek lower altitudes or latitudes as the austral winter approaches, by migrations much shorter than those of many birds in the Northern Hemisphere.

Antbirds live in pairs in thickets and forest undergrowth, or they glean insects from the foliage of broad-leaved trees in the lower levels of tropical forests. They fly well but appear rarely to fly far, and are not likely to become long-distance migrants. The colonists of North America after the retreat of the ice sheets are more mobile birds: flycatchers that catch insects on long aerial sallies; wood-warblers that flit through the treetops gleaning caterpillars; hummingbirds that roam widely as flowers bloom profusely here and there. All these birds that depend so largely upon insects, or flowers and insects, could survive in northern lands only in the warmer months when insects are active and flowers yield nectar. Most of these birds became only temporary residents at latitudes where winters are severe; with cosmopolitan swallows and swifts, they comprise the bulk of the passerine and near-passerine migrants.

Why did birds whose ancestors resided comfortably in warm lands adopt the perilous and strenuous lives of long-distance migrants? Certainly they did not with forethought impose this burden upon their descendants. Nature, it is said, abhors a vacuum; it fills any space of land or sea, however barren, bleak, or dark, with the most advanced organisms that can survive there. As the continental glaciers slowly receded, the regions left bare were gradually covered with grasses, shrubs, and trees that offered summer homes to birds that too densely populated more southerly regions (Williams and Webb 1996). As winter approached, the pioneers returned southward to lands they had temporarily abandoned. As the ice retreated to higher latitudes where summers were shorter, the birds that followed it to extend their breeding ranges were obliged to depart earlier and to fly farther southward to find wintering territory not already occupied by their own species. Thus began the long migrations that we find today.

How does the autumnal influx of migrants in tropical habitats affect the resident birds? The newcomers often settle in niches they have left vacant during an absence of only a few months; they occupy disturbed vegetation that the residents do not prefer; or they join mixed flocks in which either they or their resident companions may be more numerous. They appear not to struggle with residents for territories, as they often do with recent arrivals of their own species who prefer to live alone while they do not breed. The proportion of migrants in avian populations during the northern winter is greatest in lands nearest the breeding grounds of the visitors. In areas of west-central Mexico, well over half the birds may be migrants. High proportions of wintering birds are also found in the Bahamas, Cuba, and Hispaniola. In southern Central America the percentage of migratory individuals diminishes to about a third of that in western Mexico or on the Yucatán Peninsula. In South America the proportion of migrants from the northern continent gradually diminishes, to become almost negligible in Ecuador, Peru, and Bolivia (Terborgh 1980).

In the northern tropics, the migrants arrive as the main breeding season ends, with the resident population greatly augmented by young of the year but with the abundance of both fruits and insects diminishing, to reach in the final months of the year a low that will persist until the rainy season begins about six months later. Although figures appear to be lacking, it is incredible that doubling the number of individuals should not affect the residents in regions where this great influx of mouths occurs. The depar-

Eastern Kingbirds

ture of the visitors in March, April, and May, when insects and edible fruits become more abundant, makes the second quarter of the year most favorable for breeding by the resident birds. At the northern terminus of the migrations, where the travelers arrive as the nesting season begins, they greatly increase the breeding population but appear to have little effect on resident birds, which belong to different families with different ways of foraging. Migration greatly increases the number of birds Earth can support.

Compared with the tropical residents to which they are most closely related, the migrants are more solitary, more adaptable, more aggressive, and shorter-lived. They do not enjoy the yearlong companionship of continuously mated residents or cooperative breeders. They must adapt to different climates and different habitats in their summer and winter homes, although they may choose vegetation types as similar as they can find at both ends of their journeys. Many compete strenuously for territories twice a year instead of only once, or only once in a lifetime, as many tropical residents do. A few, including Eastern Kingbirds and Cedar Waxwings, migrate in social flocks; others avoid solitude by joining a mixed company of tropical forest birds.

By regurgitating or defecating viable seeds while they travel northward, frugivorous migrants probably helped to bring plants to lands scraped bare by continental glaciers. Insectivores, especially wood-warblers and vireos, save burgeoning trees from defoliation by teeming insect larvae.

Among the beneficiaries of the migratory habit are all people who enjoy nature, especially bird-watchers. Migrants are harbingers of spring in northern lands where winters are often harsh and gloomy. They embellish northern woods and meadows with colorful plumage and cheerful songs. To record the dates of their arrival and departure keeps watchers happily engaged in healthful outdoor activity. An unexpected visitor, often a migrant bird that has wandered from its course, excites bird-watchers with a welcome addition to their lists of species seen. Migratory birds, who bring thoughts of the distant lands where they winter, promote bird protection, but not enough. We still callously and avoidably allow too many birds to dash out their lives against picture windows and high towers, while we try to prevent the extinction of vanishing species in distant lands that we shall never see.

EPILOGUE: THE BIRDS I LOVE 🐚

Visitors to our nature reserve ask which is my favorite bird. Occasionally I lightly reply: "Tanagers and woodpeckers." At other times I respond more thoughtfully: "I have many favorite birds, but I do not love all birds equally." Preferences for birds are as diverse as the temperaments of the people who pay attention to them. Some like birds merely because many are beautiful and sing sweetly. As household pets they are companionable. Some bird-watchers are most attracted by raptors, perhaps only because they are big and easy to see; others, of a more sanguinary temperament, admire their efficiency as predators. I am unimpressed by the bigness of animals; the largest are mites on the cosmic scale, even the most powerful pitifully weak compared with our big machines. Moreover, adulation of bigness and power seems thoughtless and vulgar, the cause of many of humanity's woes. Some of the most admirable creations, both natural and human, are small and finely organized.

Although I share the widespread admiration of birds' beautiful plumage and am happy in the wild places where I go to see them, this is not what chiefly attracts me to birds. Flowers are no less beautiful and are easier to approach closely and enjoy; many butterflies are lovely and less elusive than birds. What draws me strongly to birds is their behavior—their characters, I might say. The capacity to care, devotedly and consistently, is to me the most laudable aspect of animals.

To call our own species "the animal that cares" is the noblest epithet that we can apply to humanity, greater praise than the designations of "the rational animal" or "the tool-using animal." To be sure, caring is very sporadically developed among people, and many individuals hardly deserve this epithet; but the same might be said about reason, which is often misused, or about skill in making or handling tools. Creativity is closely allied to caring; to create anything well we must certainly care about it. Among animals, as among humans, caring and creativity are unequally distributed; in many, even of the warm-blooded vertebrates, these attributes are almost totally lacking. Birds excel all other nonhuman vertebrates in caring and creating, and this is what attracts me so strongly to them.

More than any other animals that I know, birds care for their bodies, bathing frequently, spending a considerable proportion of their time arranging and oiling their wonderful vesture of feathers. Many care for their mates, preening them, often reciprocally, and/or feeding them. As builders of nests, only social insects, notably wasps, can compare with birds in the diversity and complexity of their creations. Many birds not only build nests but continue to maintain them. Most commonly, they keep them clean, removing wastes and, as well as they can, invading insects, especially ants. Builders of some of the most elaborate nests, such as the castlebuilders or spinetails (members of the Neotropical ovenbird or hornero family) constantly patrol their big, enclosed structures, tucking falling twigs into place, bringing fresh materials, promptly closing a gap in the wall, such as ornithologists make as the only way to examine eggs and nestlings. In addition to building nests for reproduction, many birds, notably wrens, make special dormitory nests.

Birds care for their young in more diverse ways than do other vertebrates, except dutiful human parents. After patiently incubating their eggs for from ten days to several months, they brood the nestlings to keep them warm, with their bodies shield them from strong sunshine, and, especially the altricial species, work hard to nourish them. After the young leave the nest, the adults guide and continue to feed them for weeks or months, while, mainly from parental example, they learn behavior that promotes survival. As night approaches, their elders lead them to a safe roost or to the nest in which they were reared, if not to one built specially for their comfort. In most species of birds, the two parents cooperate closely in rearing the young, the father feeding and guarding them if not also incubating the eggs and brooding the young, as in many avian families. The young of many constantly resident birds remain with their parents on the family territory for one or more years, helping to rear their younger brothers and sisters, in a cooperative breeding association. Only in the most united human families do the generations work so closely together.

Among ourselves, caring has profound psychic consequences. It leads the mind and its affections outward from the self, giving fresh interests and new attachments. We wish to know more about whatever receives our care. The longer anything, living or lifeless, receives our devoted attention, the more we love it.

The psychic effects of caring and creating in birds remain to be explored. That caring generates strong attachments is evident when apprehensive parent birds risk their lives attacking humans or other animals that actually or apparently threaten their young. Given the frequency of predation on nests by animals too strong to be resisted, natural selection could hardly promote such rash behavior, which may result in the destruction of both parents and progeny. Not birds who boldly confront pillagers of their nests, but those who prudently restrain their zeal and live to nest again, are likely to contribute most to the perpetuation of their kind. The manifold activities of preparing a nest and rearing a brood should sharpen intelligence, even if in the main they follow innate patterns which, however inclusive they become, can hardly provide detailed guidance amid all the diversities of complex natural situations. Intelligent adjustments are frequently needed.

Certain birds that neither incubate eggs nor attend nestlings demonstrate great capacity for caring. Among them are the megapodes or mound builders of Australia, New Guinea, and neighboring islands. One of these unique birds, the Mallee Fowl of arid western Australia, rakes together a great mound of earth and fallen vegetation, in the midst of which the female of a single pair lays a succession of big eggs. They are maintained at an almost constant temperature favorable for incubation by the skillful management of the heat of fermentation and solar radiation. The strenuous construction and care of these large incubation mounds occupies the pair, mostly the male, through much of the year. When the superprecocial chicks hatch, they work their way upward to the surface of the mound without parental assistance and wander off alone, never receiving an adult's attention.

Male bowerbirds, also of New Guinea and Australia, build little tepees, huts, Maypoles, or avenues, all of interlaced twigs. Each belongs to a single adult, who adorns his bower with colorful flowers, fruits, and human artifacts where available. He keeps his display fresh by removing wilted flowers and shriveling berries and bringing others. Some of these arrangements, notably those of the severely plain Brown Gardener Bowerbird of western New Guinea, are truly charming, a source of wonderment and delight to the few naturalists who have been privileged to see them in their remote forests. Females visit the bowers for the fertilization of their eggs, then rear their broods unassisted.

The peaceful coexistence of many different species is another endearing aspect of avian life. A mixed flock wandering through a tropical forest may contain a score or more species of diverse families and ways of foraging, each going harmoniously about its business; if conflicts were frequent and severe, the flock would disintegrate. In a garden with enough trees and shrubbery for nest sites, a diversity of birds can raise their broods in amity, with no greater misbehavior than pilfering materials from neighbors' unfinished nests. Occasionally a helpful bird feeds a neighbor's young, or two pairs jointly attend their broods.

Birds serve the plants that nourish them. Hummingbirds, honeycreepers, sunbirds, lorikeets, and many others pollinate the flowers that yield them nectar. Bees, butterflies, and other insects pollinate more flowers than do birds, but many bird-adapted flowers would set few seeds without the fecundating visits of birds.

A great variety of frugivores disseminate the seeds of plants that offer them fruits. After digesting off the pulp of berries or arillate seeds, they regurgitate or defecate viable seeds, thereby spreading widely the plants whose bounty they enjoy. (Parrots, which prefer embryos to fruit pulp, do not participate in this exchange of benefits, but they have other points in their favor.) Insectivorous birds, many of which are also fruit eaters, perform an indispensable service in reducing the numbers of insects which, without this check, would defoliate trees and shrubs that nourish frugivorous animals. Although the birds are probably unaware that they help to reproduce the plants whose fruits they eat, this service must be credited to them; just as we praise a lovely human face, although this is a gift of nature rather than a product of deliberate efforts.

Industrious woodpeckers carve many holes that eventually become nesting cavities or dormitories of birds and small mammals unable to make them for themselves. I believe it no exaggeration to say that the activities of birds benefit a greater diversity of organisms than do those of any other division of the animal kingdom.

These, then, are the birds I admire, love, and do what I can to protect: They are caring-creative animals, attentive to their mates, builders of nests that are often beautiful or elaborate, usually keeping them clean, faithful parents, good neighbors, serviceable to the plants that nourish them, all in addition to delighting our eyes with their beauty and cheering us with their songs. Most of the birds that I know well have several of these points in their favor. No other class of animals contributes so much to the beauty and interest of our planet, and to the stability of our terrestrial ecosystems, while making such small demands upon their productivity. Of the approximately nine thousand species of birds, only a small minority make themselves objectionable by becoming nest pirates or parasites, agricultural pests, or preying heavily on other birds more worthy of our love and protection.

Caring makes the more lovable birds akin to the more lovable humans; both care and create in due proportion to their intelligence, breadth of interests, strength, and manipulative skill. It is distressing to see birds that care so devotedly for their nests and young harassed by animals that care for nothing, especially snakes, the chief pillagers of nests in tropical and temperate lands. Happily, many birds soon recover from their bereavement to try again and again to rear fledglings, by their admirable perseverance keeping ecosystems flourishing and cheering us by their continuing abundance.

In childhood I was strongly attracted to feathered creatures, as was Jean Henri Fabre (1924) to those with six or eight legs. As with him, this dominant love has persisted into life's tenth decade. As I review my seventy years of bird study, nearly all in the Neotropics, I am comforted by remembering that I have never intentionally harmed, for science or otherwise, an adult bird or its young, although I was responsible for the deaths of two or three raptors preying upon birds I was studying and/or trying to protect. In the evening of life, I am distressed by the thought that humankind, as a whole, lacks the generosity to freely share an exceptionally favored planet with even the more compatible of the free creatures that surround us. Earth did not become habitable for the benefit of a single species.

BIBLIOGRAPHY ❧

Amadon, D. 1959. "The Significance of Sexual Differences in Size among Birds." *Proceedings of the American Philosophical Society* 103:531–36.

Andrle, R. F. 1967. "The Horned Guan in Mexico and Guatemala." *Condor* 69:93–109.

Belcher, C., and G. D. Smooker. 1934–37. "Birds of the Colony of Trinidad and Tobago," parts 1–4. *Ibis.*

Bent, A. C. 1932. *Life Histories of North American gallinaceous Birds.* U.S. National Museum Bulletin no. 162.

———. 1937. *Life Histories of North American Birds of Prey,* part 1. U.S. National Museum Bulletin no. 167.

———. 1940. *Life Histories of North American Cuckoos, Goatsuckers, Hummingbirds and Their Allies.* U.S. National Museum Bulletin no. 176.

———. 1942. *Life Histories of North American Flycatchers, Larks, Swallows and Their Allies.* U.S. National Museum Bulletin no. 179.

Blanchard, B. 1941. "The White-crowned Sparrows (*Zonotrichia leucophrys*) of the Pacific Seabord: Environment and Annual Cycle." *University of California Publications in Zoology* 46:1–178.

Carriker, M. A., Jr. 1910. "An Annotated List of the Birds of Costa Rica Including Cocoa Island. *Annals of the Carnegie Museum* 6:314–915.

Cherrie, G. K. 1916. "A Contribution to the Ornithology of the Orinoco Region." Museum of the Brooklyn Institute of Arts and Sciences, *Science Bulletin* 2:133a–374.

Crawford, R. L. 1981. "Bird Casualties at a Leon County, Florida, TV Tower: A 25-year Migration Study." Tall Timbers Research Station Bulletin no. 22.

Davis, T. A. W. 1958. "The Displays and Nests of Three Forest Hummingbirds of British Guiana." *Ibis* 100:31–39.

Dawson, W. L. 1923. *The Birds of California,* vol. 2. San Francisco, Calif.

Delacour, J., and D. Amadon. 1973. *Curassows and Related Birds.* New York: American Museum of Natural History.

Delannoy, C. A., and A. Cruz. 1988. "Breeding Biology of the Puerto Rican Sharp-shinned Hawk (*Accipiter striatus venator*)." *Auk* 105:649–62.

De la Peña, M. R. 1979. *Aves de la Provincia de Santa Fe.* Provincia de Santa Fe: Ministerio de Acricultura y Ganadería.

Emmons, L. H. 1990. *Neotropical RainForest Mammals: A Field Guide.* Chicago, Ill.: University of Chicago Press.

Erickson, M. M. 1938. "Territory, Annual Cycle, and Numbers in a Population of Wren-Tits (*Chamaea fasciata*)." *University of California Publications in Zoology* 42:247–334.

Fabre, J. H. 1924. *Insect Adventures*. Retold for young people by Louise Seymour Hasbrouck. New York: Dodd, Mead.

ffrench, R. 1973. *A Guide to the Birds of Trinidad and Tobago*. Wynnewood, Pa.: Livingston Publishing.

———. 1982. "The Breeding of the Pearl Kite in Trinidad." *Living Bird* 19:121–31.

Fogden, M. P. L. 1972. "The Seasonality and Population Dynamics of Equatorial Forest Birds in Sarawak." *Ibis* 114:307–43.

Friedmann, H. 1933. "A Contribution to the Life History of the Crespin or Four-winged Cuckoo, *Tapera naevia*." *Ibis*, July, pp. 532–39.

Friedmann, H., and L. F. Kiff. 1985. "The Parasitic Cowbirds and Their Hosts." *Proceedings of the Western Foundation of Vertebrate Zoology* 2:226–302.

González-García, F. 1995. "Reproductive Biology and Vocalizations of the Horned Guan *Oreophasis derbianus* in Mexico." *Condor* 97:415–26.

Goodwin, D. 1967. *Pigeons and Doves of the World*. London: British Museum of Natural History.

Greenberg, R. 1980. "Demographic Aspects of Long-Distance Migration." Pp. 493–504 in *Migrant Birds in the Neotropics: Ecology, Behavior, Distribution, and Conservation*, ed. Allen Keast and E. S. Morton. Washington, D.C. Smithsonian Institution Press.

Greenlaw, J. S. 1967. "Foraging Behavior of the Double-toothed Kite in Association with White-faced Monkeys." *Auk* 84:596–97.

Haverschmidt, F. 1962. "Notes on the Feeding Habits and Food of Some Hawks of Surinam." *Condor* 64:154–58.

———. 1968. *Birds of Surinam*. Wynnewood, Pa.; Livingston Publishing Co.

Howell, T. R. 1957. "Birds of a Second-Growth Rain Forest Area of Nicaragua." *Condor* 59:73–111.

Hudson, W. H. 1920. *Birds of La Plata*. 2 vols. London: J. M. Dent.

Kiff, L. F., and A. Williams. 1978. "Host Records for the Striped Cuckoo from Costa Rica." *Wilson Bulletin* 90:138–39.

Lack, D. 1954. *The Natural Regulsation of Animal Numbers*. Oxford: Clarendon Press.

Laughlin, R. M. 1952. "A Nesting of the Double-toothed Kite in Panama." *Condor* 54:137–39.

Lemke, T. O. 1979. "Fruit-Eating Behavior of Swallow-tailed Kites (*Elanoides forficatus*) in Colombia." *Condor* 81:207–208.

Lindström, Å. 1989. "Finch Flock Size and Risk of Hawk Predation at a Migratory Stopover Site." *Auk* 106:225–32.

Loetscher, F. W., Jr. 1952. "Striped Cuckoo fed by Rufous-and-White Wren in Panama." *Condor* 54:169.

Lorenz, K. Z. 1952. *King Solomon's Ring*. London: Methuen.

Marchant, S. 1960. "The Breeding of some S. W. Ecuadorean Birds." *Ibis* 102: 349–82.

Mason, F. 1985. "The Nesting Biology of Some Passerines of Buenos Aires, Argentina." Pp. 954–72 in *Neotropical Ornithology*, ed. P. A. Buckley, M. S. Foster, E. S. Morton, R. S. Ridgely, and F. G. Buckley. Ornithological Monographs no. 36. Washington, D.C.: American Ornithologists' Union.

McDonald, D., and K. Winnett-Murray. 1989. "First Reported Nests of the Black-breasted Wood-Quail (*Odontophorus leucolaemus*)." *Condor* 91:985–86.

Mitchell, M. H. 1957. *Observations on Birds of Southeastern Brazil*. Toronto: University of Toronto Press.

Morton, E. S., and S. M. Farabaugh. 1979. "Infanticide and Other Adaptations of the Nestling Striped Cuckoo *Tapera naevia*." *Ibis* 121:212–13.

Murton, R. K. 1965. *The Wood-Pigeon*. London: Collins.

Narosky, S., R. Fraga, and M. de la Peña. 1983. *Nidificación de las aves argentinas (Dendrocolaptidae y Furnariidae)*. Buenos Aires: Asociación Ornitológica del Plata.

Ridgely, R. S. 1976. *A Guide to the Birds of Panama*. Princeton, N.J.: Princeton University Press.

Robbins, M. B., and D. A. Wiedenfeld. 1982. "Observations at a Laughing Falcon Nest." *Wilson Bulletin* 94:83–84.

Rowley, J. S. 1966. "Breeding Records of the Birds of the Sierra Madre del Sur, Oaxaca, Mexico." *Proceedings of the Western Foundation of Vertebrate Zoology* 1 (3): 107–204.

Sick, H. 1984. *Ornitológia Brasileira*. 2 vols. Brasilia: Editora Universidad de Brasilia.

————. 1993. *Birds in Brazil: A Natural History*. Trans. W. Belton. Princeton, N.J.: Princeton University Press.

Skutch, A. F. 1947. "A Nesting of the Plumbeous Kite in Ecuador." *Condor* 49:25–31.

————. 1954. *Life Histories of Central American Birds*. I. Pacific Coast Avifauna no. 31. Berkeley, Calif.: Cooper Ornithological Society.

————. 1958. "Life History of the Violet-headed Hummingbird." *Wilson Bulletin* 70:5–19.

————. 1960. *Life Histories of Central American Birds*. II. Pacific Coast Avifauna no. 34. Berkeley, Calif.: Cooper Ornithological Society.

————. 1964. "Life Histories of Hermit Hummingbirds." *Auk* 81:5–25.

————. 1965. "Life Histories of Two Tropical American Kites." *Condor* 67:235–46.

————. 1969. *Life Histories of Central American Birds*. III. Pacific Coast Avifauna no. 35. Berkeley, Calif.: Cooper Ornithological Society.

————. 1971. *A Naturalist in Costa Rica*. Gainesville: University of Florida Press.

————. 1972. *Studies of Tropical American Birds*. Publications of the Nuttall Ornithological Club no. 10. Cambridge, Mass.

————. 1979. *The Imperative Call: A Naturalist's Quest in Temperate and Tropical America*. Gainesville: University Press of Florida.

————. 1980. *A Naturalist on a Tropical Farm*. Berkeley: University of California Press.

————. 1981. *New Studies of Tropical American Birds*. Publications of the Nuttall Ornithological Club no. 19.

————. 1983. *Birds of Tropical America*. Austin: University of Texas Press.

————. 1985a. *Life Ascending*. Austin: University of Texas Press.

————. 1985b. "Clutch Size, Nesting Success, and Predation on Nests of Neotropical Birds, reviewed." Pp. 575–94 in *Neotropical Ornithology*, ed. P. A. Buckley, M. S. Foster, E. S. Morton, R. S. Ridgely, and F. G. Buckley. Ornithological Monographs no. 36. Washington, D.C.: American Ornithologists' Union.

————. 1992. *Origins of Nature's Beauty*. Austin: University of Texas Press.

Slud, P. 1964. *The Birds of Costa Rica: Distribution and Ecology*. Bulletin of the American Museum of Natural History, vol. 128.

Snow, D. W. 1968. "The Singing Assemblies of Little Hermits." *Living Bird* 7:47–55.

————. 1982. *The Cotingas*. London: British Museum of Natural History.

Snow, D. W., and A. Lill. 1974. "Longevity Records of Some Neotropical Land Birds." *Condor* 76:262–67.

Stiles, F. G., and A. F. Skutch. 1989. *A Guide to the Birds of Costa Rica*. Ithaca, N.Y.: Cornell University Press.

Stiles, F. G., and L. L. Wolf. 1979. *Ecology and Evolution of Lek Mating Behavior in the Long-tailed Hermit Hummingbird*. Ornithological Monographs no. 27. Washington, D.C.: American Ornithologists' Union.

Stoddard, H. L., Sr., and R. A. Norris. 1967. "Bird Casualties at a Leon County, Florida, TV Tower: An Eleven-Year Study." Tall Timbers Research Station Bulletin no. 8.

Sutton, I. D. 1955. "Nesting of the Swallow-tailed Kite." *Everglades Natural History* 3:72–84.

Terborgh, J. W. 1980. "The Conservation Status of Neotropical Migrants: Present and Future." Pp. 21–30 in *Migrant Birds in the Neotropics: Ecology, Behavior, Distribution, and Conservation*, ed. Allen Keast and E. S. Morton. Washington, D.C.: Smithsonian Institution Press.

————. 1983. *Five New World Primates: A Study in Comparative Ecology*. Princeton, N.J.: Princeton University Press.

Van Tyne, J. 1944. "The Nest of the Antbird *Gymnopithys bicolor bicolor*." University of Michigan Museum of Zoology Occasional Papers no. 491:1–5.

Wagner, H. C. 1954. "Versuch einer Analyse der Kolibribalz" (An attempt to analyze hummingbirds' displays). *Zeitschrift für Tierpsycholozie* 11:182–212.

Weatherhead, P. J., S. G. Sealy, and R. M. R. Barclay. 1985. "Risks of clustering of thermally-stressed swallows." *Condor* 87:443–44.

Wetmore, A. 1968. *The Birds of the Republic of Panama*, part 2. Smithsonian Miscellaneous Collections 150 (2).

Wiley, R. H. 1971. "Song Groups in a Singing Assembly of Little Hermits." *Condor* 73:28–35.

Williams, T. C., and T. Webb, III. 1996. "Neotropical Bird Migration during the Ice Ages: Orientation and Ecology." *Auk* 113:105–18.

Willis, E. O., and E. Eisenmann. 1979. "A Revised List of the Birds of Barro Colorado Island, Panama." *Smithsonian Contributions to Zoology* 291:1–31.

Wolfe, L. R. 1954. "Nesting of the Laughing Falcon." *Condor* 56:161–62.

INDEX ✿

Note: Pages with illustrations are indicated by italics.

Cuckoo, Striped: appearance, 98, *100;* diet, 99; egg hosts, 99–102; egg sizes, 101; feather movements, 98, 102–103; hatchlings, 102; range, 98, 102; vocalization, 99, 102

curassows, 117, 119, 182

Davis, T. A. W., 77, 83
Dawson, W. L., 129
Delacour, Jean, 124
Delannoy, Carlos A., 30
De la Péna, M. R., 48
Diana (author's broody hen): chachalaca hatching, 185; death, 188; feeding of chachalacas, 186, 187; protection of chachalacas, 187–88
Dollo's law of loss, 111

eggshell disposal, 40
Eisenmann, E., 97
Elaenia: Lesser, 197; Mountain, 197; Yellow-bellied, 146, 197
El General valley: breeding season, 42, 91–92; landscape changes, 65, 98; red-winged grasshoppers, 179–80
El Triunfo Biosphere Reserve: Horned Guan in, 117–19
Emmons, Louise H., 165
Erickson, Mary, 197
Euphonia, Yellow-crowned, 9

Falcon, Barred Forest-, 89
Falcon, Laughing. *See* Guaco (Laughing Falcon)
Farabaugh, S. M., 100–101, 103
feeding frequency: and diet, 144; and weather, 145–46
feeding of nestlings, raptors, 30–31
ffrench, Richard, 30, 47, 100–101, 132, 160, 163
finches: as cuckoo egg hosts, 99–100; palm tree fruit, 5. *See also* Salator, Grayish

Five New World Primates (Terborgh), 165
Flowerpiercers, Cinnamon-bellied, 60
Flycatcher: Boat-billed, 156–57, 161; as cuckoo egg hosts, 100–101; life expectancy, 201; and migratory patterns, 196, 202; Ochre-bellied, 73; Rusty-margined, 157; White-headed Marsh-Tyrant, 99, 100–101; Yellow-olive, 110. *See also* Flycatcher, Gray-capped; Flycatcher, Piratic; Flycatcher, Vermilion-crowned; Kiskadee, Great
Flycatcher, Gray-capped: nest building, 105, 107, 108–109, 111–12; nest protection, 106–107, 110, 112; range, 109; vocalization, 110. *See also* Flycatcher; Flycatcher, Piratic; Flycatcher, Vermilion-crowned; Kiskadee, Great
Flycatcher, Piratic: appearance, 104, *106, 108;* migratory pattern, 104, 140; nest predation, 105–108, 110–11; range, 104, 109; species success, 112; vocalization, 104–105. *See also* Flycatcher; Flycatcher, Gray-capped; Flycatcher, Vermilion-crowned; Kiskadee, Great
Flycatcher, Social. *See* Flycatcher, Vermilion-crowned
Flycatcher, Vermilion-crowned: appearance, *108,* 157; nest building, 105, 107, 108–109, 111–12, 161, 162; nest protection, 106–107, 110, 112; range, 109; vocalization, 109. *See also* Flycatcher; Flycatcher, Gray-capped; Flycatcher, Piratic; Kiskadee, Great
Fogden, M. P. L., 201
Foliage-gleaner, Buff-fronted, 99, 100–101
Friedmann, H., 100–101
frugivores: aggression, 81; seed dissemination, 209

geese, migration, 196
Gnatcatcher, Tropical, 29

González-García, Fernando, 117, 118
Goodwin, Derek, 129
grasshopper, red-winged, 179–80
Greenberg, Russell, 201
Greenlaw, Jon S., 150
Grosbeak, Blue-black, 120
Grouse, Ruffed, 124–25
Guaco (Laughing Falcon): appearance, 23, *24*, 32; egg clutch, 25, 32; incubation activities, 25–28, 29–30; nesting failures, 30–32; nest sanitation, 29; nest sites, 23, 24–25, 32; parental behavior, 24, 28, 30–31, 33; range, 23; resident companions, 28–29, 33; snakes as food, 26–27, 32, 33; temperament, 32–23; vocalizations, 27–28, 29, 30, 32–33
Guan, Black: appearance, 122, *123;* nest, 124; range and habitat, 122; size, 125; vocalization, 124; wing rattling, 122–23, 124. *See also* Guan, Crested; Guan, Horned
Guan, Crested: appearance, 120, *121;* as Horned Guan egg substitute, 119; range, 122; size, 125; vocalization, 124; wing drumming, 120–21, 123, 124. *See also* Guan, Black; Guan, Horned
Guan, Horned: appearance, 114–15, *116;* captive breeding, 119; egg clutches, 118; flight silence, 115–16; incubation activities, 118–19; mating behavior, 117–18; nests, 118; range, 117; vocalization, 114–15, 117. *See also* Guan, Black; Guan, Crested
Guatemala: breeding season, 60; Horned Guan, 117; Mountain Trogon, 4; Resplendent Quetzal, 12; Striped Cuckoo, 102; White-eared Hummingbird, 49, 59
Guimet, M., 62
gular flutter, 184

harmony as bird virtue, 208–209
Haverschmidt, F., 26, 48, 100–101, 132, 163

Hawk: Red-tailed, 138–39; Sharp-shinned, 30–31
Hermit, Little: feeding behavior, 76–77; hedge habitat, 63; as nest neighbors, 72; singing and the seasons, 64–65; singing assemblies, 52, 78. *See also* Hummingbird; *other individual species*
Honduras: Grayish Salator in, 47–48
honeyeaters (Australia), 81
honeyguides (Africa), 102
Howell, Thomas R., 32
Hudson, W. H., 158, 160–61, 162, 163
Hummingbird: Adorable Coquette, 62; Amethyst-throated, 60; Band-tailed Barbthroat, 63, 83; Beryl-crowned (Blue-chested), 52, 62, 81–82; Blue-throated Goldentail, 62, 63, 64–65; breeding season in El General, 91–92; Broad-tailed, 49, 128; Bronzy Hermit, 83; Brown Violet-eared, 62; Buff-browed, 77–78; Costa's, 128–29; Green Hermit, 76, 81; Green Violet-eared, 49, 52, 60, 62; and hedge habitat, 61, 62, 63; and migratory patterns, 202; observation of humans, 74; Purple-crowned Fairy, 90–91; Ruby-throated, 128; Rufous, 63; singing assemblies, 52, 63, 128; Snow-breasted, 62; White-necked Jacobin, 62; White-tipped Sicklebill, 81; wing sounds, 128–29. *See also individual species*
Hummingbird, Long-billed Starthroat: appearance, 90, *92;* breeding season in El General, 91–92; egg clutches, 94; eggshell removal, 95; feeding behavior, 90–91; fledglings, 96–97; flitting behavior, 97; incubation activities, 94–95, 97; mating behavior, 94; nest building, 92–95; nestlings, 95–96; parental behavior, 58, 95–97; range and habitat, 90; roosting behavior, 91; vocalization, 91. *See also*

Hummingbird, Long-billed Starthroat (*cont.*)

Hummingbird; *other individual species*

Hummingbird, Long-tailed Hermit: appearance, 75, *82;* bathing behavior, 77; copulation, 80–81; displays, 79–80; egg clutches, 84; feeding behavior, 75–76, 81–82; habitat, 62, 75; incubation activities, 85–86; nest construction, 82–86; nestlings, 86–88; nest sanitation, 86, 88; nest success, 88–89; observation of humans, 74–75, 88; parental behavior, 87–88; as pollinators, 77; range, 75; roosting behavior, 78; singing assemblies, 75, 77–79, 81; vocalization, 77. *See also* Hummingbird; *other individual species*

Hummingbird, Rufous-tailed: aggressiveness, 81–82; hedge habitat, 62; nest construction, 55, 73; parental behavior, 58; singing and seasons, 63, 64–65; singing assembly, 52. *See also* Hummingbird; *other individual species*

Hummingbird, Scaly-breasted: feeding behavior, 90–91; hedge habitat, 62; parental behavior, 58; singing and seasons, 63, 64–65. *See also* Hummingbird; *other individual species*

Hummingbird, Violet-headed: appearance, 61, *64;* egg clutches, 69; fledglings, 66, 72–73; hedge habitat, 61, 62–63; incubation actvities, 69–70, 71; nest construction, 66–69, 73; nestlings, 70–71; observation of humans, 71–72; parenting behavior, 71, 73; singing and seasons, 63–65; singing assemblies, 63, 65–66. *See also* Hummingbird; *other individual species*

Hummingbird, White-eared: appearance, 49, *51;* egg clutch, 54, 60; fledglings, 59–60; habitat preference, 49–50; incubation activities, 54–56,

60; nest building, 53–54, 56, 59, 60; nesting success, 59–60; nestlings, 56–57, 58–59; nest sanitation, 57–58; parental behavior, 56–57, 58, 59; range, 49; singing assemblies, 50–51, 52–53, 78; vocalization, 50, 51–52, 59–60. *See also* Hummingbird; *other individual species*

Hummingbirds' Brook *(La Quebrada de los Gorrones),* 67

insect eating as bird function, 209
In Solomon's Ring (Lorenz), 31

jacaranda trees, 23

Kiff, L. F., 100–101
Kingbird: Eastern, *204, 205;* Tropical, 132, 138
Kiskadee, Great: aggressive character, 156; appearance, 156–57, *159;* egg clutches, 162–63; feeding behavior, 157–59; habitat, 157; incubation activities, 163–64; migratory pattern, 157; nest construction, 161–62; parental behavior, 164; range, 157; vocalization, 159–61, 163. *See also* Flycatcher
Kite, Double-toothed: appearance, 150, *151,* 152; diet, 150; fledgling behavior, 155; incubation activities, 151; nest construction, 150–52; nestling behavior, 152, 153–55; parental behavior, 152–55; range and habitat, 150; vocalization, 154. *See also* Kite, Plumbeous; Kite, Swallow-tailed
Kite, Pearl, 30–31
Kite, Plumbeous: appearance, 140–41, *143,* 148; egg clutches, 149; feeding behavior, 141–42; feeding patterns and weather, 144–46; fledgling behavior, 147–48; migratory pattern, 149; nest construction, 149; nestling behavior, 141, 144, 147, 154; nest site, 141; parental behavior, 141, 142–44, 146–48;

range, 149; vocalization, 148. *See also* Kite, Double-toothed; Kite, Swallow-tailed

Kite, Swallow-tailed: aggression toward raptors, 138–39; appearance, 130, *134;* and death in milk tree, 139; feeding behavior, 89, 130–33; incubation activities, 136, 138; migratory pattern, 139–40, 149; nest building, 133–36, 152; nestling behavior, 137–38; parental behavior, 136–38; roosting behavior, 139; socialbility, 138; vocalization, 136. *See also* Kite, Double-toothed; Kite, Plumbeous

Laca (author's chachalaca): appearance, 185–86, *186,* 189, 190, 191; attachment to humans, 189, 190–91; domestic hatching, 182, 185; egg clutch, 192; feeding behavior, 186, 187; and mirror image, 192; perching behavior, 187; at play, 189, 190; response to Diana's death, 188–89; response to predators, 187–88; roosting behavior, 186–87, 188, 190, 191–92; vocalization, 187, 190; and wild chachalacas, 192–93. *See also* Chacha (author's chachalaca); Chachalaca, Gray-headed

Lack, David, 44

Land, Hugh C., 101–102

La Selva reserve: Long-tailed Hermit in, 78–81

latitude effect, 163, 197–98

Laughlin, Robert M., 150

Lemke, Thomas O., 133

Leon County, Florida, 199

liana vine and trees, 112–13

Life Histories (Bent), 132

lights (warning) and migration, 199

Lill, A., 201

Lindström, Å., 196

Loetscher, F. W., Jr., 100–101

Lorenz, Konrad, 31

Los Cusingos (author's farm): dead trees, 5; loss of bird species, 4; stilt palms, 179

Mallee Fowl (Australia), 208

Manakin: appearance, 125; displays, 80; Orange Collared, 125–27, *126;* range, 125; Red-capped, 127; White-bearded, 201

Marchant, S., 32

marmosets, similarities to birds: appearance, 165–66; feeding behavior, 168, 169; reproduction and child rearing, 166, 169; sleeping behavior, 168; territory defenses, 166–68, 169; vocalizations, 168, 169

Mason, F., 163

McDonald, David, 19

Mexico: Horned Guan in, 117–19; Long-billed Starthroat Hummingbird in, 94; migratory bird populations, 203

migratory birds: and cooperative breeding, 138; departure signals, 195; egg clutches, 197–98; hemisphere patterns, 195–96; impact on resident birds, 203–204; life expectancy, 201; mating systems, 197; Neotropical species representation, 201–202; nest building, 197–98, 200; nesting success, 198–99, 200; nestling feeding requirements, 198; overview, 204–205; and receding glaciers, 201–202, 203; sex-related color, 201; territorial claims, 196–97, 199–200; travel mortality, 196, 199, 200–201

Mitchell, M. H., 160

mobbing behavior, 149–50

monkeys, Capuchin: as guaco neighbors, 29; and kite feeding, 150; palm tree fruit, 5, 25

monkeys, titi: similarities to birds, 168–69

monkeys, squirrel: similarities to birds, 169

Morton, E. S., 100–101, 102

season on, 60; hummingbirds on, 49, 59

Skutch, Alexander F.: *Birds of Tropical America*, 5, 185; *Guide to the Birds of Costa Rica*, 124; *Life Histories of Central American Birds I*, 48; *Life Histories of Central American Birds III*, 43, 44; *A Naturalist in Costa Rica*, 24; *A Naturalist on a Tropical Farm*, 77; *New Studies of Tropical American Birds*, 11; *Origins of Nature's Beauty*, 166; *Studies of Tropical American Birds*, 11

Slud, Paul, 124

Smooker, G. D., 47, 100–101, 149, 163

snakes: as guaco food, 26–27, 28, 32; as predators, 31, 33, 68, 72, 164, 210

Snow, David W., 52, 128, 201

Snowcaps, 62

songs, learning of, 52

Sparrow: Black-striped, 99–101, 102, 150; White-crowned, 197

species success and deficiencies, 112–13

Spinetail: Chotoy, 99, 100; as cuckoo egg hosts, 99, 100; nest building, 207; Plain-crowned, 101; Rufous-breasted, 101–102; Yellow-throated, 99, 100, 101

squirrels, red-tailed, 25

Stachytarpheta hedges, 61, 62

Stiles, F. Gary, 78, 80, 81–82, 124

Stoddard, H. L., Sr., 199

Suriname: Great Kiskadee in, 163; Striped Cuckoo in, 101

Sutton, Ivan D., 137, 138

Swallow: Barn, 196; Black-capped, 52; migration, 196, 202

swifts, migration, 196, 202

Tamarin, Cotton-top, 166, *167*

tamarins, similarities to birds: appearance, 165–66, *167*; feeding behavior, 168; reproduction and child rearing, 166, 169; sleeping behavior, 168; territory defenses, 166–68, 169; vocalizations, 168

Tanager: Blue-gray, 104; Golden-hooded, 131–32; Green Honeycreeper, 149; and migratory patterns, 202; palm tree fruit, 5, 175–76; plumage color and migration, 201; Summer, 200

tayra (black weasel) as predator, 24, 33

Terborgh, John, 165, 203

termitaries as trogon nests, 5, 11

Térraba Valley, Costa Rica: Great Kiskadee in, 156

Texas: Great Kiskadee in, 162

thornbirds: as cuckoo egg hosts, 99, 100–101

Thorntail, Green, 62

Thrush, Garden (Clay-colored Robin), 42, 104, 131

Tinamou, Great, 21

titi monkeys, similarities to birds, 168–69

Toucan: Chestnut-mandibled, 151, 176; Fiery-billed Aracari, 176; habitat, 89; Rainbow-billed, 120

Trinidad: Grayish Salator in, 47–48; Great Kiskadee in, 163; Striped Cuckoo in, 101

Trogon: appearance, 3; Black-throated, 14; diet, 3; historical persistence, 4; Mountain, 4; nest construction, 4–5; non-fighting character, 3; vocalization, 3. *See also* Trogon, Slaty-tailed; Trogon, Violaceous

Trogon, Slaty-tailed: appearance, 5–6, *6*; and chicken shelter, 7–8; nest building, 4–7, 8, 16. *See also* Trogon; Trogon, Violaceous

Trogon, Violaceous: appearance, 8, *10*; incubation activities, 12–13; nest building, 9–12, 14–15; nestling behavior, 14; parental behavior, 13–14; and Piratic Flycatcher nest predation,